How can company leaders and employees negotiate their different religious and spiritual commitments in the workplace? At a time of international debate over religious conflict and tolerance, workforces in various parts of the world are more diverse than ever before. Religion and spirituality are, for many employees, central to their identities. From the perspective of the employer, however, they can be distracting or divisive influences. This book analyzes the current interest in religion and spirituality in US companies. It provides conceptual distinctions and comparative examples (from the pluralistic contexts of India and Singapore) to trace the myriad ways that religion is present at work. It offers a model of *respectful pluralism*, asserting that the task of effective and ethical leadership in organizations is not to promote a single spiritual or religious framework but to create an environment in which managers and employees can respectfully express their own beliefs and practices.

DR. DOUGLAS A. HICKS is Assistant Professor of Leadership Studies and Religion at the Jepson School of Leadership Studies, University of Richmond, in Virginia. He is author of *Inequality and Christian Ethics*, published by Cambridge University Press in 2000. His articles have appeared in *The Leadership Quarterly*, *The Journal of Religious Ethics*, *World Development*, and *The Journal of Ecumenical Studies* and he contributed to the CD-ROM *On Common Ground: World Religions in America*. An ordained minister in the Presbyterian Church (USA), he is an editor, with J. Thomas Wren and Terry L. Price, of the forthcoming three-volume reference work *The International Library of Leadership*.

RELIGION AND THE WORKPLACE

Pluralism, Spirituality, Leadership

DOUGLAS A. HICKS

CAMBRIDGE
UNIVERSITY PRESS

PUBLISHED BY THE PRESS SYNDICATE OF THE UNIVERSITY OF CAMBRIDGE
The Pitt Building, Trumpington Street, Cambridge, United Kingdom

CAMBRIDGE UNIVERSITY PRESS
The Edinburgh Building, Cambridge, CB2 2RU, UK
40 West 20th Street, New York, NY 10011–4211, USA
477 Williamstown Road, Port Melbourne, VIC 3207, Australia
Ruiz de Alarcón 13, 28014 Madrid, Spain
Dock House, The Waterfront, Cape Town 8001, South Africa

http://www.cambridge.org

© Douglas A. Hicks 2003

First published 2003

Printed in the United Kingdom at the University Press, Cambridge

Typeface Adobe Garamond 11/12.5 pt.   *System* LATEX 2ε   [TB]

A catalogue record for this book is available from the British Library

ISBN 0 521 82240 8 hardback
ISBN 0 521 52960 3 paperback

Contents

Acknowledgments

Writing this book would have been impossible without the superb research and editorial assistance by four individuals at the University of Richmond: Cassie Price King, Elizabeth H. Rickert, and Amanda D. Nelson, at the Jepson School of Leadership Studies, and Lucretia McCulley, at the Boatwright Memorial Library. I want to communicate to them my profound appreciation for their conscientious and creative efforts. I also thank Noreen Cullen at the interlibrary loan office for enabling us to track down obscure sources.

Kevin Taylor and his associates at Cambridge University Press have been most helpful in bringing the book to press. From the book's inception, Kevin supported the central concept and encouraged me to shape the argument in ways that have improved greatly upon my own proposed idea.

Many colleagues at Richmond and elsewhere in the US, India, and Singapore were careful and critical readers of the text. I express my abiding gratitude especially to individuals who read major portions of the manuscript: Catherine L. Bagwell, Joanne B. Ciulla, Carolyn C. Gerber, Gill R. Hickman, Terry L. Price, Thomas E. McCollough, Jr., and Jonathan B. Wight. Valuable comments on specific chapters were provided by William J. Everett, Mary McClintock Fulkerson, Devesh Kapur, Anne E. Monius, and K. M. Thiagarajan. For excellent advice on one or more dimensions of the book, I also want to thank Maylin Biggadike, Richard A. Couto, Frank E. Eakin, Jr., Diana L. Eck, Asghar Ali Engineer, Elizabeth A. Faier, Daniel R. Finn, Grove Harris, Azizah al-Hibri, Fredric Jablin, Robert A. Johnson, Jr., Becky R. McMillan, Robert G. Moore III, Ellie Pierce, and Kenneth P. Ruscio. I also thank the students in my Leadership and Religious Values class at the University of Richmond, spring 2002, for their incisive comments on the first half of the manuscript.

Earlier versions of three chapters were presented at academic conferences: the International Leadership Association annual meeting (2001), the Art of Teaching Leadership, Administration, and Finance conference sponsored by the Claremont School of Theology and the Lilly Endowment, Inc. (2002), and the American Academy of Religion annual meeting, Religion and the Social Sciences section (2002).

Chapter 3 (with parts from chapters 4 and 9) is reprinted, in modified form, from *The Leadership Quarterly*, Vol. 13, Douglas A. Hicks, "Spiritual and Religious Diversity in the Workplace: Implications for Leadership," pages 63–80, copyright 2002, with permission from Elsevier Science.

Parts of chapters 8 and 9 are reprinted, in modified form, from *The Journal of Religious Leadership*, Vol. 2/1 (Spring 2003), Douglas A. Hicks, "Religion and Respectful Pluralism in the Workplace: A Constructive Framework," copyright 2003, with permission from the journal.

I am grateful for research support provided by grants from the Jepson School of Leadership Studies (2000–2002) and by a summer stipend from the National Endowment for the Humanities (2001). I also acknowledge an earlier research grant from the Harvard Pluralism Project (1994) that allowed me to make my initial foray into the complexities of religious diversity in American public life.

Finally, I express my deepest appreciation to Catherine L. Bagwell, not only for reading every page of the manuscript, but, more importantly, for her constant love and support.

Introduction

I am writing this introduction during December. This religiously charged month is a fitting time to contemplate religious diversity in the workplace, especially in the United States. Because a majority of US citizens are Christian, or were at least raised in that tradition, Christianity has enjoyed a culturally privileged status in this country. Christmas is not only a religious holiday but a national and consumeristic one as well. December has become "the holiday season." More noticeably than at other times of the year, company leaders struggle with whether and how to respect the diverse religious commitments of their employees. The interreligious calendar is full of festivals in December. This year Chanukkah falls during the first week of the month, and Ramadan culminates with the feast of Eid al-Fitr on the 6th. Many Buddhists mark Bodhi Day two days later, and Wiccans celebrate Yule on the 21st. The Christian season of Advent leads up to Christmas on the 25th. Kwanzaa, a cultural festival observed by African Americans, starts the following day and continues until New Year's Day. Should American companies celebrate them all? What about atheists who do not have a holy day and, like some of their co-workers, believe these holidays have no place at work?

When Christians constitute a majority of employees, some managers find it acceptable – and traditional – for the office to celebrate Christmas. But that reinforces what Jews, Muslims, and others already know: Christianity enjoys preferential status in many companies. When bosses disguise Christmas parties as "holiday" parties but retain the tree and the carols, the practice is not genuinely inclusive. Other managers try an avoidance strategy – no cards, no trees, no parties. This dodges some problems but fails to recognize that faith of one sort or another is essential to many workers. Besides, employees have come to expect some kind of festivity as a perk for their labors. Some company leaders attempt a promising route of displaying diverse symbols in the reception area, but this raises the question of which traditions should be represented.

In this book I suggest a framework called *respectful pluralism* as an approach to challenges such as this "December dilemma." Respectful pluralism means resisting company-sponsored religion and spirituality while allowing employees to bring their own religions to work. From a moral standpoint, the presence of a Christmas tree in the lobby is markedly different than the display of a crèche, a menorah, or a Buddha on an individual's desk. Workers can decorate their personal office areas with religious symbols. Company leaders, rather than promote any religious worldview, should create a culture of mutual respect that allows diverse employees to work together constructively. My framework will not solve all problems (especially in December) but it offers guidance for companies that are serious about diversity and respect.

Religion and the Workplace: Pluralism, Spirituality, Leadership draws upon scholarship in religion, management, and leadership to tackle the disparate issues of religion and the workplace. At a time of international tension and public debate over the interrelationships of religion, conflict, and discrimination, workforces in various parts of the world are more diverse than ever before. Individual religious beliefs and practices are, for many employees, central to their respective identities. Yet, from the perspective of the employer, workers who wear religious garb, hold on-site Bible studies, or request time off for prayers or holy days can be a divisive or distracting influence.

The standard approaches in leadership studies, organizational culture, and human resource management pay inadequate attention to religious beliefs and practices at work. In models of the secular workplace, religion is clearly a "private" matter and should be excluded from "private" sector workplaces. My analysis argues that labeling either religion or business as private is descriptively inaccurate and morally problematic. The religious commitments of employees find their way into the workplace in one way or another, whether or not managers or scholars acknowledge it. Managers should create conditions under which employees are able to express their religion at work within certain moral constraints.

In contrast, advocates of "spiritual leadership" recognize that the workplace is not properly understood or managed as a secular sphere, but they depend upon an untenable dichotomization of spirituality (which is welcome at work) and religion (which is not welcome). Despite the fact that many practitioners accept such a spiritual–religious distinction, problems with its conceptual and practical applications persist. Most accounts of spiritual leadership disguise genuine differences of perspective and potential conflict behind happy (and often false) commonality. In addition, too many scholars and corporate leaders portray spirituality as the latest leadership tool to be used in the quest for increased efficiency and profitability.

In recent public discussions about corporate scandals marked by leaders' deception, greed, and corruption, journalists and scholars have called upon American corporate leaders to demonstrate more social responsibility, exercise servant leadership, and cultivate a moral character. Some commentators assert that bringing more "faith" or "soul" or "values" (and these terms are often thrown about interchangeably) into the workplace is a ready solution. Such perspectives overlook the diversity of moral values – *which* values? – and they make a facile assumption that people from religious and spiritual backgrounds are more likely than their co-workers to act ethically.

In the United States, a solid majority of citizens claim Christianity as their "religious preference." (Fewer than half, however, are regular participants in a congregation.[1]) A voluminous literature of popular and scholarly works advises Christians on how to live out their faith at work. Most of these authors rightly note that Christian theological and moral traditions have a great deal to say about economic life. Few of them, however, pay proper attention to the religious diversity of co-workers or to the problematic nature of culturally established Christian workplaces.

If the respective fields of leadership and management studies have avoided religion, the academic discipline of religious studies has overlooked the workplace. Scholars' most in-depth examinations of religion in public life have addressed politics or civil society. In the US, these discussions focus on "civil religion" in presidential pronouncements, predominantly legal debates over religious and government institutions ("church and state"), and the potential relationship of religious involvement and social capital. In terms of religion and the economy, religious ethicists have analyzed the "meaning of work," the social responsibility of corporations, and questions of distributive justice. Scholars of religion have devoted scant direct attention, however, to religion and the workplace. Increasingly, the workplace has become a significant and public sphere in which people of diverse religious perspectives encounter one another; it thus merits scholarly attention.

The structure and size of private-sector workplaces, arguably, are as varied as religious expression by employees. Multinational corporations can be larger than all but the most powerful national economies; small businesses might employ as few as a handful of people. Clearly, the latter companies do not encounter the full array of challenges and opportunities related to

[1] George Gallup and D. Michael Lindsay, *Surveying the Religious Landscape: Trends in U.S. Beliefs* (Harrisburg, PA: Morehouse Publishers, 1999).

diversity, but in workplaces of all kinds, some issues of leadership, diversity, and religion arise.

Supporters of models such as the secular workplace, spiritual leadership, and Christian preference will encounter challenges in this book. They will take issue with some points of my analysis, because I argue that each of those views is significantly flawed. At the same time, these scholars and practitioners will also find areas of agreement or complementarity with their perspectives. I intend my criticisms to be constructive and hope that the ensuing debates will contribute to workplace policies and cultures that respect, on equal terms, employees of all backgrounds.

I believe it is important to provide a word about my own background. I am a professor with an undergraduate degree and graduate coursework in economics, a Master of Divinity degree, and a Ph.D. in religious studies. My current academic position includes a joint appointment in leadership studies and religious studies. My religious tradition is Presbyterian (Protestant, Christian) and I am a minister in the Presbyterian Church (USA). I have sought *not* to frame the book in explicitly Christian language. It is my hope that readers of various academic, professional, and religious backgrounds will find the analysis to be accessible and relevant to their work. I discuss the methodological issues of my approach and the nature of my moral argument in chapter 8.

Some of the most vocal critics of my perspective will probably be Christian readers who believe the analysis to be unduly harsh about the preferential status that Christians enjoy in US society and workplaces. Although I do not state my criticism of Christian privilege in theological terms, I believe that faithful Christians should have no interest in imposing their beliefs or practices upon others and they should want to receive no advantage in public life or the workplace because of their religion. As I show in the comparative examination of India and Singapore, persons of the majority tradition often receive official or unofficial privilege in public institutions; my moral argument, based on a view of equal respect owed to all persons, rejects such preferential practices in the workplace, whether they are afforded to Christians, Hindus, adherents of Chinese religions, or anyone else.

RELIGION AND THE WORKPLACE: WHAT IS AT STAKE AND
WHAT LIES AHEAD

I will use the remainder of the introduction to name the book's central questions and provide an overview of the analysis and argument. The book is structured in three parts. Part I (chapters 1 through 4) addresses current realities of religion and spirituality in American society and its workplaces. Part II (chapters 5 through 7) offers distinctions, concepts, and comparative examples in order to delineate more precisely the myriad ways in which religion is present in contemporary workplaces. Finally, Part III (chapters 8 and 9) presents a moral argument for respectful pluralism and discusses how such a framework can constructively address the conflicts that inevitably arise in diverse organizations.

Making sense of religion and spirituality in the workplace requires an understanding of the changes in US society in the post-World War II period that have come to bear on religion in public life and the workplace. Chapter 1 examines how developments in immigration policy, especially in 1965, significantly widened the scope and degree of religious (and racial, ethnic, and cultural) diversity in the United States. More recently, the responses to the events of September 11, 2001, brought the questions of religiously based conflict and religiously based discrimination to the center of public debate. How has the changing American context transformed the relationship of religion and business in the past fifty years?

How has the current interest in religion and, especially, spirituality in the workplace arisen? What factors have contributed to the corporate interest in spirituality? Chapter 2 attributes the recent interest in spirituality to demographic, economic, and religious trends in the US and to transformations in the nature and organization of work. Some of the factors that have led people to embrace spirituality in the workplace are positive, while others are morally troubling. Is it possible to determine how much of the current interest entails genuine respect for workers and their needs and, in contrast, how much reflects companies' efforts to take advantage of employees?

How can businesses adapt to increasing religious and spiritual diversity? Chapter 3 asserts that the literature on spirituality and work tends to emphasize the sameness or commonality that is supposedly at the root of spirituality – rather than the religious particularity that appears at first glance to be (and often is) divisive. Employees from different religious and spiritual perspectives may well be able to find significant common ground, but commonality should not simply be assumed.

Is religious expression more controversial, difficult, or incomprehensible than other kinds of potential conflict among co-workers? Chapter 4 considers individual-level and institutional-level issues concerning religion in relation to conflicts based on spiritual, political, and cultural expression at work. A variety of recent cases that have received media attention serve as examples. Are there ways to address conflict without subscribing to a reductionist view of religious difference?

Part II begins with chapter 5, which offers a map of various ways in which *individual* employees express their religious commitments differently from one another. What does it mean to "be religious at work"? Some persons, coming from minority traditions, wear distinctive garb that sets them apart from most of their co-workers. Other employees, for various reasons, keep their beliefs and practices to themselves and are thus not overtly religious at work, but their commitments still fundamentally influence their actions. Some employees do not identify as religious or spiritual; many (but not all) of these persons would prefer a secular workplace. Chapter 5 traces the variety of religious and spiritual forms, among other kinds of diversity, in the workforce.

Chapter 6 analyzes the *institutional* roles of religion in the workplace. What happens to religious diversity when an organization supports a religion *of* the workplace? The chapter draws upon the concepts of civil religion and established religion in the political sphere in order to draw analogies to institutionalized beliefs and practices in the workplace. The case of "corporate chaplains" is considered as a curious and problematic intersection of workplace spirituality and established Christianity.

Chapter 7 explores religion, public life, and the workplace in India and Singapore. These two very different societies experience tremendous degrees of religious diversity, each contrasting explicitly with a neighboring Islamic state. Given their distinct histories, how have India and Singapore shaped a pluralistic identity? My analysis offers neither of these nations as a wholly positive model for addressing diversity in the US society or workplace – indeed there are morally problematic features with each. Yet this cross-national examination informs the examination of the US context.

My constructive proposal for respectful pluralism is developed and applied in Part III, comprised of chapters 8 and 9. Given the complexities detailed in earlier chapters, can a moral framework give adequate guidance to company leaders who wish to respect the diverse religious, spiritual, political, and cultural identities of employees? What can employees expect from their companies and what can companies rightly ask of their employees? This moral framework presupposes the legal minimums of religious expression guaranteed by US laws, and it argues that a level of respect higher than the legal minimum guarantees is due to employees. Chapter 8 outlines the moral argument for respectful pluralism and applies the framework to specific scenarios in the workplace.

Chapter 9 asserts that respectful pluralism connects to various themes of leadership studies, such as organizational culture, ethics, diversity, and critical thinking. What requirements does the framework place on leaders? Is constructing respectful pluralism itself an act of leadership? Chapter 9 concludes with a discussion of some limitations of my perspective and some central implications and areas for future research on religion and the workplace.

How can leaders and followers negotiate religious differences in their workplace? Respectful pluralism is a framework, not a specific blueprint, for addressing inevitable conflicts that result from religious, spiritual, and other differences in the workplace. Pragmatic and moral issues that are context-specific will require that the view be adapted to fit well in any actual organization. Nonetheless, at a time in which Americans have endorsed a vision of a national community in which people of many faiths (and no professed faith) are invited to participate in all spheres of society, this framework of respectful pluralism can contribute to a conversation about religion and spirituality at work and in other spheres of public life. I hope that readers living outside the US may also see applications and insights for understanding diversity in their own contexts.

PART I

Analyzing current realities

CHAPTER I

The changing American context

The challenge of negotiating religion and the workplace fits within a wider public context in which citizens debate the meaning of terms like religion, spirituality, ethics, diversity, commonality, conflict, and unity. This chapter explores changes in US public life that make an analysis of religion and the workplace fascinating, messy, and timely.

US citizens and leaders now confront challenges that few people had envisioned before the devastating events of September 11, 2001. Talk of religion in its myriad forms swirls in the public conversation about that tragic day and responses to it. Extremists who claimed a religious motivation for their terrorism too vividly demonstrate the power of religious ideas and commitments on adherents to produce disastrous effects. For their part, however, the overwhelming majority of US Muslim leaders and followers responded with firm rejections of any depiction of Islamic faith that supports the killing of civilians. Many commentators drew the painful image that the terrorists had hijacked Islam itself.

In the face of the attacks, religious people and nonreligious people united across boundaries to rescue the trapped, heal the sick, and comfort those who were mourning. A prayer service in the National Cathedral in Washington brought together religious and political leaders who drew upon many civic and religious traditions to mourn the dead.[1] The following weekend a memorial event for grieving families, held in Yankee Stadium and broadcast across America, testified even more fully to the tremendous religious diversity of contemporary America.[2] The event offered the prospect that political, civic, and religious leaders could draw upon various traditions to unite for a common cause. Mixed (somewhat

[1] Rene Sanchez and Bill Broadway, "A Kinship of Grief: With Prayers and Patriotism, a Nation Comes Together," *Washington Post*, September 15, 2001.
[2] Robert D. McFadden, "In a Stadium of Heroes, Prayers for the Fallen and Solace for Those Left Behind," *New York Times*, September 24, 2001.

11

strangely) with popular entertainers' songs and politicians' remarks, the religious portions of the event rivaled the World's Parliament of Religions with a rich variety of prayers, songs, colorful vestments, styles of speech, and languages.

The challenge now facing the United States is whether Americans will succeed – even as the specter of terrorism makes heightened caution a prudent and appropriate response – in celebrating and protecting the tremendous religious diversity that has reshaped the nation in the past four decades. Will US citizens muster the strength and develop the critical skills to live peaceably – at work, in schools, in politics – with people of all religious traditions?

These recent events increase the urgency of such a question for America, but they do not raise completely new issues. As Diana Eck and her colleagues at Harvard's Pluralism Project have documented, America's "religious landscape" has changed dramatically. Eck contends that America is now the world's most religiously diverse nation, at least in terms of the number of active traditions and communities.[3] Long before the events of September 2001, Americans had been moving in the direction of greater religious tolerance and acceptance, even while experiencing periodic setbacks of misunderstanding, discrimination, and violence.

It is worth focusing briefly on the tradition that has received significant (if often unwanted) media attention and public scrutiny recently – namely, Islam. For their part, Muslims in the United States have long shared public spaces with people of other religious communities. They also have experienced, throughout recent decades, harassment and vandalism. American Muslims suffered each time a high-profile act of terrorism was committed somewhere in the world. Prior to the attacks of September 11, 2001, Eck noted the following:

Even while American Muslims create mainstream mosques and Islamic centers, register to vote, and become active participants in the American democratic process, newspapers bring to American homes the images of Islamic Jihad and other terrorist organizations, their rifle-toting leaders and their hideouts, creating a view of Islam as dangerous, subversive, highly political, and anti-American. When a terrorist attack occurs elsewhere in the world, American Muslims may well be among the first to condemn the attack and to speak of terrorism as anti-Islamic, but their

---

[3] Diana L. Eck and the Pluralism Project at Harvard University, *On Common Ground: World Religions in America CD-Rom* (New York: Columbia University Press, 1997); Diana L. Eck, *A New Religious America: How a "Christian Country" Has Now Become the World's Most Religiously Diverse Nation* (San Francisco: Harper San Francisco, 2001).

voices are usually not heard, let alone magnified by the popular press. American Muslims may also be among the first to feel the repercussions, as their mosques are pelted with stones.[4]

Eck's account was prescient, though she had referred to terrorism "elsewhere in the world." When the strike occurred in the United States, some American Muslims – along with Sikhs, Hasidic Jews, and Christian Arabs mistaken for Muslims – not only experienced repercussions against their places of worship, but, in multiple cases, were beaten or murdered.[5]

Although the number of Muslims in America has grown drastically since the 1965 Immigration and Naturalization Act, Muslims have been part of the United States since the earliest colonial days. African slaves brought Islam to the Americas. Scholar Allan Austin has estimated that "10% of West Africans sent to America from 1711 to 1808 were, to some degree, Muslim."[6] Competing strands of Islam existed and developed among African Americans; the early twentieth century marked a turn to more explicit claims to Islamic traditions.[7] In the present day, adherents of the Nation of Islam, led by the controversial figure Louis Farrakhan, are dwarfed in numbers by followers of W. D. Mohammed, who advocates a more orthodox form of Islam. Eck claims that African Americans comprise 25 to 40 percent of the contemporary Muslim community in the United States. Immigrants and converts make up the rest.[8]

The diversity within the American Muslim community itself is immense. When the lens is widened to examine all traditions in America – including the "homegrown" strands and those "world religions" that have been strengthened in recent decades by immigration – it becomes apparent that the varieties of religious expression have transformed and will continue to transform America. When extremists claim a religious motivation, they gain the public spotlight; yet there are many deeper, and potentially positive, trends taking place beyond the headlines.

---

[4] Eck, *A New Religious America*, 223.

[5] Elizabeth Bell, "Central Valley Town Gropes with Specter of Hate Slaying; Arab American Shot in His Reedley Store," *San Francisco Chronicle*, October 4, 2001; Kelly Ettenborough, Adam Klawonn, and Christina Leonard, "Valley Mourns Apparent Backlash Killing," *Arizona Republic*, September 17, 2001; Gustav Niebuhr, "Christian Arabs, Too, Are Harassed," *The New York Times*, October 15, 2001; "Flight Diverted Due to Confusion over Prayer," *Reuters Online*, October 15, 2001.

[6] Allan D. Austin, *African Muslims in Antebellum America: A Sourcebook*, vol. 5, *Critical Studies on Black Life and Culture* (New York: Garland Publishers, 1984), 35. See also Albert J. Raboteau, *Slave Religion: The "Invisible Institution" in the Antebellum South* (Oxford University Press, 1980), 5–7.

[7] For a broad overview of the strands and institutions of African American Islam in the twentieth century, see Eck, *A New Religious America*, 251–60.

[8] Ibid., 260.

THE WORLD TRADE CENTER AND THE CHANGING
AMERICAN WORKPLACE

Public attention to religion vis-à-vis the World Trade Center has focused on the beliefs – and actions – of the suicidal hijackers. The discussion has tended to overlook another significant reality. The World Trade Center was one of the most religiously diverse collections of workplaces in one of the most religiously diverse cities in the United States. Precise figures about the backgrounds of the victims, of course, are not known (and never will be known). Reliable data, however, point to the fact that these people were citizens of over sixty countries, with some reports placing the number as high as eighty. An American Red Cross chaplain at Ground Zero stated that, taken together, the victims' families speak some 180 languages.[9]

In terms of religion, of the tens of thousands of people who worked at the World Trade Center as of September 11, 2001, the Council on American–Islamic Relations reported that 1,200 Muslims were employed there.[10] Other media reports conservatively placed the number of Jews employed in the World Trade Center at 4,000. Office workers and visitors who died in the attack included Muslims, Christians, Jews, Hindus, Buddhists, Sikhs, and people of no professed religion.[11] The corps of volunteer chaplains who responded to support victims' families was comprised of hundreds of pastoral leaders, including Christian ministers and priests, Jewish rabbis, Muslim imams, and Buddhist monks.[12]

Located in Northern Virginia just outside Washington, DC, the Pentagon serves as the headquarters of the US Department of Defense, a (government) workplace of military personnel and civilians. The US military now employs chaplains from a range of religious traditions, including at least nine Muslim chaplains.[13] Forty military chaplains were among the very first to respond to the tragedy of September 11 and then to perform

---

[9] Telephone interview with Greg Bodin, then head of the Spiritual Care Center of the American Red Cross, October 3, 2001.

[10] Glenda Cooper, "A Muslim Family in N.Y. Fears for a Son Who Loved America," *New York Times*, September 18, 2001.

[11] Ibid.; Telephone interview with Fr. Joe O'Donnell, October 8, 2001. O'Donnell is a Catholic priest who succeeded Greg Bodin in leading the Spiritual Care Center of the American Red Cross in providing pastoral care to victims' families. The "Portraits of Grief" that appeared in issues of *The New York Times* from September through December 2001 made direct reference to victims' identities as Catholics, Protestants, Jews, Muslims, Hindus, and Buddhists.

[12] O'Donnell interview, October 8, 2001. O'Donnell also reported that both the New York City Fire Department and the New York Police Department are predominantly Catholic, but they also include people from many religious backgrounds.

[13] Eck, *A New Religious America*, 356.

rituals to mourn the dead. These leaders included Protestant and Catholic clergy, rabbis, and an imam. Military and civilian victims killed in the attacks also came from a range of religious backgrounds.[14]

In the shocking aftermath of September 11, it was more "newsworthy" to focus on the stated beliefs and actions of the terrorists than to focus on the faith backgrounds of the victims. In a long-term view, however, it is equally important to recognize that people of many religious traditions lived and worked together peaceably in the very buildings that were targeted by the extremists. In that respect, the coverage of these tragedies mirrors wider public coverage of religion in the United States: religiously motivated violence receives more attention than quiet religious understanding or cooperation.

The religious diversity of employees in the World Trade Center in particular reflected the very cosmopolitan nature of the firms and agencies located there. One of the reasons the victims represented so many religious traditions, of course, was that they hailed from all regions of the world. At the same time, the diversity found at the World Trade Center is a reflection of present-day New York City, one of the most religiously and demographically complex cities in the world. The wave of immigration into the United States since 1965 has affected all parts of the US, but New York, long an ethnically and religiously rich center, has been dramatically transformed. New York, once a settlement in which "the only permitted form of public worship was Dutch Reformed Christianity," is now

home to many American religious landmarks, including one of the first U.S. temples built according to ancient Hindu guidelines, the upper East Side's ultramodern Islamic Cultural Center of New York, the first Jain temple in North America, and the nation's largest Christian Cathedral, St. John the Divine Protestant Episcopal Church.[15]

In the aftermath of September 11, commentators noted that the dream of religious freedom associated with Ellis Island and the Statue of Liberty had not been disrupted by the attacks. New York was and is home to a myriad of religions.

The forces of globalization suggest that workplaces across the United States – not to mention other parts of the world – are moving toward the reality of dramatic religious diversity among employers and employees. The symbolism of the new global economy and its workforce was understood,

---

[14] E-mail correspondence from US Army Chaplain Donna Weddle, September 26, 2001, and October 18, 2001.
[15] Eck, *On Common Ground,* essay on "New York City."

surely, by those who plotted the destruction of the World Trade Center. Although most companies and office complexes will not achieve the degree of diversity of that cosmopolitan workforce in the near future, it is evident that many companies will face increasingly complex religious demographics among their employees.

It is this dimension of the post-September 11 period that most clearly frames the inquiry of *Religion and the Workplace*. While it has been a gradual change, the tremendous increase in religious and spiritual diversity has transformed all aspects of American public life, including the workplace.

RELIGION IN A LAND OF IMMIGRANTS

The date July 4, 1965, marked the beginning of a new and broad period of immigration. On that day, President Lyndon Johnson signed the Immigration and Naturalization Act as he stood at the foot of the Statue of Liberty. Prior waves of immigration had arrived predominantly from Europe. Africans had come against their will as slaves in earlier centuries. Latin Americans from Mexico and further south could immigrate by land, but long-standing conflict between the United States and Mexico served to constrain that immigration. Asian immigration to America experienced a slow, steady increase during much of the nineteenth century, but, beginning in the late nineteenth century, strong anti-Asian sentiment slowed the Asian influx to a trickle. The Chinese Exclusion Act of 1882 marked the beginning of a period that restricted Asian immigration in general – Japanese and Korean as well as Chinese. The 1924 Johnson–Reed Act severely tightened all immigration to the United States and assigned quotas by country. In 1923 the Supreme Court upheld an old statute declaring that "orientals" were not "free white men" and, thus, could not be citizens. In that particular case, Bhagat Singh Thind, a Sikh who was a US veteran of World War I and a naturalized US citizen, was stripped of his citizenship.[16] During the four decades immediately preceding 1965, the small immigrant stream hailed almost entirely from Europe.[17]

The variety of religious expression has multiplied in the decades following 1965. Numbers alone do not capture the diversity of the new landscape, but they provide some perspective. While estimates vary broadly, there are now millions of Muslims in the United States. Scholars debate figures between

[16] Eck, *A New Religious America*, 59–60.
[17] Eck, *On Common Ground*, essays on "Asians and Asian Exclusion," "Xenophobia: Closing the Door," and "A New Multi-Religious America" (sections co-authored by Rebecca K. Gould and Douglas A. Hicks); Eck, *A New Religious America*, 6–7.

1.8 and 6 million Muslim adults and children.[18] Together, Asian American and white Buddhists total as many as 4 million people, and roughly 1 million Hindus reside in the United States.[19] Jews number approximately 6 million persons, ranging from Hasidic Jewish persons living in relatively closed communities to Reform and secular Jews. In surveys, 86 percent of all Americans still claim Christianity as their "religious preference."[20] The Christian community, however, has become increasingly diverse in recent years. For example, while the majority of the over 30 million Hispanic Americans are Catholic, the number of evangelical Protestant Hispanic Americans is on the rise. This latter group, supplemented by increasing numbers of Protestant Asian Americans, comprises a kind of reverse missionary impact on the country whose Protestants long supported outreach efforts in Latin America, Korea, China, and other areas.

The workplace has been at the forefront of institutions affected by this post-1965 broadening. The presumed Christian homogeneity (sometimes politely widened to the "Judeo-Christian tradition"[21]) no longer fits demographic or religious reality. To be sure, such an assumed uniformity always excluded minority expressions, including Native American traditions and many aspects of African American religions. Whether this diversity is a challenge to confront or an opportunity to welcome is up for debate. Both aspects should be accorded their full due.

RELIGION AND LEADERSHIP IN THE AMERICAN WORKPLACE

Two articles from *Fortune* magazine provide snapshots of public discussion about religion and the workplace before and after the post-1965 wave of immigration. Seen together, these essays illustrate just how much has

---

[18] A recent study by the Graduate Center of the City University of New York estimates there are 1.8 million Muslims; a report commissioned by the American Jewish Committee estimated 1.9 million but acknowledged another method that estimated 2.8 million (Gustav Niebuhr, "Studies Suggest Lower Count for Number of US Muslims," *New York Times*, October 25, 2001). Diana Eck uses the widely quoted estimate of 6 million (Eck, *A New Religious America*, 2–3). Critics of the lower number cite the difficulties of locating and aggregating people from various Muslim traditions, including African American and immigrant groups.

[19] Eck, *A New Religious America*, 2–3.

[20] George Gallup and D. Michael Lindsay, *Surveying the Religious Landscape: Trends in US Beliefs* (Harrisburg, PA: Morehouse Publishers, 1999), 16.

[21] The problems of citing a "Judeo-Christian" tradition are well developed in the literature of religious studies. The label "Judeo-Christian" tends to assume, at the expense of Judaism, that Christians and Jews believe essentially the same things. Besides glossing over the very real and important theological and liturgical differences, it tends to subsume Jewish traditions within an umbrella that is dominated by Christian ideas and practices. See Arthur Allen Cohen, *The Myth of the Judeo-Christian Tradition* (New York: Harper & Row, 1969).

shifted in fifty years. A 1953 article by Duncan Norton-Taylor bore the title "Businessmen on Their Knees."[22] In 2001, Marc Gunther published an article entitled "God and Business" in the same magazine.[23] Understanding the differences and the similarities in these two articles can help set a historic frame for the contemporary analysis of religion and the workplace. It is also important to consider aspects of spirituality and religion and the workplace that both articles omit.

Norton-Taylor's essay sets the 1953 context by noting a "religious phenomenon" of increased church attendance and heightened general interest in religious matters in the post-war United States. Businessmen shared this new enthusiasm for religion and they sought to apply their beliefs to their work. The de facto focus of the article is not on religion in general, but on the Christian faith of a growing group of businessmen. They had created new Bible study groups and were even engaging co-workers through "evangelizing." Norton-Taylor notes that Christian men's groups had formed around the country with names such as "Christ Bearers," "Fishermen's Clubs," and the "Christian Business Men's Committee."[24]

Behind the local movement in Pittsburgh, which Norton-Taylor discusses at length, was an Episcopal priest, Dr. Samuel Moor Shoemaker, rector of the Calvary Episcopal Church. Shoemaker is portrayed as innovative for the efforts he took, not only to attend solely to the Sunday activities at the church, but also to prod his parishioners to connect their Christian faith to their labors in the business world.

For many other observers, such a "phenomenon" should not be seen as particularly surprising. After all, the idea that Christian (or other religious) commitments are not for worship time alone, but are guiding principles for living one's life, is not new or particularly revolutionary. But Norton-Taylor has framed his article with the claim that "[a] man's religion used to be a private matter."[25] Even if businessmen professed Christian faith before the period of religious renewal, Norton-Taylor seems to suggest, they did not usually discuss it at work. The novelty, then, is found in the explicit and intentional talk about religion in the workplace by Christian businessmen, and in the formation of groups that crossed congregational and denominational lines.

The 1953 discussion focuses almost exclusively on Protestant business leaders. Presbyterians and Episcopalians receive most of the attention, with mention of a few Methodists. Catholics get passing attention. Beyond

---

[22] Duncan Norton-Taylor, "Businessmen on Their Knees," *Fortune*, October 1953.
[23] Marc Gunther, "God & Business," *Fortune*, July 9, 2001.
[24] Norton-Taylor, "Businessmen on Their Knees," 140–41.   [25] Ibid., 141.

the Christian traditions, a rabbi is quoted in general terms, and there is one reference to "a revival of Judaeo-Christian passion."[26] In 1953, then, religion in the workplace generally means Christian – namely, Protestant – faith.

The article examines high-ranking businessmen who held formal positions of authority in their companies. Norton-Taylor reports that the Rev. Dr. Shoemaker approached the members of the Pittsburgh Golf Club with his seminar on "How to Become a Christian."[27] The leaders featured are those, as the byline states, "at a peak of their worldly strength and success,"[28] a group comprised of board chairmen and company presidents. These positional leaders managed to combine Christian faith and worldly success.

That the intended audience of this movement of Christian faith consists of executives is supported by the discussion of how to take Bible studies to workers on the assembly line. Norton-Taylor cites one worker at US Steel who became fed up by his fellow workers' labor strike. The company president supported the worker's idea to begin a Bible study among his fellow workers. The article notes that, at another company that had been holding prayer meetings, "[t]here hasn't been a strike . . . in eleven years."[29] US Steel decided to spend $150,000, the article reports, to distribute *Guideposts* magazine to its workers. *Guideposts* was edited by Norman Vincent Peale, whose Protestant theology of uplifting messages and socially disengaged faith would not have challenged the basic assumptions of the American corporation. Norton-Taylor discounts the anticipated charge that this program was an attempt to pacify workers:

It would be a little ridiculous to raise the old Marxist charge that management is using religion to drug gullible workers. Management knows by this time that organized labor is not that gullible.[30]

Norton-Taylor implies that, because it would be obvious this program might be an effort to pacify workers, it must not be so. Whatever the motives of US Steel for supporting the program, the example provides evidence that the discussion of religion in the workplace in 1953 had a top-down approach, aimed at Christians in management who could carry the religious discussion to their workers.

These managers were men. In 1953, women comprised only 30.6 percent of the labor force, and many women who were in the private sector held secretarial positions. Given that women now comprise 46.5 percent of the

[26] Ibid., 254, 256.   [27] Ibid., 248.   [28] Ibid., 140.   [29] Ibid., 253.   [30] Ibid., 254.

labor force, this demographic transition has broadened the discussion of religion and spirituality in the workplace.[31]

The reference to "spirituality" in the 1953 article means the everyday expression of Christian faith as lived out in the workplace, home, and community. For example, within a discussion of whether the new religious enthusiasm reflects "the meaning of the agony of Christ" and "the meaning of true religion," Norton-Taylor refers to "Protestant clergymen [who] were inclined to see just such a true *spirituality* at work."[32] Importantly, there is no suggestion that spirituality is somehow distinct or separate from organized religion – a distinction that took on prominence in more recent public and scholarly discussions.

The spirituality and leadership discourse looked quite different in 2001. The focus broadened beyond Christianity and beyond men. Yet parallel to the 1953 article, Marc Gunther's contemporary essay in *Fortune* begins with a discussion of a "spiritual revival" and a "groundswell of believers [who are] breaching the last taboo in corporate America" by bringing God and spirituality into business. In the current epoch, however, the movement includes people influenced by all of the world's religions and by various New Age expressions.

Norton-Taylor's account of the 1950s had focused on Protestant Christendom and included passing acknowledgment of Catholicism and Judaism. In contrast, Gunther's article profiles the stories of six people for whom religion, faith, or spirituality has made a significant difference in their business lives. They include a Mormon man, a Presbyterian woman, a Buddhist man, a "traditional" Catholic man, a "fully Jewish" man influenced by a number of other traditions, and an African American Catholic man who collaborates with a former Jew converted to Buddhism.

For each of these figures, Gunther examines how his or her religious or spiritual practices have affected the ways they do business. As already noted, diversity is the norm. For some, faith has made them question the kinds of work they do; a few have refused to work on their sabbath day; others have decided to contribute to their community through their business. One person criticizes the long hours that he works, but another states that he has greatly increased his work hours for eleven months of the year in order to take an annual month-long retreat in India. As Gunther describes it, the effects of faith on these individuals are generally positive, though for at least one person, "God and business . . . sometimes . . . collide

---

[31] Data were obtained from the US Department of Labor, Bureau of Labor Statistics, Historical Data, http://www.bls.gov/cps/cpsatabs.htm, accessed February 15, 2003.
[32] Norton-Taylor, "Businessmen on Their Knees," 254, emphasis added.

head on."[33] Even this man, however, is presented as a highly successful businessperson.

Women are now part of the faith-in-the-workplace story. Their presence in the labor force has contributed to the increased religious diversity and willingness to talk about "private" matters in the public space. After all, women's massive entrance into the workforce made problematic the simple distinctions between the domestic sphere and public spheres upon which much of modern liberalism depends.[34]

By 2001, religion and spirituality have been distinguished and even separated. Gunther's description of one man, Richard Levy, is illustrative:

> Levy, who is Jewish, had long been interested in philosophy and religion, particularly the Eastern traditions; he has, for example, practiced tai chi, a physical discipline rooted in Taoism. Like many baby-boomers, *Levy has fashioned his own brand of spirituality, which draws from a number of religious traditions.* "For me, spirituality is a very individual issue," he says. "Although I consider myself fully Jewish, I'm not a member of a synagogue. Those of us who are less affiliated have to uncover our own path, and that's hard. Especially when, at the same time, we are CEOs of fast-growing companies."[35]

Levy articulates clearly (and the author Gunther seems to concur) that spirituality pertains to the individual. Spirituality is what individual people construct, and discover, and perhaps practice. It does not require religious affiliation. It is possible to be spiritual without being religious.

Unlike the predominant theme in 1953, when religion at work was rooted in the practices of a faith community (for example, the church or synagogue), the contemporary movement of spirituality and leadership does not require such institutional religious affiliation on the part of business leaders or their employees. In fact, spirituality in the workplace becomes, for many businesspeople, an alternative form of religious affiliation.

It is significant to note that people who profess their own brand of spirituality usually do not arrive at it on their own. In addition to religious leaders and traditional holy texts that may have influenced them, a host of "spiritual corporate consultants" currently make their living talking about spirituality in the workplace and undoubtedly influence business leaders and employees. If the Protestant minister was the old paradigm of a spiritual guide, today's paradigm is the executive trainer. Bookstores are stocked with best-selling texts about work, leadership, and spirituality, with titles such

[33] Gunther, "God & Business," 78.
[34] See, for instance, Iris Marion Young, *Justice and the Politics of Difference* (Princeton University Press, 1990).
[35] Gunther, "God & Business," 76, emphasis added.

as *Spirit at Work, Leading with Soul,* and *Synchronicity: The Inner Path of Leadership.*[36] If it is true that a growing number of business leaders are discovering themselves and their inner spirituality, they can buy any number of texts that tell them what they are likely to find. Indeed, these texts have become the latest trend in effective workplace leadership. Have they also created a new kind of religious orthodoxy?

Not all people who talk about spirituality at work have renounced organized religion, to be sure. For some people featured in Gunther's article, their religious practice and affiliation in a faith community remain a fundamental part of their identity. One leader, Dick Green, is part of a Chicago-based group of Catholic businesspeople who call themselves "Business Leaders for Excellence, Ethics, and Justice." This group was founded as a critical response to the US Catholic Bishops' pastoral letter on the economy,[37] which they saw as too negative in its assessment of capitalism. Despite the disagreement with the church statement, this group and its members remain critically engaged in the life of the Catholic church.[38]

Thus the discourse about religion and the workplace has not shifted simply from traditional religion (especially Christianity) in the workplace to individual New Age spirituality in the workplace. Rather, now there is a diversity of forms of expression in business. Adherents include practicing religious followers of all strands of Christianity, Judaism, Islam, Hinduism, Buddhism, Wicca, and New Age religions; individuals of no professed faith; and as many different practitioners of "individual spirituality" as there are individuals.

For all of the differences noted here between the contexts of 1953 and 2001, some important similarities remain. First is the assumption that the workplace is essentially a secular sphere – at least until religious or spiritual people seek to transform it. Only four decades prior to 1953, however, scholars such as the Social Gospel theologian Walter Rauschenbusch spoke of "Christianizing the social order," which included the application of Christian principles to American business.[39] Although Rauschenbusch was impressively thoughtful about just how to apply Christian ideas to the

---

[36] Jay Alden Conger, ed., *Spirit at Work: Discovering the Spirituality in Leadership*, first edn., The Jossey-Bass Management series (San Francisco: Jossey-Bass, 1994); Lee G. Bolman and Terrence E. Deal, *Leading with Soul: An Uncommon Journey of Spirit*, first edn. (San Francisco: Jossey-Bass, 1995); Joseph Jaworski, *Synchronicity: The Inner Path of Leadership*, ed. Betty S. Flowers, first edn. (San Francisco: Berrett-Koehler Publishers, 1996).

[37] National Conference of Catholic Bishops, *Economic Justice for All: Pastoral Letter on Catholic Social Teaching and the U.S. Economy* (Washington, DC: United States Catholic Conference, 1986).

[38] Gunther, "God & Business," 78.

[39] Walter Rauschenbusch, *Christianizing the Social Order* (New York: Macmillan, 1912).

workplace, there was little public debate at the time that questioned whether "Christianizing" was a positive thing to do. Just a year before Rauschenbusch published *Christianizing the Social Order*, Frederick Winslow Taylor issued his *The Principles of Scientific Management*, marking the beginning of the modern, autonomous business sphere in society.[40]

The contemporary spirituality and leadership discussion often proceeds without this wider historical frame of the de facto Christian establishment in American society that predated it. This oversight avoids the question of whether Christian influences remain part of the workplace environment even when Christians do not explicitly evangelize. The 1953 framework involved "recovering" such a Christian influence upon business, without acknowledging that the influence was part of the culture all along. The 2001 discussion also fails to note the predominance of Christian symbols and influences in the business realm and in society as a whole – or the possible problems of such a reality for an increasingly diverse workforce. Instead, the contemporary literature seems to celebrate the mutual interaction of a variety of religious and spiritual practices and ideas, all on an ahistorical and equal footing. Does it not matter that Christian symbols and ideas and holidays continue to have culturally established status in US workplaces and wider public life? Precisely how it matters is the more difficult issue.

Another similarity between the 1953 and 2001 articles is that they each profile positional leaders – persons who have brought their religion or spirituality into the workplace via the executive suite or the management floor. Gunther calls the contemporary phenomenon a grassroots movement, but by this he means that he sees no person or group of persons orchestrating a national movement. Gunther examines how religion and spirituality pertain to those people with formal positions of authority in particular workplace organizations. Like Norton-Taylor, he portrays formal leaders as the ones who introduce faith into the workplace – as if religion and spirituality would otherwise be absent.

There are various problematic aspects of this framework. First, the almost exclusive featuring of people who have reached positions of influence contributes to the narrative that faith leads to success. Although many (but not all) authors insist that the interest in religion and spirituality is *not* associated with the end of increasing profit, the very structure of the discussion is biased to suggest that religion contributes to material success.

[40] Frederick Winslow Taylor, *The Principles of Scientific Management* (New York: W. W. Norton, 1911). The story of the movement toward more humanistic models of management is found in Joanne B. Ciulla, *The Working Life: The Promise and Betrayal of Modern Work* (New York: Times Books/Random House, 2000).

Few if any stories spotlight people who have given up positions of power –
or renounced the business sector altogether – because of their faith. Even
those persons who have stood up for their faith and paid some price in terms
of their career have found ways to recover and to be financially successful.

Another problem with the exclusive emphasis on people in formal positions is that, by default, it neglects consideration of workers or followers. Is
it that such persons do not have faith? Do they need their bosses to introduce them to religion or spirituality? Do bosses become "spiritual guides,"
as at least a few articles suggest in all seriousness?[41] There are, of course, reasonable alternate explanations for what is occurring. Perhaps authors and
journalists simply find it more interesting to cover the faith of successful
managers than to profile the faith of assembly line workers, secretaries, or
middle managers. Such a preference would be related to the success bias
noted above. Or there is yet another possible explanation: workers may
be more constrained than managers to express their religious views in the
workplace. That is, they may be less inclined to have such conversations
with managers or co-workers because they feel more vulnerable than their
bosses. Whatever the cause or set of causes for the focus on formal leaders
in these articles, it is important to expand the analysis to include followers
as well as leaders and to study the ways in which religion and spirituality
in the workplace concern both followers and leaders.

Both essays in *Fortune* neglect other important aspects of religion and
the workplace. The approach in each article is to analyze the faith of individuals. For example: how does a faithful Presbyterian manager live out his
belief in Jesus when hiring and firing? How should a Buddhist organize her
time and priorities and treat her co-workers? We do not see more difficult
issues addressed concerning, for example, religious dress or speech in the
workplace, such as: may a Sikh employee wear his turban or his *kirpan*
(ritual dagger) at work? May an employee protest a company product by
appeals to Jewish teachings? Neither article offers a detailed analysis of the
organizational culture and structure and their impact upon the expression of
religion and spirituality. A focus on the institutional level would ask a variety of questions such as these: does a particular corporation create a secular
atmosphere? Does the company, rather, promote an effective establishment
of Christianity? (Tests: Does it play Christmas carols over the loudspeaker in
December? Is the company closed on Good Friday or Easter Monday?) Do
the managers pay for and require attendance at spirituality seminars? Does
the organization have and uphold a nondiscrimination policy to protect

---

[41] See ch. 3 below.

people of "minority" religions? These questions address the *institutional*, and not just the *individual*, aspects of religion and spirituality in the workplace. Leadership can create or stifle the institutional space for individual religious expression.

Finally, neither article confronts the challenges of religious diversity directly. A product of its context, the earlier article assumes, without seeing a need for justification, that Protestant Christianity is the paradigmatic religion within a wider Christian tradition. Norton-Taylor suggested in 1953 that Protestants were bringing their faith back into the workplace; Catholics and Jews were welcome to do the same, with the assumption that their practice looked similar to the Protestant model. Forty-eight years later, Gunther's article is indeed broad by comparison in choosing and describing six protagonists; in this way, Gunther certainly gives a taste of the contemporary variety of religious and spiritual expression. Yet his treatment of these six leaders gives no consideration to the possibility that any of the traditions or expressions – whether Christian, Buddhist, or New Age – could be at odds with one another or might lead to conflict in the workplace. While Norton-Taylor, for instance, at least saw a dilemma in 1953 about whether Christians should evangelize in the workplace, Gunther chooses not to address such a potentially divisive question. Rather, there is an assumption that the disparate religions coexisting in the workplace will lead to better performance on the part of leaders – and indeed to more enlightened leadership and a pleasant work environment. Religious and spiritual expressions may well lead to a richer workplace, but that conclusion should only be drawn after the challenges and potential conflicts have been fully considered.

CONCLUSIONS

The examination of the articles from *Fortune* has introduced many of the issues about religion, leadership, and the workplace to be explored in the following chapters. The articles suggest that many individuals seek to integrate their working lives with religious or spiritual ideas and practices for a multitude of reasons. The diversity of religious commitments and expressions deserves close attention, along with an analysis of organizational values and culture. Thus, when different people speak about "faith in the workplace," or "spirit at work," or "the soul of business," they often are referring to quite distinct conceptions and realities. Indeed, understanding how various advocates of these concepts, including conservative Christians, liberal Christians, orthodox Jews, Muslims, Wiccans, and New Age individuals, can manage to use similar language but mean many different things is one of the tasks of this inquiry.

The voluminous literature on religion, spirituality, and leadership tends to be a-contextual. That is, it overlooks factors that provide important information for understanding the contemporary interest in this phenomenon. The popularity of talking about religion, spirituality, and even leadership in the workplace is part of wider US trends in religion and society. The tremendous increase in diversity of religious traditions represented among Americans has broadened the public conversation. At the same time, many Americans have moved their spiritual quest for self-fulfillment, meaning, and purpose outside of the confines of organized religion. For some people, this has meant leaving their church, synagogue, or mosque altogether; for others, it has entailed enriching or expanding their religious faith by learning from other traditions. The study of leadership and management has shifted from a more rationalistic model to include attention to the whole person – which for some scholars reaches to the spiritual and religious dimensions of the human person. The movement toward bringing matters religious and spiritual into the workplace is not an isolated one; it is, rather, part of the wider trends of a changing American society.

CHAPTER 2

The corporate interest in spirituality

Since the late 1980s, interest in spirituality and leadership has mushroomed. Books, magazines, and videos on spirituality at work or spirituality for business leaders have become a tremendously profitable industry for publishers.[1] Parachurch and other new organizations have joined "corporate chaplains" in bringing faith to the office. "Consultants" and "corporate trainers" from a variety of perspectives – New Age, Christian, Buddhist, Hindu, interfaith, and every combination thereof – have built a specialty field.

Scholars refer to the developments since the late 1980s not merely as a trend, but as a movement. How and from where did this new (or resurgent) interest arise? Is it a result of positive societal and corporate changes that have led to a discovery of a spiritual dimension of work? Are there reasons to be concerned about this so-called movement because it results from, or exposes, other more troubling developments in work and society?

Scholars from many disciplines and approaches have pointed out a vast array of factors which may have affected the current interest in workplace spirituality and religion. These factors include demographic and religious changes in US society, overall improvements in the US standard of living, and a variety of transformations in the workplace itself. This chapter suggests that no single cause or simple answer can account for the phenomenon and that many different elements have played some part in focusing attention on spirituality and religion in organizations. Although positive factors are involved, many less benign factors – factors that the proponents of workplace spirituality do not adequately acknowledge – are also at work.

[1] Thomas J. Billitteri, "Finding the Spirit at Work: In Their Quest for Peace and Fulfillment, Today's Harried Workers Can Get Help from Many New Books," *Publishers Weekly*, May 19, 1997, 48.

Spirituality talk

The most often cited demographic change contributing to an increased interest in spirituality, in the workplace and elsewhere, is that the baby boomer generation has reached midlife.[2] This population cohort, those men and women born between 1946 and the early 1960s, is so large that its characteristic attitudes and behaviors have had a disproportionate impact on almost every American institution, including the workplace. According to standard views of religion in the life cycle, young adults have relatively little interest in religious or spiritual matters, but, as they reach middle age, their interest in faith heightens.[3] From the life-cycle perspective, the aging of the boomer-dominated workforce has been a prime factor in the rise in spirituality in the office. The boomers experienced a spiritual awakening of sorts in the late 1980s and the 1990s. As a generation, they had abandoned the church in large numbers and, while some have returned, many others have sought to grow spiritually outside of religious institutions or communities.

Wade Clark Roof, a sociologist of religion, penned a seminal examination of faith and the boomers entitled *A Generation of Seekers: The Spiritual Journeys of the Baby Boom Generation.*[4] This 1993 book has been cited sympathetically by a number of scholars of leadership, including Jay Conger, Craig Johnson, and Judith Neal.[5] Roof contends that, to understand

---

[2] Jay Alden Conger, ed., *Spirit at Work: Discovering the Spirituality in Leadership*, first edn., The Jossey-Bass Management series (San Francisco: Jossey-Bass, 1994), 3–4; Judith A. Neal, "Spirituality in Management Education: A Guide to Resources," *Journal of Management Education* 21/1 (1997): 121; Sandra W. King and David M. Nichol, "A Burgeoning Interest in Spirituality and the Workplace: Exploring the Factors Driving It," *Business Research Yearbook* (1999): 719.

[3] One examination of the changes in religious and spiritual attitudes through different periods of the life cycle appears in Robert C. Fuller, *Religion and the Life Cycle* (Philadelphia: Fortress Press, 1988). Fuller includes an interesting discussion of the "search for meaning" (pp. 68–72) as a fundamental element in the midlife transition, marked by having children and increasing one's awareness of human limitations.

[4] Wade Clark Roof, *A Generation of Seekers: The Spiritual Journeys of the Baby Boom Generation* (San Francisco: Harper San Francisco, 1993); see also Wade Clark Roof, *The Spiritual Marketplace: Baby Boomers and the Remaking of American Religion* (Princeton University Press, 1999).

[5] Conger, *Spirit at Work*, 3–4; Craig E. Johnson, *Meeting the Ethical Challenges of Leadership: Casting Shadow or Light* (San Francisco: Sage, 2001); Neal, "Spirituality in Management Education: A Guide to Resources," 122. It is important to note that each of these three prominent scholars cites Roof's discussion of spirituality – specifically, Roof's discussion of the spiritual views of "Mollie," one of the representative boomers on whom Roof focuses: "Mollie's spirituality arises out of her own experience. In its truest sense, spirituality gives expression to the being that is in us; it has to do with feelings, with the power that comes from within, with knowing our deepest selves and what is sacred to us,

contemporary society and its leaders, it is necessary to understand the baby boomers:

[Boomers] enjoy enormous social and economic influence: They now own small businesses, occupy seats on corporate boards, and are rapidly moving into the front offices, taking on leadership and power positions. Across the country they are the volunteers filling posts in civic and community organizations. With the election of Bill Clinton and Al Gore, baby boomers now occupy the nation's highest offices . . . [The boomer generation] now comprises the bulk of our new leaders (in politics, business, education, religion, and so on).[6]

Like his predecessor in the White House, George W. Bush is also a baby boomer. With their influence and sheer numbers (accounting for almost a third of the total US population), boomers have brought their "seeking" into the workplace, especially via their leadership positions. Boomers are the prime market for books and seminars on spirituality in the workplace.[7]

As Roof has shown, the variety of religious and spiritual commitments of this generation is broad and disparate:

The term [spirituality] now conveys much more clarity and creativity: Boomers speak of creation spirituality, Eucharistic spirituality, Native American spirituality, Eastern spiritualities, Twelve-Step spiritualities, feminist spirituality, earth-based spirituality, eco-feminist spirituality, Goddess spirituality, and men's spirituality, as well as what would be considered traditional Judeo-Christian spiritualities.[8]

Thus the language of spirituality may be widespread, but it is not clear that boomers are seeking, or speaking about, the same things.

The talk of spirituality has been embraced by participants in formal religious institutions (churches, synagogues, mosques, temples, etc.) and by those who do not participate in such congregations. One of the remarkable aspects of the interest in spirituality talk is that many churchgoers, other religious adherents, and their leaders have employed it in shaping their message and programs.[9] Indeed, many would claim that it is nonreligious persons who are misappropriating the term. Among many nonmembers of religious groups, however, the personal spiritual quest, including exploration in the workplace, has become an alternate form of communal life. That is, employees who do not belong to religious congregations lack an

---

with, as Matthew Fox says, 'heart-knowledge' " (Roof, *A Generation of Seekers*, 64). Conger, Johnson, and Neal each attribute to Roof the definition Roof attributes to "Mollie." (None of the leadership scholars includes the first sentence included above in their quotations of Roof's text.) Roof's own view on spirituality is more complex.

[6] Roof, *A Generation of Seekers*, 3–4, 8.   [7] Billitteri, "Finding the Spirit at Work," 48.
[8] Roof, *A Generation of Seekers*, 243; see also Roof, *Spiritual Marketplace*.
[9] See Roof, *Spiritual Marketplace*, esp. pp. 93–96.

explicitly faith-based community with which to engage in conversation about their faith (not to mention to meditate, pray, or worship). They explore their spirituality in the other institutional contexts, like the workplace, in which they participate.

The proportion of Americans who are not members and who are not active participants, respectively, of religious congregations has increased in recent decades. In his study of American civic engagement, Robert Putnam concludes that, since the 1960s, church membership has experienced a slow decrease of about 10 percent. Putnam goes on to argue that actual engagement – regular participation – in religious activities has declined by as much as 50 percent.[10] Thus, Americans' search for spirituality has shifted significantly, but not totally, from religious institutions to other kinds of communities and contexts. Baby boomers, both inside and outside of faith-based communities, have embraced spirituality talk.

Immigration and widening diversity

The sheer number of religious traditions represented in the US following the 1965 Immigration and Naturalization Act has resulted in novel encounters in society and in the workplace. This demographic development has contributed to the spiritual quests undertaken by boomers and members of other generations alike. Eastern traditions and spiritualities have offered ways for religious seekers to explore religious and spiritual experiences without accepting the institutions and commitments of their parents' religions. Unfamiliar traditions such as Buddhism, Hinduism, and Chinese religions seem to have an exotic appeal for many boomers that Methodism, Episcopalianism, and Catholicism do not possess. These new traditions have increased the "supply" of religious resources by introducing alternate (though not necessarily incompatible or incommensurable) traditions from which seekers can "choose."[11] While some people have converted to Islam, Buddhism, and other world religions now commonly found in America,[12] the vast majority of seekers have not converted but have instead drawn upon practices or concepts of these traditions to construct their own individual or personal spirituality.

In addition to the literal migration of religious newcomers since 1965, the wider phenomenon of globalization has transformed the spiritual resources

---

[10] Robert D. Putnam, *Bowling Alone: The Collapse and Revival of American Community* (New York: Simon & Schuster, 2000), 69–72.

[11] Roof, *Spiritual Marketplace*, 89–90.

[12] Diana L. Eck, *A New Religious America: How a "Christian Country" Has Now Become the World's Most Religiously Diverse Nation* (San Francisco: Harper San Francisco, 2001).

available to Americans. People connected to the Internet have access to texts and information about a myriad of religious traditions and have the chance to discuss spiritual matters with others around the world. Roof makes the point in this way:

Once perceived as worlds apart, the distance between Jerusalem and Benares has greatly shrunk: people move more freely between religious worlds via travel, reading, television, and other media. Religious symbols, teachings, and practices are easily "disembedded," that is, lifted out of one cultural setting, and "re-embedded" into another. Meditation techniques imported from India are repackaged in the United States; Native American teachings extracted from their indigenous context pop up in other settings . . . Yet depth to any tradition is often lost, the result being thin layers of cultural and religious meaning. What often follows is pastiche, collage, religious pluralism *within* the individual, bricolage, mixing of codes, religion à la carte, to cite some of the terms now in vogue describing how the individual is thrust into a position of having to pull religious themes together from a variety of sources.[13]

This type of change is not a demographic change per se; rather, it reflects an increased immigration of ideas and practices. Yet it complements the post-1965 demographic changes by promoting the presence and availability of different religious symbols and spiritual paths. This variety expands the range of choices that individuals confront as they seek to construct their own spirituality, but it also tends to de-contextualize ideas and rituals from the wider narratives in which they make sense.

New Age traditions

One of the most significant and complicated developments in American religion that contributes to interest in spirituality at work and elsewhere is the rise of New Age traditions. Indeed, along with a new public Christian evangelicalism, New Age language fundamentally shapes discussions of contemporary workplace spirituality.

What is New Age religion? In her critical overview, Catherine Albanese traces many of the aspects of a New Age movement that coalesced in the 1970s. These roots point to a variety of ideas and practices emphasizing a new era of self-discovery, integration, and harmony. While its pre-history is based in movements of metaphysical religion like Transcendentalism and Christian Science, New Age religion also contains elements of Jungian psychology, transpersonal psychology, the human potential movement, parapsychology, holistic medicine and healing, astrology, and

---

[13] Roof, *Spiritual Marketplace*, 73.

environmentalism. In addition, New Age religion has borrowed selectively from Native American traditions, and the already noted influx of people and ideas of Eastern religious traditions has had a profound impact on expanding New Age ideas. Significantly, the employment of aspects of Buddhism, Hinduism, Sikhism, and (Islamic) Sufism added legitimacy to New Age ideas.[14]

It is important to acknowledge, then, that the New Age religion refers to many distinct phenomena. Albanese offers a helpful distinction between the *ordinary* and *extraordinary* aspects of New Age spirituality:

On the one hand, there are those thinkers with environmental, transformational, and holistic-health agendas, and, on the other, those "actors" who have immersed themselves in New Age practices such as channeling and work with crystals.[15]

In this frame, the ordinary refers to those practices and concepts that involve integrating or enhancing everyday human reality; extraordinary elements require viewing a "transcendent world of entities." The New Age language of the participants common to both ordinary and extraordinary forms and the common rejection – though with selective appropriation! – of traditional religion have shaped American society, including the workplace.

The noninstitutional or quasi-institutional nature of New Age practice has made it conducive to expression at the office. Most adherents do not belong to formalized New Age congregations. Instead, they tend to emphasize individual faith expression while also participating in short-term or ad hoc groups and communities in a fluid way.[16] New Age adherents are much more likely to claim to be "spiritual" rather than "religious." The view that New Age religion is not exclusive or dogmatic but universal makes it seem less divisive or confrontational in the workplace. The mixing and matching of various New Age and other religious ideas is a prime example of "choosing" one's faith that defines the current era of American religion and spirituality. Scholars of spirituality and leadership tend to accept as unproblematic the idea that individuals can simply cobble together ideas and practices from other traditions without attending to the context or community in which these ideas and practices had coherence. In my view, this uncritical stance toward a-contextual choice seems particularly striking when discussing a tradition such as New Age that emphasizes integration and holism.

Albanese posits a new kind of rigid orthodoxy that is appearing in New Age traditions.[17] This helps to account for the strikingly uniform themes

---

[14] Catherine L. Albanese, *America: Religions and Religion*, third edn. (Belmont, CA: Wadsworth, 1999), 350–59.
[15] Ibid., 361.   [16] Ibid., 368.   [17] Ibid., 350–69.

in the literature on spirituality and leadership (for example, wholeness, integration, self-help, human potential, mysticism) and their resonance with New Age concepts. While New Age adherents would emphasize their individual journeys, many such journeys bear a strong resemblance to one another and to an emerging orthodoxy in popular and scholarly writings on spirituality and leadership.

A public Christian evangelicalism

Although New Age participants and Christian evangelicals are highly critical of each other, important similarities are evident in the two groups' language and religious expression. Evangelicals and New Age adherents both embrace a language of spirituality, personal exploration, and journey.[18] The New Age movement involves more dogmatism and ritualized practice than adherents would acknowledge; conversely, evangelicals embrace, as do New Age proponents, the language of healing and transformation. Both movements are "spiritually democratic" – promoting the voice and agency of individual believers.[19] Perhaps most important for workplace spirituality, both groups see the importance of applying one's spiritual beliefs and experiences to common aspects of life, including work. In Albanese's language, "the extraordinary guides – and transfigures – everyday life for believers, New Age and Christian evangelical alike."[20] The distinction between New Age and evangelical expressions of faith and work, however, should not be lost due to a common use of spirituality talk. Nash and McClennan, for instance, properly note the important differences in practice between living out one's Christian faith at work and the use of the language of spirituality by proponents of the "spirituality in the business movement."[21]

Christian engagement in public life, of course, is by no means a new reality in modern America, and evangelicals have played a central role in that public involvement. The social reformations of the nineteenth and early twentieth centuries were informed and, to a great extent, motivated by faith-inspired leaders.[22] Many reformers were Christian women who applied

[18] Roof, *A Generation of Seekers*, 117–48.
[19] Albanese, *America: Religions and Religion*, 388–89.   [20] Ibid., 388.
[21] Laura L. Nash and Scotty McClennan, *Church on Sunday, Work on Monday: The Challenge of Fusing Christian Values with Business Life* (San Francisco: Jossey-Bass, 2001).
[22] In his discussion of the limits of public reason, John Rawls acknowledges the importance of Christians in the abolitionist movement and the fundamental contribution that their faith-based "comprehensive" vision made to oppose injustice (within a context in which he claims that "public reason" was not "complete"). See John Rawls, *Political Liberalism, The John Dewey Essays in Philosophy No. 4* (New York: Columbia University Press, 1993), 247–54; see also John Rawls, "The Idea of Public Reason Revisited," *University of Chicago Law Review* 64 (1997).

their faith to address social ills.[23] It would be impossible to understand the US civil rights movement without considering the fundamental role played by African American churches (and other Christian and Jewish congregations) in contributing ideas of liberation, freedom, and equality and in contributing institutional support by providing meeting places, funding, and committed people.[24] The new public evangelicalism has arisen in response to a perceived loss of Christian morality from American public life. The rise in political prominence – the significance of which has been the subject of fierce debate – is just one result of an increasing mobilization in many Christian circles. Many evangelicals perceive that the US (and the globalizing world) is slowly sliding away from God and toward religious and moral relativism, the decline of families, and a general permissiveness and lack of discipline and order.

Christian engagement in public life, including the workplace, is not restricted either to evangelicals or fundamentalists. In addition to the social activism on both sides of the political spectrum, mainline and moderate Christians have also sought a prominent voice in public life.[25] It is unfair to classify the overall increase in public Christian engagement as wholly reactionary or as the brainchild of Christian fundamentalists. Mitroff and Denton, in their typology of "models for fostering [corporate] spirituality," make such a mistake. They relegate the treatment of Christian workplace spirituality to a chapter entitled "Taking Over Your Company for Christ: The Religion-Based Organization." They depend upon a publication by W. H. Nix, *Transforming Your Workplace for Christ*, to suggest that Christians in general are interested in converting all co-workers and storming their corporations to accomplish a religious coup of the company.[26] Religious belief, in the Christian evangelical movement and beyond, is not

[23] Constance Buchanan, *Choosing to Lead: Women and the Crisis of American Values* (Boston: Beacon Press, 1996); Evelyn Brooks Higginbotham, *Righteous Discontent: The Women's Movement in the Black Baptist Church, 1880–1920* (Cambridge, MA: Harvard University Press, 1993).

[24] Aldon Morris, "The Black Church in the Civil Rights Movement: The SCLC as the Decentralized, Radical Arm of the Black Church," in *Disruptive Religion: The Force of Faith in Social Movement Activism*, ed. Christian Smith (New York: Routledge, 1996); see also Richard Couto, "Narrative, Free Space, and Political Leadership in Social Movements," *Journal of Politics* 55 (1993); Christian Smith, "Correcting a Curious Neglect, or Bringing Religion Back In," in *Disruptive Religion: The Force of Faith in Social Movement Activism*, ed. Christian Smith (New York: Routledge, 1996).

[25] Ronald F. Thiemann, *Religion in Public Life: A Dilemma for Democracy* (Washington, DC: Georgetown University Press, 1996); Robert Wuthnow and John H. Evans, eds., *The Quiet Hand of God: Faith-Based Activism and the Public Role of Mainline Protestantism* (Berkeley: University of California Press, 2002).

[26] Ian I. Mitroff and Elizabeth A. Denton, *A Spiritual Audit of Corporate America: A Hard Look at Spirituality, Religion, and Values in the Workplace*, first edn, The Warren Bennis Signature series (San Francisco: Jossey-Bass, 1999).

adequately described when scholars of management simply discount all of it as reactionary, confrontational, or hostile.

Christian thinkers from a variety of perspectives have become interested in integrating the various aspects of life with their faith; they articulate it differently as applying worship to work, bridging Sundays and Mondays, or living out their Christian vocation in a secular workplace.[27] Scholars writing from faith-based frameworks have tended to reject the "spiritual takeover" model that Denton and Mitroff employ in favor of less "extreme" and "objectionable" models of generic spirituality.[28] In order to distance themselves from the model, many have downplayed particularistic language that refers specifically to Christian doctrines and have chosen a language of faith that they believe adherents of other traditions could also embrace. Even the well-known approach of "servant leadership" stems from Robert Greenleaf's attempt to draw deeply from Christian themes, in conversation with Eastern traditions, in a way that is applicable to many leaders.[29]

Christians in general, and evangelicals in particular, tend not to acknowledge the problems with either the past or present-day cultural establishment of Christianity. Nor have they taken fully into account the current reality of religious diversity (including nonbelievers and secularists as well as other religious traditions) in the United States in their proposals for a recovery of religion, spirituality, or values in the workplace. Even broad-minded calls for faith-based renewal of civic life or the workplace often seem to equate religion with Christianity.

The visible signs of disestablishment of Christianity in recent decades have galvanized Christian evangelicals in particular to reclaim a prominent public voice. The workplace has become a major staging ground for this expression. The fact that many evangelicals have opted to use the language of spirituality instead of emphasizing Christian theological language has contributed to their relative invisibility in the analysis of workplace spirituality.

Together, the aging of the baby boomers and their interest in spirituality and the influx of immigrants with the accompanying confluence of a variety of religious ideas have contributed to disparate and frequent spiritual

---

[27] A few different perspectives on Christian faith and leadership include Nash and McClennan, *Church on Sunday, Work on Monday*, William E. Diehl, *Thank God It's Monday!* (Philadelphia: Fortress Press, 1982), and Gregory F. Pierce, *Spirituality @ Work: 10 Ways to Balance Your Life on-the-Job* (Chicago: Loyola Press, 2001). The Avodah Institute, founded and coordinated by David Miller, seeks to help Christian business leaders integrate faith and work. See http://www.avodahinstitute.org.

[28] Mitroff and Denton, *A Spiritual Audit of Corporate America*, 58.

[29] Robert K. Greenleaf, *Servant Leadership: A Journey into the Nature of Legitimate Power and Greatness* (New York: Paulist Press, 1977).

encounters in various institutions of public life. The boomers' flight from religious institutions, the influx of world religions in the US, the coalescence of New Age traditions, and a heightened desire of evangelicals to apply their faith at work all combine to make the workplace a more important context for spiritual expression, exploration, and potential conflict. Along with these demographic and religious changes, a variety of social and economic factors also deserve consideration, a task to which we now turn our attention.

AN INCREASED STANDARD OF LIVING

Climbing the ladder of needs?

A number of scholars in psychology, sociology, and business predict that, as the standard of living in a society goes up, interest in nonmaterial or even spiritual matters also increases. With material gains, the time and energy required to meet basic human needs decreases, and people tend to shift their focus to meeting other kinds of need. Maslow's hierarchy of needs is often cited in the leadership literature as important for understanding the motivation of leaders and followers alike.[30] The literature on spirituality and leadership generally classifies spirituality as a higher-order need, most often in relation to *self-actualization*, the top tier of Maslow's pyramid. According to such a view of meeting needs, the heightened interest in spirituality has accompanied, and is partly explained by, the rise in average incomes in the postwar period. Tischler, for instance, takes a wide historical "socio-economic" view in claiming that the interest in spirituality in business is a result of the postmodern age of relative affluence and the satisfaction of basic needs (at least in the developed world). In agrarian times, he asserts, a majority of the population struggled for subsistence, but the transformations that accompanied industrialization brought wealth and flexible social structure to the populace. Now many Western societies have advanced "to a post-industrial society that focuses on individual achievement and self-actualization growth for as many people as possible in a socially, economically, and environmentally sustainable and responsible manner."[31] That reality, Tischler suggests, allows persons to nurture their spirituality.

[30] Abraham H. Maslow, *Motivation and Personality* (New York: Harper, 1954); James MacGregor Burns, *Leadership* (New York: Harper Torchbooks, 1978), esp. 61–80; Richard L. Hughes, Robert C. Ginnett, and Gordon J. Curphy, *Leadership: Enhancing the Lessons of Experience*, third edn. (Boston: Irwin McGraw-Hill, 1999), 395–96.
[31] Len Tischler, "The Growing Interest in Spirituality in Business: A Long-Term Socio-Economic Explanation," *Journal of Organizational Change Management* 12/4 (1999).

Tischler's sweeping thesis is problematic for a number of reasons. First, economic data show that most of the gains in real per capita income growth for US citizens occurred in the first three decades of the postwar period and not in the past three decades. The median family income figure, for example, increased in real terms by only 10 percentage points between 1979 and 1997[32] – and it is the period since 1980 in which the interest in spirituality and leadership has been greatest. Tischler claims that "[i]n the USA and most of Western Europe in the 1990s, even when [they are] laid off most people are not going to starve to death if they are out of work for several months or even for a year or more."[33] This may be a reasonable contrast to earlier times or poorer societies, but it appears to be an imprecise argument to account for the workplace spirituality movement and its marked rise in the late 1980s. Further, it is not clear that the American or European populations prior to the Industrial Revolution – not to mention the Asian, African, or Latin American populations of today – should be seen as any less spiritual or self-actualized than contemporary people. Such a grand historical narrative, therefore, is not particularly helpful.

Does money buy happiness?

A related but less ambitious effort to interrelate rising American affluence and the interest in spirituality is located in another body of social–scientific literature. In recent decades a number of scholars have engaged in debate over the question, Does money buy happiness?[34] Sociologists and economists have demonstrated, in broad terms, that *relative* income does, in fact, have a significant impact on one's reported happiness or satisfaction with one's life. At the same time, *overall* societal levels of reported happiness have remained almost unchanged over the post-World War II years, even when national income per capita has increased dramatically. These social scientists tend to argue that economic growth in developed economies has occurred far above the income levels required to meet Maslow's lower-order

---

[32] Paul Krugman, "For Richer," *New York Times* Magazine, October 20, 2002.

[33] Tischler, "The Growing Interest in Spirituality in Business," 274.

[34] Richard J. Easterlin, "Does Money Buy Happiness?," *The Public Interest* 30 (1973); Richard J. Easterlin, "Does Economic Growth Improve the Human Lot?," in *Nations and Households in Economic Growth: Essays in Honour of Moses Abramowitz*, ed. Paul A. David and Melvin W. Reder (New York: Academic Press, 1974); Richard J. Easterlin, "Will Raising the Incomes of All Increase the Happiness of All?," *Journal of Economic Behavior and Organization* 27 (1995); Robert Frank, *Luxury Fever: Why Money Fails to Satisfy in an Age of Affluence* (New York: Free Press, 1999); other references are surveyed in Douglas A. Hicks, "Inequality, Globalization, and Leadership: 'Keeping Up with the Joneses' across National Boundaries," *The Annual of the Society of Christian Ethics* 21 (2001).

needs of subsistence and security. For most Americans the increase in income in the postwar years allowed not just subsistence but also affluence.
This discussion suggests a growing disaffection with American affluence
and the subsequent search for other sources of happiness. With this trend
has come increased questioning of whether income improvements can be
a guarantor of happiness – and an accompanying focus on other spheres of
life.[35]

In a similar vein, some scholars of leadership and spirituality have emphasized that spirituality is a rejection of the excessive materialism of contemporary society.[36] Such a development is consistent, in general terms, with
the realization that obtaining material goods only goes so far in meeting
one's needs. The quest for spirituality in the workplace, on this view, is part
of the search beyond income for human fulfillment, meaning, and purpose,
but, unlike the simple Maslowian view, the interest results not from having
met basic needs but from having been unsatisfied by material excess.

The commodification of spirituality?

A less benign interpretation of workplace spirituality would explain much
of the movement not as a rejection of materialism, but as itself a manifestation of the marketized society that is under criticism. That is, spirituality
is the latest item to be commodified and packaged for sale. Proponents
of this explanation cite the proliferation of merchandise associated with
the "spirituality industry" – its books, tapes, seminars, programs, music,
and so on[37] – as a line of products that generates tremendous profits. This
aspect of the current boom in spirituality – its commercial development
as a new market – should not be underestimated. It is consistent with the
general shift in the global economy from heavy manufactured goods, to
lighter goods, to services and entertainment.[38] Such an analysis acknowledges an economic transformation similar to the one Tischler noted, but
the interpretation of the factors contributing to the interest in spirituality
is distinct. For Tischler, the spiritual quest is driven by the healthy pro-
gression in individuals' ability to achieve higher-order needs; in contrast,
the largely supply-driven view of economic transformation understands
the spirituality movement as a result of the perceived needs promoted by

---

[35] Hicks, "Inequality, Globalization, and Leadership."
[36] Gilbert W. Fairholm, *Perspectives on Leadership: From the Science of Management to Its Spiritual Heart*
(Westport, CT: Quorum, 1998), 124–25; Rabindra N. Kanungo and Manuel Mendonca, "What
Leaders Cannot Do Without: The Spiritual Dimensions of Leadership," in *Spirit at Work: Discovering
the Spirituality in Leadership*, ed. Jay Alden Conger (San Francisco: Jossey-Bass, 1994), 162–65.
[37] See Roof, *Spiritual Marketplace*, 98–100.
[38] Benjamin R. Barber, *Jihad Vs. McWorld* (New York: Ballantine Books, 1995).

would-be sellers of goods and services. Supporting the view of commodifica-tion of spiritual goods and services does not require arguing that spirituality itself is an invented need. It emphasizes, rather, that marketers try to con-vince people that the goods and services they are promoting will actually meet such a need.

It is not possible to state definitively whether the interest in spirituality and religion in the workplace is a rejection of the culture of material-ism or just the latest expression of it. Arguably, it is both. Indeed, the spirituality-and-leadership rubric is so broad that it is not possible to make this assessment for the movement as a whole. It is hard to deny, however, that publishers and other media companies have profited a great deal from the market products associated with spirituality and leadership in the work-place. If the quest for spirituality reflects an effort to escape materialism, it has not succeeded in realizing that end.

TRANSFORMATIONS IN WORK AND SOCIETY

Transcending Taylorism

A central development in the US workplace over the course of the twentieth century was the rejection of the rational and mechanistic view of labor typi-fied by Frederick Winslow Taylor's "principles of scientific management," or Taylorism, and the increasing recognition that workers are motivated by more than rationality or narrowly considered self-interest. Time-and-motion studies could only go so far in increasing efficiency.[39] Spirituality, according to some scholars, is simply another facet of the human character which warrants consideration when viewing the human – whether worker or boss – as a whole person.[40]

Jerry Biberman and Michael Whitty outline such a "paradigm shift" in their article "A Postmodern Spiritual Future for Work."[41] They argue that the "spiritual paradigm" replaces the earlier "modern paradigm" in which human persons were viewed simply as rational animals that could

---

[39] The stages and contours of these transformations are well explained in Joanne B. Ciulla, *The Working Life: The Promise and Betrayal of Modern Work* (New York: Times Books/ Random House, 2000), esp. pp. 90–168.

[40] Ciulla (ibid.) discusses the recent turn to spirituality as part of "the search for something more" on pp. 219–24. She is critical of many spiritual practices at work for reasons that complement my own account. While Ciulla tends to prefer that religion or spirituality be expressed apart from the workplace, my approach seeks to forge a framework in which workers are free to express their genuine religious and spiritual convictions to a significant degree.

[41] Jerry Biberman and Michael Whitty, "A Postmodern Spiritual Future for Work," *Journal of Organizational Change Management* 10/2 (1997); See also Fairholm, *Perspectives on Leadership*.

be conditioned to be efficient. In that earlier view, people are motivated by self-interest and competition with other workers. The spiritual paradigm broadens the account of human nature and human motivation. It incorporates the developments in understanding the workplace not merely as a conglomeration of individuals (leaders and employees) but in terms of team dynamics and interrelationships.[42] Biberman and Whitty's description of the postmodern, spiritual workplace typifies various frameworks of leadership studies that portray leadership as a spiritual relational process or system. However, much about the spiritual paradigm is not really spiritual at all, unless one applies an all-encompassing definition to the term. It is possible to reject the modern, mechanistic paradigm without including matters explicitly religious or spiritual. The current attention in leadership studies on teams, interdependence, systems theory, and organizational culture and values complements many of the themes emphasized in workplace spirituality. This reality helps account for how spirituality talk has readily entered a sphere of society purported to be wholly secular, but whether spirituality as a term should be seen to encompass and even subsume these other phenomena deserves fuller attention.

One important and relevant trend in leadership and management is what Gill D. Robinson calls "person-centered management" or Jeanne Plas labels "person-centered leadership."[43] Under differing terminology, scholars argue that "the whole person" comes to work. That is, the identity and background of the worker or employer influence a person's potential and actual contribution to a production process. Hickman and Lee describe person-centered management as "an approach that focuses on the employee as a complex, multifaceted individual whose functioning in the workplace is not isolated from his or her functioning as a total person."[44] Various scholars of spirituality and leadership have invoked similar approaches to emphasize that people do not, alas cannot, leave their beliefs and commitments at the workplace door. Many of these scholars, however, only go part way with Hickman's insight on the whole person; they admit generic *spirituality* talk, but insist that *religion* is divisive for the workplace.[45]

To the extent that person-centered management has been implemented, it entails a positive development for employees. The new conception of

[42] Biberman and Whitty, "A Postmodern Spiritual Future for Work."
[43] Gill D. Robinson, "Person-Centered Management," *Black Women of Achievement Magazine* 1 (1998); Jeanne M. Plas, *Person-Centered Leadership: An American Approach to Participatory Management* (Thousand Oaks, CA: Sage, 1996).
[44] Gill Robinson Hickman and Dalton S. Lee, *Managing Human Resources in the Public Sector: A Shared Responsibility* (Fort Worth: Harcourt College Publishers, 2001), 138.
[45] See ch. 3 below.

work transcends treating people as machines or simply as means to the ends of profitability. To the extent that spirituality talk and explicit use of religiously based ethical perspectives on humane working conditions have contributed to workers' rights and protections, faith-based perspectives at the workplace have had positive effects. This is not to say, of course, that employers have not utilized progressive concepts, including spirituality talk, to produce newer, subtler ways to dominate workers. Joanne Ciulla's discussion of "bogus empowerment," for example, reveals that high-profile attention to new management concepts often does not translate into real improvements in the agency or voice of workers.[46] Thus, it is necessary to consider some of the potentially detrimental effects when employers introduce spirituality or religion into a workplace in ways that are coercive to some or all employees. As the language of empowerment has been employed to give a false sense of agency or control to workers, so, too, spirituality talk has the potential to take unfair advantage of workers. Although phrases like person-centered leadership can help employees to enjoy a better working environment, these phrases can also allow bosses to make unreasonable demands that impinge upon workers' personal time or home life. Like other concepts and ideas about good organizational leadership, spirituality talk can be abused.

Women entering the workplace

Another important factor contributing to the interest in spirituality in the workplace is the increased participation of women in the business world. Wuthnow's analysis of the Economic Values Survey of US workers suggests that traditional religious teachings have contributed to keeping women out of the workplace:

Religious teachings have often been interpreted in such a way that women were encouraged either not to participate in the labor force at all, or if they did participate, to subordinate such activities to household duties not expected of their husbands. While many of these traditional teachings have been challenged, there is still some evidence that the more religiously committed a woman is, the less likely she is to participate in the labor force, or to do so full-time.[47]

Wuthnow determined, however, that, once they do enter the labor market, women are more likely than men to discuss faith in their workplace.[48]

---

[46] Joanne B. Ciulla, "Leadership and the Problem of Bogus Empowerment," in *Ethics: The Heart of Leadership*, ed. Joanne B. Ciulla (Westport, CT: Praeger, 1998).
[47] Robert Wuthnow, *God and Mammon in America* (New York: Free Press, 1994), 43.
[48] Ibid., 74.

(Albanese also suggests that women are more likely than men to participate in New Age spirituality at work and elsewhere.[49]) The same public–private distinction that relegated women to the private sphere also kept religion and spirituality out of the public sphere. Why is this so? Women are less likely to hold a "religion in private" ethic, and they tend to be more open to speaking about their faith. It is also worth considering that traditionally women have been excluded from leadership positions in Christian, Jewish, and other congregations.[50] Women's expression of their faith within those religious institutions has been subject to the constraints of orthodoxy imposed by predominantly male leaders. It would not be simple, of course, to establish causally that women therefore tend to seek opportunities outside of religious institutions to express their faith, but it is a question deserving further study. What does seem clear is that women's broad entrance into the workplace has contributed to the discussion of spirituality in the workplace.

At the same time, the predominant emphasis in the literature on studying the faith of leaders (i.e., CEOs and high-profile founders of companies), coupled with the continued relative exclusion of women from top corporate positions, has resulted in men being cited more often than women as the heroes of workplace spirituality. Though different in their spiritual and religious beliefs and approaches, CEOs Tom Chappell (Tom's of Maine), C. W. Pollard (ServiceMaster), Max De Pree (Herman Miller), and S. Truett Cathy (Chick-Fil-A) are frequently touted as role models of spiritual leadership. No "great women" have yet attained such prominence in the spirituality and the workplace literature. In this sense, gender divisions play out in this movement in ways that parallel both religious institutions and many prominent social movements: women comprise the majority of the participants, but men get the credit and the high-profile leadership positions.[51]

Seeking but not finding spirituality at work?

The fascination with spirituality in the workplace arose at a time in which other important institutions of civic life were declining. Robert Putnam's seminal work in this area reveals that the social bonds that unite individuals into civic communities beyond the immediate family have weakened in

---

[49] Albanese, *America: Religions and Religion*, 367.

[50] Mark Chaves, *Ordaining Women: Culture and Conflict in Religious Organizations* (Cambridge, MA: Harvard University Press, 1999).

[51] Ibid.; Jo Ann Gibson Robinson, *The Montgomery Bus Boycott and the Women Who Started It*, ed. David J. Garrow (Knoxville, TN: University of Tennessee Press, 1987); Gill R. Hickman and Georgia Sorenson, "Invisible Leadership: Acts on Behalf of a Common Purpose," in *Building Leadership Bridges*, ed. C. Cherrey and L. R. Matusak (College Park, MD: James MacGregor Burns Academy of Leadership, 2002).

recent decades. Putnam employs the vivid description of Americans who are "bowling alone": more Americans are bowling today than twenty years ago, but membership in bowling leagues has fallen by 40 percent since 1980.[52] This image reflects the broader decrease in participation in civic organizations, neighborhood groups, parent–teacher associations, scouting groups, labor organizations, and religious institutions. This decline of civic engagement has led to a decrease in *social capital*, those networks and norms of trust that increase the quality of social relations within a society.[53]

In the sphere of the workplace, Putnam acknowledges that there is some evidence for increased social activities, bonds, and friendships at the office. Workplace spirituality meetings and prayer groups fit within this rubric. He notes that team building and related activities "became all the rage in management circles" in the 1980s and 1990s. Many scholars of workplace spirituality emphasize, as Putnam does, that people have turned to workplace spirituality because other kinds of civic associations have diminished in quality and importance.[54] But Putnam mounts strong evidence to show that, in overall terms, workplace bonds have not replaced the social capital lost by declining civic or religious participation. He offers empirical evidence to assert that workplace friendships, on average, do not have the depth or endurance that even neighborhood friendships do. While workplaces have made worker-friendly changes that create a sense of community, managers have also implemented technological monitoring (such as e-mail monitoring and surveillance cameras) and made other changes that require workers to guard what they say and do.[55] Thus Putnam's analysis suggests that workplace spirituality may be part of a quest for community due to the qualitative and quantitative decline of other kinds of social association. At the same time, it points to the limitations that workplace relationships can have in fulfilling social or spiritual needs. It is worth exploring whether the instrumental nature of workplace relationships, constrained by the pay-for-work nature of the market, makes impossible, or at least significantly undermines, the intrinsic nature of spiritual or religious growth.

Nourishing or pacifying hungry souls?

On a related note, scholars emphasize that employees are searching for meaning, purpose, and even spirituality in their workplaces in response to

---

[52] Putnam, *Bowling Alone*, 111–13.   [53] Ibid., 19–20.

[54] King and Nichol, "A Burgeoning Interest in Spirituality and the Workplace: Exploring the Factors Driving It," 718, 721.

[55] Putnam, *Bowling Alone*, 87–92.

an era of increased job insecurity.[56] An environment of downsizing and re-engineering has discouraged many workers from investing in relationships with co-workers who might not be co-workers for long.[57] Spiritual interest has heightened, in this view, in response to downsizing, as workers "hunger for jobs that nourish their souls and that provide some sense of meaning in the chaotic and unpredictable workplace."[58] To the extent that such a view is accurate, workplace spirituality has become a kind of opiate that helps dull the new reality of workplace instability. Stating this issue in Marxian terms emphasizes the problematic nature of such a corporate phenomenon. Some scholars note their concern about developments that have produced an insecure workplace, but most accept employment instability uncritically as part of the reality of the competitive workplace. They choose to highlight the positive feature, namely, that, if and when employees face the pink slip, at least they can do so with a happy spirit. It should be clear that this type of spirituality talk can play an exploitative role in pacifying vulnerable workers.

Motivating good, efficient workers

Much of the literature on spirituality is framed in terms of creating a work environment that is conducive to high morale and, in turn, high productivity. After all, the paradigm shifts from the modern worker, to total quality management, to teams, even to a spiritual frame, have occurred largely in response to improved understandings of how best to motivate employees. Many scholars make no apologies when they claim that spirituality "will help companies realize a multitude of significant benefits" and "get the maximum return possible" from their workers and other inputs.[59] The "value-added" benefit of spirituality in the workplace, it is often argued, will accrue to both individual workers and to the organization as a whole. In other words, it is a fortunate coincidence that spirituality in the workplace contributes to the well-being of workers and to the profits of the firm.

Although this claim may be true in some, or even many, specific instances, a number of problematic dimensions to the claim in general are apparent. First, the literature seems to suggest that having more spiritual workers will make one's company more economically successful. The claim

---

[56] King and Nichol, "A Burgeoning Interest in Spirituality and the Workplace: Exploring the Factors Driving It," 720–21.
[57] Putnam, *Bowling Alone*, 87–89.
[58] Neal, "Spirituality in Management Education: A Guide to Resources," 122.
[59] Fairholm, *Perspectives on Leadership*, 118.

that spirituality leads to profitability is an assumption that should not be made a priori. Rather, it deserves careful scrutiny on descriptive and normative grounds. Second, much like Ciulla's worries about the language of empowerment, perhaps there is legitimate cause for concern that organizations may be promoting "bogus spirituality." At a minimum, the spiritual messages or programs offered – or simply supported – by organizations should be examined critically. Consider this thought experiment: would an organization support an expression of spirituality that called into question some fundamental aspect of the organization's purpose? How critical or "radical" could a spiritual message be before it was no longer supported by the company's leaders? When spirituality is defined instrumentally in terms of productivity, critical or prophetic faith-based expressions are defined away.

Working weekends

A final factor contributing to the rise in workplace spirituality is the overall increase in working hours for the US population. The economist Juliet Schor calls this labor phenomenon "the overworked American" problem.[60] Schor has shown that, in the 1970s and 1980s, the average labor force participant increased his or her total working time – the sum of hours on the job and hours doing household labor – by over 160 hours per year. That is, the average working person had squeezed in the equivalent of an additional four weeks of full-time labor during each year.[61] The increased burden of labor hours for men and women – particularly given the latter group's influx into the formal labor market and continued responsibilities at home – has led to a significant loss of hours in which men and women may engage in activities outside of the workplace. Importantly, this is a dimension of the decline in social capital Putnam outlines so well in his book. Scholars of workplace spirituality have similarly noted the tensions workers feel between commitment to their employer and to other spheres of life.[62] As one vivid example, consider Herman Lea, featured in a front-page article in *The Wall Street Journal*: "Juggling Act: More Plants Go 24/7, and

[60] Juliet Schor, *The Overworked American: The Unexpected Decline of Leisure* (New York: Basic Books, 1992).

[61] Ibid., 35. Schor also notes that the percentage of unemployed and underemployed persons, especially men, has made the overall trend for all Americans slightly more complex. For the adult population as a whole, the average increase in total hours worked per year has risen by 47 hours per year. Schor, *The Overworked American*, 36–41.

[62] Heather Hopfl, "The Making of the Corporate Acolyte: Some Thoughts on Charismatic Leadership and the Reality of Organizational Commitment," *Journal of Management Studies* 29/1 (1992).

Workers Are Left at Sixes and Sevens."[63] Working for Goodyear Tire and Rubber Company in Danville, Virginia, Lea discerned a calling from God in 1996 to become a Christian preacher. He would serve as an occasional preacher at churches in the Danville area, but, when Goodyear changed its production and employment schedules to keep the plant open twenty-four hours a day, seven days a week, Lea was required to work a few Sundays per month. He is able to preach only on those Sundays when he is not required to work at Goodyear. Other workers interviewed for *The Wall Street Journal* indicate similar inabilities to be counted on for civic meetings or family commitments in the evenings or on weekends. For these employees, time spent at work has crowded out civic, family, and religious time.

Many employees and employers have increasingly brought spirituality to the workplace because they do not have time to spend in religious communities. It is important to see this contextual reality – the overworked American problem – as a contributor to the increased interest in workplace spirituality. If people bring their whole person to work, and they work long hours, they may not have the energy or time to engage in other important spheres of life. Spiritual and religious concerns may be more likely to surface in the workplace when people have little time or energy to take them anywhere else.

CONCLUSIONS

Through this wide-ranging analysis at the societal and the workplace levels, I have sought to shed light on the host of factors that have contributed to recent interest in workplace spirituality. In overall terms, scholars have paid particular attention to the aging of the baby boomers, the rejection of Taylorism, and spirituality as a response to an insecure workplace. Other factors have received less emphasis, including immigration and globalization, public Christian evangelicalism, women's expanded presence in the labor force, the commodification of spirituality, and the potential for exploiting spirituality to fuel profits.

Throughout this chapter, I have sought to point out the problematic aspects of the interest in spirituality in the workplace, while at the same time recognizing the potentially positive aspects of the development. On the positive side, we should recognize that employers and employees alike can draw upon resources of religious and spiritual traditions for cooperation,

[63] Timothy Aeppel, "Juggling Act: More Plants Go 24/7, and Workers Are Left at Sixes and Sevens," *Wall Street Journal*, July 24, 2001.

mutual understanding, personal satisfaction, and the creation of a just working environment. Workplace seminars addressing religious worldviews in response to the September 2001 terrorism – for instance, Ford Motor Company's discussion of Islam and religious tolerance for its employees[64] – offer examples of how using the workplace as a public forum can lead to positive outcomes. The commitment to treat workers as whole persons, and not merely as inputs to a production process, can lead to genuine and beneficial progress toward creating a humane workplace. Yet such spirituality talk can also be employed to the detriment of workers or to distract employees and scholars from more pressing problems. For instance, instead of emphasizing the availability of spiritual resources to help workers cope with downsizing, scholars could offer a critical perspective on the painful realities of downsizing itself and the often unequal power balance between management and labor that allows some firms to downsize without proper attention to the impacts on employees' lives. Corporate spirituality and values statements should not mask the unjust and immoral business practices that thrust Enron and WorldCom into international headlines. Putnam's work on social capital and civic engagement suggests that trying to find spirituality in the workplace will ultimately fail because of the fundamentally instrumental nature of workplace relationships. The long hours that many Americans now work may create the need and the opportunity for people to discuss religious ideas at work, but the problem of excessive work hours is also worthy of scholars' and leaders' attention.

It is not possible to specify the precise impact of each of the factors noted above on the new interest in spirituality in the workplace. The account of societal and workplace trends outlined here avoids viewing the interest in workplace spirituality as an isolated or a-contextual reality. It also cuts against the grain of viewing workplace spirituality as a matter limited to a few individual leaders who have discovered spirituality talk and then let it trickle down into their companies. It is necessary to analyze in more detail the many conceptions and practices that scholars have classified as spirituality and religion in the workplace. We will see that spirituality and religion at work have widely disparate meanings for different people, due in no small measure to the complex trends and contributing factors outlined in this chapter.

---

[64] Danny Hakim, "Ford Motor Workers Get on the Job Training in Religious Tolerance," *New York Times*, November 19, 2001; see ch. 9 below.

CHAPTER 3

Which spirituality in the workplace?

Scholarly and popular authors of leadership talk more about *spirituality* than about *religion* in the workplace. Their writings tend to accept uncritically a strict distinction between spirituality and religion. In this frequently repeated view, religion is institutional, dogmatic, and rigid; spirituality is personal, emotional, and adaptable to an individual's needs. Spiritual language, symbols, and rituals should be acceptable in the workplace, but religious talk and action remain unacceptable. Adherents of this approach to workplace leadership tend to downplay the potentially contentious nature of things spiritual, even as they maintain that religious matters are divisive.

This chapter critically examines the spirituality–religion dichotomy. The chapter builds a case to argue that the mantra "spirituality unites, but religion divides" is much more problematic than scholars or proponents of spiritual leadership would have us believe. Further, the chapter asserts that the corresponding definitions of spirituality are too broad to be coherent and that the frequent emphasis on the potential of spirituality to create unity or common ground in the workplace overlooks difficult issues.

The ensuing critical exploration of the spirituality and leadership literature will help clarify the myriad issues of the increasingly diverse contemporary workplace. Acknowledging the complex nature of the phenomena (and the difficulties of imposing a simple distinction) will allow for more rigorous analyses of the role of religion and spirituality in the workplace.

DEFINING SPIRITUALITY IN OPPOSITION TO RELIGION

For many scholars of leadership and management, the definition of spirituality is offered by way of the *via negativa* – that is, by emphasizing that it is not religion. Jay Conger's lead essay in the widely read book *Spirit at Work* contains a section entitled "Spirituality and Religion: Is There a Difference?" Conger answers his own question in the affirmative. Other

bad

leadership scholars do the same. Ron Cacioppe discusses spirituality in this way:

The meaning of the term spirituality is often misunderstood and can have negative connotations for many people. Spirituality is often seen in the same context as organized religion, with particular beliefs, moral rules and traditions. Spirituality, however, is not formal, structured, or organized. Organized religion has more of an external focus where spirituality involves a person looking inward and therefore is accessible to everyone whether religious or not. Religion often has salvation as its major aim. Spirituality is above and beyond any specific religious denomination and seeks to find and experience the common principles and truths that each religion offers.[1]

Narottam Bhindi and Patrick Duignan express a similar sentiment:

[We] make a plea for the restoration of spirituality in leadership. By spirituality a partisan religious view is not meant, but that individuals and groups should experience a sense of deep and enduring meaning and significance from an appreciation of their interconnectedness and interdependency, and from their feelings of being connected to something greater than the self.[2]

In their recent book, *A Spiritual Audit of Corporate America*, Mitroff and Denton claim an empirical basis for building a leadership framework around the opposition between spirituality and religion. They maintain that the majority of managers whom they surveyed or interviewed are receptive to spirituality in the workplace but opposed to religion in the workplace.[3]

In general, the participants differentiated strongly between religion and spirituality. They viewed religion as a highly inappropriate form of expression and topic in the workplace. They saw spirituality, on the other hand, as a highly appropriate subject for discussion [at work].[4]

---

[1] Ron Cacioppe, "Creating Spirit at Work: Re-Visioning Organization Development and Leadership – Part I," *Leadership & Organization Development Journal* 21/1 (2000): 51.

[2] Narottam Bhindi and Patrick Duignan, "Leadership for a New Century: Authenticity, Intentionality, Spirituality and Sensibility," *Educational Management & Administration* 25/2 (1997): 126.

[3] Ian I. Mitroff and Elizabeth A. Denton, *A Spiritual Audit of Corporate America: A Hard Look at Spirituality, Religion, and Values in the Workplace*, first edn., The Warren Bennis signature series (San Francisco: Jossey-Bass, 1999), 39–42; Ian I. Mitroff and Elizabeth A. Denton, "A Study of Spirituality in the Workplace," *Sloan Management Review* Summer (1999): 86.

[4] Mitroff and Denton report a return rate of 6.6 percent of the questionnaires mailed out to HR executives. They note: "We don't know at this point if the responses are typical of HR executives in general, although they do match the responses of the HR executives we interviewed in person." Mitroff and Denton, "A Study of Spirituality in the Workplace," 85; Mitroff and Denton, *A Spiritual Audit*, 35. It would not be surprising if the persons who returned the survey were, as a whole, predisposed favorably to the spirituality and leadership movement which, as is discussed in the text, frequently makes the spirituality–religion distinction.

There is little doubt that this opposition between spirituality and religion is a commonly held one, not simply among leadership scholars, but also among those leaders and followers who are proponents of spirituality in the workplace. The fact that such a view has wide currency, of course, does not make it either correct or helpful for understanding effective leadership in diverse organizations.

According to the frequently stated framework of spiritual leadership, spirituality holds the potential to bring together a workforce or organization. Jerry Biberman and Michael Whitty concisely state an underlying assumption of the literature: "A basic workplace spirituality can be the common ground for the new work community."[5] When it is opposed to religion – defined as partisan and rigid – spirituality then stands for those unifying and adaptable values that all people are supposed to hold. Spirituality is assumed to be a dimension of the human being that is shared by all persons. Anticipating the charge by critics concerned about the potentially divisive nature of spirituality, leadership scholars invoke the religion–spirituality dichotomy to state that, if a practice or belief is controversial, it is probably religious and not simply spiritual. They thereby define away any possible conflict.

Many accounts of spiritual leadership accept as unproblematic the view that it is possible to cull religions for their essential insights, while leaving behind the other parts of tradition and communal practices that might create disagreement or simply be inconvenient for modern, busy individuals. Appeal to particular religions in a religiously diverse context is "not energy giving, but divisive" and "can encourage distrust," according to Gerald Cavanagh.[6] Cavanagh does not allow for the possibility that people from different religious traditions might be able to communicate their differences to one another without reducing traditions to their "core values." Rather, after noting that not all aspects of the spirituality movement are helpful, he asserts that Christians and Jews can find common ground with the "positive features" of workplace spirituality. The points that are "congruent with traditional Judeo-Christian traditions" are these:

• People in the movement generally have a belief in God.
• Emphasis on quiet, prayer and contemplation in one's life.
• Emphasis on the centrality of people and listening to others. This generally results in better relations with family and colleagues.

[5] Jerry Biberman and Michael Whitty, "Editorial: Twenty-First Century Spiritual Paradigms/ Possibilities for Organizational Transformation," *Journal of Organizational Change Management* 12/3 (1999): 170.
[6] Gerald F. Cavanagh, "Spirituality for Managers: Context and Critique," *Journal of Organizational Change Management* 12/3 (1999): 190.

- A commitment to better relations among peoples, and to help bring greater peace and harmony in the world.
- The movement is optimistic about the perfectibility of human nature and business culture; they are convinced that people and the world can become better.
- Commitment to a sustainable environment, so to pass on a better world to future generations.[7]

This approach fails to acknowledge that the distinctive traditions of Christianity and Judaism entail complex and varied religious ideas and practices, nor does it recognize the various constructive and critical resources these two faiths might allow adherents to bring to leadership and the workplace. Rather, these six ideas become the elements of workplace spirituality to which Christians or Jews could give their assent. Cavanagh acknowledges the argument of legal scholar Stephen Carter that contemporary American public life tends to trivialize or to be hostile to religion.[8] Despite the fact that Cavanagh cites Carter approvingly, however, Cavanagh's own reductionist approach contributes to the trivialization of religion in the leadership literature.

In the various frameworks of spiritual leadership, good leaders are those people who are able to unite an organization around spiritual values. Gregory Konz and Frances Ryan even call for leaders to make a "role shift from manager to spiritual guide" in order to facilitate making organizations "into places of spiritual development."[9] Models that dismiss the religious differences among leaders and followers allow for such elisions between individual spirituality and institutional spiritual leadership, enabling scholars to suggest that organizational leaders can or should be spiritual guides.

SPIRITUALITY, THE "WHOLE PERSON," AND ORGANIZATIONAL LEADERSHIP

The opposition between spirituality and religion creates a problem for analysts who acknowledge that the "whole person" comes to work. On this point, once again, Mitroff and Denton are representative. They posit that keeping spirituality and work separate is wrong-headed – and futile – because they recognize that people bring their whole selves to the workplace.

---

[7] Ibid., 191–92.

[8] Stephen L. Carter, *The Culture of Disbelief: How American Law and Politics Trivialize Religious Devotion* (New York: Basic Books, 1993).

[9] Gregory N. P. Konz and Frances X. Ryan, "Maintaining an Organizational Spirituality: No Easy Task," *Journal of Organizational Change Management* 12/3 (1999): 200–1.

In language that echoes Hickman's person-centered management,[10] they criticize the view that

> spiritual matters . . . are best dealt with outside of work, on employees' own time and in the particular way of their choosing. Armed with such rationales, most organizations kid themselves that by erecting a "Chinese wall" between the so-called private concerns of their employees and the public demands of their businesses, they can keep them strictly separated.[11]

Mitroff and Denton thus reject a framework that keeps "so-called private issues" out of the workplace domain. They propose, in effect, breaking down the Great Wall, because it is ineffective. That wall obstructs the "power and potential inherent in the soul," and it denies the reality that human beings are spiritual as much as they are physical.[12]

In the same discussion, however, Mitroff and Denton accept the view that religion in the workplace is inappropriate and out-of-bounds. They fear that workers will "proselytiz[e] for a particular religion."[13] Mitroff and Denton fail to explain why excluding religion from the workplace is not inconsistent with their view of bringing the whole person to the workplace. After giving a strong defense of spiritual expression at work, they miss or choose to avoid the fact that, for many leaders and followers, religious commitment and practices are a fundamental part of that same whole person.

On efficiency grounds, Mitroff and Denton might well respond that, if religious expressions were admitted, the ensuing conflicts would outweigh the benefits (translated into gains in productivity) of allowing that part of the whole person into the workplace. They do not provide such an argument. Even if that cost–benefit calculation were proven in particular cases, it would not address the inconsistency of including that part of the whole person called *spirituality* and excluding that called *religion*. Mitroff and Denton's view also assumes that organizational leaders are able to distinguish readily between spirituality and religion. If, as Mitroff and Denton would claim, the spiritual values capture the essence of religious values, it

---

[10] Gill D. Robinson, "Person-Centered Management," *Black Women of Achievement Magazine* I (1988); Gill Robinson Hickman and Dalton S. Lee, *Managing Human Resources in the Public Sector: A Shared Responsibility* (Fort Worth: Harcourt College Publishers, 2001).

[11] Mitroff and Denton, *A Spiritual Audit*, 5–6.

[12] In addition, to exclude spirituality from the workplace is "hypocritical": "On the one hand, corporate America declares spiritual issues strictly out-of-bounds, [but] on the other hand it tries sneaking them in through the back door and drawing heavily on them with calls for the unbridled energy and enthusiasm of its workers." They go on to note that the etymological roots of "enthusiasm" can be translated as "the god or spirit within." Ibid.

[13] Ibid., 6.

is curious that their framework depends so heavily on the opposition of the two.

Gilbert Fairholm makes a similar call for integration of the whole self within the leadership process. Fairholm maintains that leading without drawing upon the spirituality of employers and workers is to overlook the "essence of who we are."[14] Human life is about the spirit, he maintains, and spirit "must manifest itself in both our personal and professional lives."[15] But within this emphasis on the integration of all aspects of life, including spirituality and work, Fairholm includes this footnote:

While important, the religious nature of spirituality is not considered here. This aspect of spirituality is better accommodated in doctrinaire religions and their social instrumentalities. Indeed, many, including this author, would object to matters of personal religion being introduced in the workplace.[16]

Like Mitroff and Denton, Fairholm undermines his own leadership framework for the integrated person when he dismisses the possibility of appropriate religious expression by individuals within the workplace.

Acknowledging that the "whole person" somehow comes to work is not the same as saying that any kind of behaviors, attitudes, or manners of dress or speech are acceptable in the workplace. This section has simply attempted to show that the spirituality–religion distinction is not a tenable way to make such a determination of what is acceptable and what is not.

IS SPIRITUALITY UNIFYING?

I have already suggested that the very dichotomy of spirituality and religion helps reinforce the view that spirituality is unifying – and the previous paragraphs demonstrated how that opposition leads some advocates of spirituality and leadership to offer inconsistent grounds for admitting employees' spirituality, but not religion, into the workplace. But what is spirituality? Some of the scholars of and "experts" on spirituality in the workplace choose not to provide a definition of spirituality for, as they claim, it might create conflict. In such a view, offering a definition could imply the very kind of dogmatic rigidity that spirituality is meant to transcend. I assert, however, that the difficulty in defining spirituality with precision exists because of underlying tensions and ambiguities in the term itself.

---

[14] Gilbert W. Fairholm, *Perspectives on Leadership: From the Science of Management to Its Spiritual Heart* (Westport, CT: Quorum, 1998), 113.
[15] Ibid., 111.   [16] Ibid., 113.

Drawing from their surveys and interviews, Mitroff and Denton provide an eleven-point definition of spirituality. They begin, not surprisingly, with three points in opposition to religion: first, "[i]n contrast to conventional religion, spirituality is not formal, structured, or organized"; second, "[s]pirituality is not denominational"; and third, as opposed to the partisan nature of religion, "[s]pirituality is broadly inclusive; it embraces everyone."[17] The claims the authors make in their subsequent points are wideranging. Spirituality is "universal and timeless," "the ultimate source and provider of meaning and purpose," "the sacredness of everything," and "the deep feeling of interconnectedness of everything," among other things.[18]

Mitroff and Denton go to great lengths to assert that many or most people in the workplace hold such views. This claim notwithstanding, it is hard to maintain that these points do not raise fundamental theological and philosophical questions upon which people disagree. To maintain that spirituality is unifying and a source of common ground is simply to overlook the deeply contested nature of some of these statements. For example, what does it mean to define spirituality as "universal and timeless"? Does each human being experience spirituality in the same way? Are people who claim not to be spiritual people simply misguided? Does "timeless" mean that spirituality is too profound to be held within time? Does it mean that spirituality does not change over time? Can people develop and grow in their spirituality? Mitroff and Denton do not consider these questions.

The Mitroff–Denton definition raises central theological issues. Is spirituality itself a personal agent – as in "[s]pirituality is the ultimate source and provider of meaning and purpose"?[19] This is just one place in which the term *spirituality* seems to stand in as a term for *God*. Many Christians, Jews, and Muslims, at least, would maintain that God, not an abstract notion of spirituality, is "the ultimate source and provider of meaning and purpose." Another statement in the Mitroff–Denton definition raises a related issue: "[Spirituality] was there prior to and subsequent to creation."[20] Jews and Christians would make this claim about God, but not necessarily about spirituality. If *spirituality* is not simply a polite (i.e., non-divisive) way of saying *God*, what would it mean to assert that spirituality existed prior to creation, a time or realm in which, presumably, no humans and no earth existed? If *spirituality* does mean *God*, then the spirituality–religion opposition does not hold.

A person might reply that *spirituality* can mean *God* for some people but not for others; in such a view, unity is being sought by simply redefining

---

[17] Mitroff and Denton, *A Spiritual Audit*, 23.   [18] Ibid., 23–25.   [19] Ibid., 24.   [20] Ibid., 25.

potential conflicts as common beliefs. It is possible to reply, alternatively, that these questions do not need to be answered in order for spirituality to be important in people's lives. (I would agree.) But to assert without further discussion that these phrases or terms somehow create common ground is to sidestep the complex philosophical and theological issues that they pose.

Based on a reading of some one hundred articles on leadership and workplace spirituality, the groups shown in the Table below include words that occur frequently in discussions and proposed definitions of spirituality. Like Mitroff and Denton, other scholars provide a multifaceted definition of spirituality.[21] I have grouped these words into eight clusters that may help to give the list some semblance of order. Even broken down in this way, each cluster holds an immense breadth of possible meanings. The supposed common ground that spiritual leadership is intended to create is common only if the important distinctions among these terms are not acknowledged.

---

self-actualization; self-fulfillment; self-awareness; self-consciousness; self-discovery

wholeness; holism; integration; integrity; authenticity; balance; harmony

meaning; purpose

emotion; passion; feeling

life force; energy; vitality; life; intrinsic motivation

wisdom; discernment; courage; creativity

morality; values; peace; truth; freedom; justice

interconnectedness; interdependence; interrelationship; cooperation; community; teamwork

---

In the abstract, few if any of these terms are objectionable, but, as abstractions, they provide little more precision than the word *spirituality* itself does. That is, most of these words are extremely rich; yet, like spirituality, they need careful specification. Similar to the elements of the Mitroff–Denton definition of spirituality, any one of these terms or clusters of terms is philosophically and theologically complicated and contested. They parallel Christian theological discussions concerning who God is (for example, is God the ultimate concern, or is God the actively engaged sovereign and

---

[21] As one example, note the "elements of spiritual leadership" offered by Fairholm: *Perspectives on Leadership*, 138. That list by itself is nearly as broad as the list compiled herein.

transformer of human society?);[22] and who human beings are (for example, are humans creatures whose purpose is found when they submit to God's call, or are they agents who have been called by God to struggle for justice?);[23] and what faith is (for example, is faith the belief in and response to statements about God, or is it a feeling of absolute dependence?).[24] They also mirror contemporary philosophical debates about who human persons are (for example, are humans autonomous individual agents, or are they interconnected selves in community?).[25]

This discussion suggests that the claim that "spirituality creates common ground" cannot be readily established without undertaking more work at least to address the philosophical and theological difficulties of the term and its definitional components. Authors who make broad and sweeping claims about spirituality should clarify the connections and coherence of their account. Renaming perennial philosophical or theological issues does not resolve them. Indeed, the hard work of navigating potential conflicts is left for leaders and followers in the workplace (and elsewhere in public life). The common ground that spiritual leadership claims to create does not address the issues that leaders and followers might actually face in the workplace, such as the accommodation of religious dress, or the need for flexible work schedules, or a policy addressing employees (or bosses) who communicate their faith at work. To be sure, the underlying theological and philosophical debates likewise do not address the everyday work of organizational leadership. That is the point: this critique of spiritual leadership is not a call for leaders and followers to embrace a common spirituality, theology, or philosophy. On the contrary, it simply acknowledges that conflict may result amidst a diverse workforce and that appeal to abstract principles (or religious dogmas) will not solve them. Effective leadership that recognizes and steers amidst diversity is needed to help employees work together.

---

[22] Contrast the positions of Paul Tillich, *Systematic Theology*, vol. 1 (University of Chicago Press, 1951) and H. Richard Niebuhr, *Christ and Culture*, first edn. (New York: Harper & Row, 1951).

[23] Contrast the positions of Karl Barth, *Church Dogmatics: The Doctrine of Creation, the Creature*, ed. T. F. Torrance and G. W. Bromiley, trans. J. K. S. Reid, et al., 4 vols., vol. 3/3 (Edinburgh: T. & T. Clark, 1960), and Gustavo Gutiérrez, *A Theology of Liberation: History, Politics, and Salvation*, trans. C. Inda and J. Eagleson (Maryknoll, NY: Orbis Books, 1973).

[24] Contrast the positions of John Calvin, *Institutes of the Christian Religion*, ed. J. T. McNeill, trans. F. L. Battles (London: S.C.M. Press, 1961) and Friedrich Schleiermacher, *On Religion: Speeches to Its Cultured Despisers*, trans. R. Crouter (Cambridge University Press, 1996).

[25] Contrast the position presented by John Rawls in *A Theory of Justice* (Cambridge, MA: Harvard University Press, 1971) with that of Michael Sandel in *Liberalism and the Limits of Justice* (Cambridge University Press, 1982).

WHICH LEADERSHIP PRACTICES COUNT AS SPIRITUAL?
(AND WHICH DO NOT?)

What happens when we consider specific actions and interactions of leaders and followers in the workplace? This section suggests that many situations or examples of spirituality are potentially conflict-ridden – similar in kind to encounters of religion in the workplace.

In an article in *Personnel Journal*, Patricia Hardin explores the question, "What's Your Sign?: Companies Use Otherworldly Assessment Methods to Choose the Right Employees."[26] Hardin interviewed a number of business executives and human relations professionals who apply nontraditional methods to hire new employees. Their methods include reading tarot cards, consulting psychics, using Enneagrams, and analyzing handwriting samples.[27] Psychics and graphologists alike reported a steady business from employers who utilize their services. The article ran with this header: "Spirituality." Are these practices to be included under the umbrella of workplace spirituality?

What other practices fit within the spirituality rubric? When co-workers seek to analyze another worker's "aura," or to convince others to meditate at work, or to engage in sunset watching from a conference room,[28] are they engaged in spiritual practices? The abstract definitions do not provide much help in determining what actions or practices are properly spiritual. They also are limited in their ability to differentiate between what is potentially unifying and what is divisive.

These examples serve to illustrate some difficulties with determining what should be called *spirituality* and what should not be. What about practices that adherents explicitly name as *religious* – for instance, individual religious people (Christians, Jews, Muslims, etc.) who recite prayers or wear religious garb to work? Examples here include Christians who place a Bible on their desk or Christian posters in their cubicle or Muslim women who wear the headscarf, *hijab*, to work. Of course, within the spirituality–religion opposition, these cases can be defined as *religious*, and not *spiritual*, and thus deemed inappropriate in the workplace. Some leadership scholars,

[26] Patricia Hardin, "What's Your Sign?: Companies Use Otherworldy Assessment Methods to Choose the Right Employees," *Personnel Journal* 74/9 (September 1995).
[27] I do not think it necessary to consider whether each of these methods should or should not be examined in parallel fashion, since the task of this section is simply to ask if the "spirituality and leadership" umbrella extends far enough to cover these kinds of practices.
[28] Jennifer J. Laabs, "Balancing Spirituality and Work," *Personnel Journal* 74/9 (1995): 61.

though, assert that such religious expressions are not out-of-bounds as long as they are undertaken without "bothering" their co-workers. (Reasonable accommodation of religious prayer and garb is also required by law.[29])

This brief examination of practices reveals that the discussion of abstract elements of spirituality does not address the everyday leadership challenges concerning which practices should be permitted in the workplace and which should not. Legal requirements of religious accommodation are more practical than lists of spirituality, but good and effective leadership requires more than minimal adherence to laws. Through either organizational policies or through informal norms, employees should know what is acceptable religious or spiritual expression at work. Determining such a structure and culture requires the hard work of a leadership process, not reference to abstract spiritual concepts.

SPIRITUALITY OR COMMUNITY SPIRIT?

Another problematic aspect of defining the term *spirituality* concerns not those potentially coercive or controversial ideas and practices but seemingly innocuous ones. Some discussions of spiritual values do not clarify just what is spiritual about the values being discussed. In their article on "Spirit and Community at Southwest Airlines: An Investigation of a Spiritual Values-based Model," John Milliman, Jeffery Ferguson, David Trickett, and Bruce Condemi explain that Southwest's spiritual values include four elements: "a strong emphasis on community," "employees feel[ing] they are part of a cause," the "empowerment of all employees," and a cultural emphasis on "emotional and humor aspects," all of which contribute to a corporate culture of "enthusiasm and commitment."[30] Are these spiritual values? If so, what sorts of values would not be spiritual values? Is the adherence to these values an example of spiritual leadership?

Judith Neal, one of the leading scholars of workplace spirituality, lists Stephen Covey's *Seven Habits of Highly Effective People*[31] as the first

---

[29] On the legal dimensions of religious expression in the workplace, see Josh Schopf, "Religious Activity and Proselytization in the Workplace: The Murky Line between Healthy Expression and Unlawful Harassment," *Columbia Journal of Law and Social Problems* 31/1 (1997) and Michael Wolf, Bruce Friedman, and Daniel Sutherland, *Religion in the Workplace: A Comprehensive Guide to Legal Rights and Responsibilities* (Chicago: Tort and Insurance Practice Section, American Bar Association, 1998).

[30] John F. Milliman et al., "Spirit and Community at Southwest Airlines: An Investigation of a Spiritual Values-Based Model," *Journal of Organizational Change Management* 12/3 (1999). One potential issue raised by this example is the institutional nature of these spiritual values – a culture that seeks to inculcate certain (spiritual) values. Such an issue is more complex when the spiritual values are more potentially divisive than community spirit and empowerment.

[31] Stephen R. Covey, *The Seven Habits of Highly Effective People* (New York: Simon & Schuster, 1989).

recommendation on her list of "resources that help individuals integrate work and spirituality." Covey's work "is intended to move people from dependence to independence to interdependence." Neal notes that in *Seven Habits* and in his co-authored book, *First Things First*,[32] Covey contributes to understanding work and spirituality because his texts "focus on the deeper priorities in life."[33] As with the article about Southwest Airlines, we must ask if the values detailed by Covey are spiritual ones. In other words, are the insights that Covey offers to students of management or leadership best classified as spiritual in nature?

Finally, does *The Wizard of Oz* offer a tradition that provides resources for making workplace leadership more spiritual? Jerry Biberman, Michael Whitty, and Lee Robbins argue in the affirmative within their essay in a journal volume on "Spirituality in Organizations":

We believe that for organizations and individuals the key to spiritual change lies in transformation which must come from within. Using *The Wizard of Oz* as a metaphor, we explain how an organization can balance its intellect, emotionality and sense of purpose; and we recommend steps organizations can take in each area to achieve this balance.[34]

The authors draw upon the narrative of *The Wizard of Oz* itself and upon later analyses of the book and film to argue for balance and wholeness in the workplace. They assert that "[h]ope is found in the human spirit and activated through such cultural stories as that of Oz."[35] They proceed to argue that corporations should learn from Dorothy and begin to judge their success not on the single criterion of profit but on a wide range of criteria, including production and distribution.[36] In my view, it is not problematic to draw upon rich cultural narratives to develop a moral argument. Exercising the "literary imagination" can be helpful to this end.[37] Yet it is not clear from this discussion why or how this use of the literary imagination – this appeal to Oz – is a spiritual one.

It is possible to define spiritual leadership to include any appeal to the "human spirit" or "community spirit" or "team spirit." In such a case, spirituality is expansive enough to include almost any positive value or feature.

---

[32] Stephen R. Covey, A. Roger Merrill, and Rebecca R. Merrill, *First Things First* (New York: Simon & Schuster, 1994).

[33] Judith A. Neal, "Spirituality in Management Education: A Guide to Resources," *Journal of Management Education* 21/1 (1997): 129.

[34] Jerry Biberman, Michael Whitty, and Lee Robbins, "Lessons from Oz: Balance and Wholeness in Organizations," *Journal of Organizational Change Management* 12/3 (1999): 244.

[35] Ibid.   [36] Ibid., 252.

[37] Martha Nussbaum, *Poetic Justice: The Literary Imagination in Public Life* (Boston: Beacon Press, 1995).

Some scholars of spirituality and leadership, though, would surely reject one or more of these examples (i.e., the community focus of Southwest Airlines, *Seven Habits*, or *The Wizard of Oz*) as having to do with spiritual leadership. As in the previous section, this section suggests that the debate over what is spiritual or not is contested and requires further clarification. But here the issue is not those controversial practices that may be part of spiritual leadership; it is, instead, the question of naming as spiritual some arguably helpful practices of organizational leadership. In neither case does the label help leaders or followers in the hard work of resolving potential conflicts over diversity in the workplace.

CONCLUSIONS AND IMPLICATIONS

The literature on spirituality and leadership depends predominantly on an opposition between religion and spirituality that is highly problematic. At the same time, attempts to define spirituality have sought to encompass many religious ideas or concepts by renaming them as spiritual and asserting that, repackaged in nonpartisan terms, they can help build unity and common ground. Such an approach assumes that religiously particular language and practice is divisive, on the one hand, but it fails to acknowledge the analogous potential conflict over spiritual ideas and practices, on the other.

Is spirituality about personal faith and/or team spirit? What practices properly count as spiritual? What happens when some employees do not recognize a practice as spiritual, while others see it in those terms? This chapter has argued that, when discussion moves beyond abstract definitions to consider specific practices or ideas, the potential conflicts quickly come to the fore. While some practices may seem controversial or potentially coercive, other ideas and programs labeled as *spiritual* do not seem to be spiritual at all, unless the range of meanings is stretched to include almost anything that is *human*.

Many Americans speak in terms of spirituality and even understand themselves to be somehow spiritual.[38] As Wade Clark Roof's research has shown, however, people mean many different things by the term. This chapter has applied that insight to the literature on spirituality and leadership to show that, if pressed, the apparent common ground of spirituality is much rockier and more uneven than many proponents would acknowledge.

---

[38] Wade Clark Roof, *A Generation of Seekers: The Spiritual Journeys of the Baby Boom Generation* (San Francisco: Harper San Francisco, 1993); Wade Clark Roof, *The Spiritual Marketplace: Baby Boomers and the Remaking of American Religion* (Princeton University Press, 1999); Robert Wuthnow, *After Heaven: Spirituality in America Since the 1950s* (Berkeley, CA: University of California Press, 1998). See ch. 2 above.

In the quest for simplicity, descriptive or normative models should be careful not to overlook complexities and potential disagreements. If the discussion of spirituality were more carefully developed, the disparate faith expressions and potential and realized divisions would become clear. This enterprise does not require offering a single definition of spirituality, but rather it necessitates the delineation of the ways in which different leaders and followers holding different, and often divergent, views of religion and spirituality manage to work effectively together.

By showing that both the current treatment of spirituality and the avoidance of religion are flawed approaches to leadership in a diverse workplace, the analysis of this chapter suggests the need for theories that include religious differences within the purview of significant employee diversity; such diversity can be a source of both conflict and innovation. The analysis allows room for scholars working on superior-subordinate relations, employee diversity, organizational culture, and ethics to develop models that are alternatives to either the "secular workplace" model or the "spiritual leadership" model.

In my view, the very effort to oppose religion and spirituality is misguided. What is needed is a way to acknowledge, understand, and live with spiritual – and religious – differences within a given workplace context. The starting place is not an assumed common ground or an achievable unity. Rather, if cooperation, mutual understanding, or even some kind of unity is achieved, it results from open dialogue and the sharing of ideas, not by assumption or definition.

It is important to state that, in such a view, it is not necessary for all people to agree on matters spiritual or religious in order for those kinds of phenomena to have an appropriate, or even valuable, place in the workplace. But it is wrong-headed – and potentially detrimental to the workplace itself – to ignore the potential conflicts or to live in the happy fiction that all persons agree about spirituality.

Is there a way to evaluate whether particular expressions of spirituality are appropriate or inappropriate? Unlike the view that places spirituality and religion in opposition, the debates about what spiritual practices are acceptable and what religious practices are appropriate for employees in the contemporary workplace can be seen as roughly parallel. Religious traditions and languages affect some people more than others. They make sense to some persons and not to others. They may seem threatening to some and not to others. Organizations do not need to allow all spiritual or religious expressions by bosses or employees into the workplace – but the critical evaluation needed to assess their role in people's lives, their potential value, and their potential dangers should proceed on similar grounds for all matters of values, attitudes, and practices that employers and workers bring into the workplace. That is, it is not even necessary to determine whether an idea or practice is spiritual and/or religious – or for that matter, political, cultural, or social – in order to evaluate it as appropriate or inappropriate.

To be sure, more work is needed to develop the parameters for inclusion of spirituality and religion in the workplace. The current literature offers few resources for this enterprise. With the exception of the unsustainable spirituality–religion opposition, scholars have developed few descriptive or normative criteria to determine what spiritual or religious expressions are appropriate. Efforts along these lines should emphasize the insight from other areas of leadership studies, namely, that healthy organizational environments benefit not only from establishing common ground but also from engaging in respectful, honest conflict. By recognizing that faith expressions of employees are important aspects of employees' identities – and are potential sources of both cooperation and conflict – we will be better able to describe and evaluate the role of religion and spirituality in the workplace and in other contexts.

CHAPTER 4

Conflicts at work: is religion distinctive?

When scholars of organizational leadership discuss diversity in the work-place, they most often focus upon gender, race, ethnicity, nationality, age, ability–disability, and sexual orientation as principal categories. Religion does not receive prominent attention in this scholarship; many texts on leadership treat diversity without mentioning religion.[1] In terms of prac-tice, less than one in five human resource managers reported that their companies hold diversity training sessions in which religion is discussed.[2] One leading book on diversity, used in classrooms and corporate training sessions, considers religion only as a subcategory within the experiences of workers who are immigrants to the United States. A Pakistani Muslim becomes the sole "voice" of religious diversity.[3] The authors' decision to include only a Pakistani voice reinforces the view that Muslims are not Americans and Americans are not Muslims. Further, the text fails to ad-dress the challenges that many Americans who are religious – Christian, Jewish, Muslim, Hindu, Buddhist, New Age, or otherwise – confront or create in the workplace.

Why do many scholars avoid religion in their analyses of diversity and organizational leadership? Many state that religion is an inappropriate topic altogether for the workplace (and for other spheres of public life), thus re-inforcing the view of religion as a private matter. Some understand religion as a "nonrational" (often with the suggestion that it is a "primitive") phe-nomenon that has no place in the modern or postmodern secular workplace.

[1] Gary Yukl, *Leadership in Organizations*, fifth edn. (Upper Saddle River, NJ: Prentice Hall, 2002), 410–22; Gill Robinson Hickman, ed., *Leading Organizations: Perspectives for a New Era* (Thousand Oaks, CA: Sage, 1998); see essays by Offerman and Fernandez in ibid., that address diversity explicitly but do not mention religion even in their lists of diversity categories.
[2] Society for Human Resource Management Issues Management Program, "Religion in the Workplace Mini-Survey" (Alexandria, VA: Society for Human Resource Management, 1997), 5.
[3] Renee Blank and Sandra Slipp, *Voices of Diversity: Real People Talk about Problems and Solutions in a Workplace Where Everyone Is Not Alike* (New York: Amacom, 1994), 84–85, 91–94.

Other scholars may simply state that they do not have the background to address religion adequately in the discussion. Although it is not possible to account precisely for the notable absence of religion in the study of organizational leadership, I suggest that many authors overlook religion because they accept the strong opposition between spirituality and religion analyzed in the previous chapter. This perspective preempts the need to treat religion as a category of diversity, because religious particularities and differences should be transcended through "translating" religious insights into spiritual ones and thus attaining common ground.

Such an approach avoids situations in which religious expression could lead to conflict in the workplace. It is curious that much of the literature on other forms of diversity, however, is quite open to addressing conflicts. Scholars directly confront problems of misunderstanding, discrimination, and marginalization based, for example, on race, gender, or sexual orientation. They view religion differently, however. Both the reductionist view – i.e., religious differences can be reduced to other kinds of concerns, such as spirituality, culture, nationality, race, or ethnicity – and the religion-as-ultimately-divisive view lead to the same result: it is easier to focus on other categories of diversity.

This chapter offers an alternative approach. It acknowledges directly that religiously based beliefs and actions in a diverse workplace can and often will create situations of potential conflict. At the same time, the wider framework of the book asserts that negotiating conflict is a central aspect of good leadership, that is, leadership that is ethical and effective.[4] This chapter examines a variety of examples of religiously based or religiously influenced conflict in the workplace. The examples range from expression of individuals' religious commitments to decisions that companies or their leaders have to make about religious accommodation. Rather than viewing only religiously based conflicts – as if the workplace would be conflict-free if religion were kept out – this chapter also considers other conflicts in the workplace arising from political, spiritual, or cultural/aesthetic differences. None of these problems is simple to describe or to solve. One aim of the chapter, however, is to assert that religiously based differences are no more or no less complicated or threatening to a workplace than are other kinds of differences.

---

[4] See ch. 9 below. For an important essay in leadership ethics that explains good leadership in terms of both ethics and effectiveness, see Joanne B. Ciulla, "Leadership Ethics: Mapping the Territory," in *Ethics: The Heart of Leadership*, ed. Joanne B. Ciulla (Westport, CT: Praeger, 1998).

AN INCREASINGLY CONTESTED PUBLIC PRESENCE OF RELIGION

In his book *Religion in Public Life: A Dilemma for Democracy*, Ronald Thiemann delineates how contemporary US society experiences the "unresolved tension" created by the national founders' treatment of religion.[5] The authors of the Constitution and the Bill of Rights laid a framework to maintain the legal nonestablishment of religion, but they still assumed an effective cultural establishment of Christianity. They could do so because an overwhelming majority of the population hailed from a Christian background. In the 1830s, Alexis de Tocqueville observed that the multiplicity of religious sects and groups in America could fit within the "great union" of Christendom.[6] Tocqueville went on to assert that Americans agreed on basic "common beliefs" and "leading ideas." Religion – that is, in this case, Christianity – provided a common core of ideas on which nearly all Americans could agree. This commonality, in Tocqueville's view, provided stability for American democracy.[7] Although he was impressed by the variety of religious expression in America, Tocqueville also realized that this diversity was circumscribed within the category of Christianity. One could take issue with his observation that even Christians could agree upon basic essentials of faith or society. His own emphasis, to be sure, was on the variety of ideas and practices that voluntary (nonestablished) religious communities contributed to the rich texture of American democracy. Yet he believed that the common foundation of Christian belief contributed to an a priori assent to central social values.[8]

Over a century later, sociologist Will Herberg offered his influential thesis that American religion could be readily understood in terms of three categories – which became the title of his classic book, *Protestant–Catholic–Jew* (1955). He argued that all three categories were, at bottom, American

[5] Ronald F. Thiemann, *Religion in Public Life: A Dilemma for Democracy* (Washington, DC: Georgetown University Press, 1996), 33–37.

[6] Ibid., 33.

[7] Alexis de Tocqueville, *Democracy in America*, trans. George Lawrence, ed. J. P. Mayer (New York: HarperPerennial, 1969), 287–301.

[8] Tocqueville, for instance, feared that Islam could not contribute to such social values:

> Muhammed brought down from heaven and put into the Koran not religious doctrines only, but political maxims, criminal and civil laws, and scientific theories. The Gospels, on the other hand, deal only with the general relations between man and God and between man and man. Beyond that, they teach nothing and do not oblige people to believe anything. That alone, among a thousand reasons, is enough to show that Islam will not be able to hold its power long in ages of enlightenment and democracy, while Christianity is destined to reign in such ages, as in all others. (Ibid., 447)

His distinction makes sweeping and problematic claims about both Islam and Christianity.

creations of the social context peculiar to the United States. The supposed unity, for example, of the *Protestant* category transcended the more visible groupings by denomination. The category *Jew* had to counter the rifts of theology and practice among Orthodox, Conservative, and Reformed factions. While *Catholic* was perhaps the most straightforward of the three categories, Herberg points out that Roman Catholicism in America had to overcome barriers relating to ethnic, national, and linguistic differences. Herberg argued that "[t]he three religious communities – Protestant, Catholic, Jew – are America. Together, they embrace almost the entire population of this country."[9] He noted that a few nonbelievers and persons of other religions lived in the US, but in his view they were insignificant in the overall sociological picture of America in the 1950s.

Tocqueville and Herberg alike sought to identify, as a kind of moral foundation, common values that were supportive of democracy and "the American way." Neither foresaw a situation in which the diversity of religious traditions, such as that experienced in recent decades, might stretch the undisputed acceptance of common American values to a breaking point.[10]

The cultural establishment of Christianity in earlier periods made it less noticeable than it is today when Christianity (or, more broadly, a so-called Judeo-Christian tradition) operated as a quasi-official state or civil religion. The memorial services in honor of the victims of the September 11, 2001, attacks underlined just how diverse America has become. The diversity of religious expression in response to those events stands in marked contrast to the accounts of American religion described by Tocqueville or Herberg.

Many Christians have recognized and responded to the cultural disestablishment of Christianity, but they have differed in terms of how to evaluate it. Some have commented on the dangers that occur when Christianity is tied too closely to the wider culture and society. Stanley Hauerwas and William Willimon, for example, do not lament cultural disestablishment but see it as a chance for Christians to forge a distinctive and faithful identity. They call upon Christians to become "resident aliens" within the culture, persons modeling lives faithful to God within the enclaves of their church communities.[11] Other Christians mourn the fact that their tradition has lost its cultural (and political and social) hegemony; in contrast to Hauerwas

9 Will Herberg, *Protestant–Catholic–Jew: An Essay in American Religious Sociology* (Garden City, NY: Doubleday & Company, 1960), 211.
10 To his credit, Tocqueville in particular analyzed the problems of race and criticized the treatment of Native Americans and portrayed the slavery of African Americans as a fundamental flaw in the US system that might ultimately lead to its destruction. See Tocqueville, *Democracy in America*, 316–63.
11 Stanley Hauerwas and William H. Willimon, *Resident Aliens: Life in the Christian Colony* (Nashville, TN: Abingdon, 1989).

and Willimon, they would seem to prefer a return to effective Christian establishment. This latter group, part nostalgic and part defensive, tends to equate religious diversity with religious and moral relativism.[12] The cultural disestablishment of Christianity, in this view, inevitably leads to the loss of religiously based public values.

Newcomers from traditions such as Islam, Hinduism, and Buddhism do not enjoy a historical connection between their religious narratives and American public life. This plays out in the workplace, among other ways, in terms of the lack of consonance between their religious holidays and the predominant US working calendar. Many aspects of American public life, including workplace schedules and the public school calendar in most places, are structured around Christmas and, to a lesser extent, Easter. Muslims cannot say the same about Ramadan or Dhu al-Hijjah, the month of pilgrimage to Mecca. If Hindus wish to celebrate Diwali or Buddhists want to observe the Buddha's birthday, they will have to take vacation time from work. For their part, Jewish persons and groups have long experienced disadvantages both in the Christendom that Tocqueville described and within the "Judeo-Christian tradition" that is reflected in Herberg's framework. For years, Jews have faced the difficulty of trying to fit in commemoration of the high holy days in September or October – a busy time of year in American public life. One of the only days when American business shuts down almost completely is Christmas Day – leaving those Americans who do not celebrate Christmas with little choice but to have a quiet day at home.[13]

In overall terms, the cultural disestablishment of Christianity can be seen as a positive development from a variety of perspectives. For Christians, it is not necessary to adopt Hauerwas and Willimon's call to become resident aliens – as if Christians do not comprise a majority in American culture and do not continue to enjoy many advantages in US society – in order to see the opportunities of cultural nonestablishment. Such opportunities include the occasion to clarify Christian identity as well as the chance to learn from the religious expression of neighbors from other traditions. As members of minority traditions, Jews, Muslims, Wiccans, Hindus, Buddhists, Sikhs, Jains, Native Americans, and others can clearly benefit from a more genuinely equal playing field in public life, including the workplace.

[12] Note, for example, the case in which a Lutheran Church Missouri Synod official was removed from his leadership position because he participated in the interfaith service at Yankee Stadium. He was accused of "lowering" the Christian God to be as one among other gods and of worshiping with "pagans." See Daniel J. Wakin, "Seeing Heresy in a Service for Sept. 11; Pastor Is under Fire for Interfaith Prayers," *New York Times*, February 8, 2002.

[13] My point, of course, is not to criticize days of rest or relaxation, but rather to note that non-Christians have little choice in the selection of this particular Christian holy day as a national holiday. See ch. 9 below.

At the same time, the cultural disestablishment of Christianity and a more religiously diverse workforce arguably lead to greater potential for tensions.[14] When two workers discuss their faith around the water cooler, the likelihood that they are coming from the same broad tradition is lower than it was even a few decades ago. The outfits or dress that people wear to work varies widely, partly based on religion. Many people are likely to ask for vacation time to celebrate religious holidays and, at a minimum, the number and variety of those holiday dates have increased. Even as we recall the potential for positive opportunities to arise from religious encounter, it becomes important to explore the nature of potential conflicts that occur when people seek to live out their faith – diverse faiths – in the workplace.

WORKPLACE CONFLICTS: RELIGIOUS, POLITICAL, CULTURAL, AND AESTHETIC

The workplace conflicts that have received media attention in recent years are most often legal cases. The juxtaposition of religiously based instances with other types of conflict will raise questions such as these: are there issues common to the various conflicts, or are they distinguishable according to the aspect of identity (political, religious, cultural) under debate? When and how is it possible to determine if a conflict is based on religion (instead of, for example, a matter of spirituality, ethics, politics, or culture)? In what ways, if any, are religiously based challenges distinct from the other kinds of workplace tensions?

Clothing, jewelry, and dress codes

The debate on religious dress usually focuses on those religious adherents who want to wear something different than the normal dress code – whether that code is a matter of formal policy or informal cultural norms. What those policies or norms include – or how they are shaped by wider social and cultural contexts – is seldom noted. Men and women wearing jewelry with Christian symbols elicit little controversy or even notice.[15]

---

[14] It is possible to argue that these tensions were present all along within a context of explicit Christian cultural establishment. This point is well taken. The very fact that Jews, Muslims, and even atheists can now challenge this effective establishment more openly is a marker of a less hegemonic Christian influence.

[15] A recent case, however, centers around the claim of Kimberly Draper, who asserts that she lost her job in a local public library in the Louisville area because she insisted on wearing a cross-shaped pendant on a necklace (Beverly Goldberg, "Aide Says She Was Fired for Wearing a Cross," *American Libraries*, March 2002).

Cross-shaped pendants have become a part of contemporary culture and fashion. Athletes and entertainers wear prominent crosses as earrings and pendants and sometimes even wear clothing, such as a t-shirt, featuring the symbol of the cross. The fact that so many people wear this symbol for reasons other than religious devotion suggests that Christianity enjoys a position of cultural establishment.

Adherents of some Christian denominations, however, have experienced workplace controversies over their dress. In 1999, for instance, a Pentecostal Christian employee of Bridgestone/Firestone, Inc. sued the company for denying her a promotion to a position in which she would be required to wear pants or overalls. She claimed that her faith required her to wear a long skirt as a matter of modesty. The company argued that the central issue in the case was one of safety and not of religion. In response, the employee offered to wear a fire-retardant skirt, but Bridgestone/Firestone responded that this would still violate their "comprehensive safety program."[16]

The media have focused attention recently on the religious garb of Muslims and Sikhs. Many Muslim women uphold a religious commitment to wear *hijab*, a loose-fitting outfit of clothing that customarily includes a headscarf. A host of employers have protested this garb – for reasons ranging from appearance to uniform policies to safety concerns. In their 2001 report on civil rights and the accommodation of Muslims in public life, the Council on American–Islamic Relations (CAIR) reported that 23 percent of the cases of discrimination in the workplace and other public settings involved the wearing of headscarves by Muslim women.[17] One of the most prominent cases in recent years was that of Rose Hamid, a flight attendant with US Airways. Hamid's growing commitment to Islam led her to follow her understanding of Islamic law and wear a headscarf on the job. When she returned to work from a medical leave of absence, she wore a scarf with her flight attendant uniform, citing her intensified religious commitment. US Airways, citing the importance of a common uniform, relegated her to unpaid leave when she refused to remove the scarf. She filed a religious discrimination complaint with the US Equal Employment Opportunity Commission (EEOC) and the airline later settled the case. She moved to another job in the company in which a uniform was not required.[18]

---

[16] "Company, Employee at Odds over Religious Dress Code," *Fort Worth Star Telegram*, August 8, 1999.

[17] Mohamed Nimer, "Accommodating Diversity: The Status of Muslim Civil Rights in the United States 2001" (Washington, DC: Council on American–Islamic Relations, 2001), 5.

[18] Julie Gannon Shoop, "Keeping the Faith: Advocates Seek Protection for Religious Rights at Work," *Trial* 33/11 (1997).

Even before the 2001 terrorist attacks, US airports were a common site of controversy about women's headscarves and other religiously motivated dress. Airlines, rental car agencies, and airport security firms were workplaces of significant religious, cultural, and national diversity. Further, in the context of airport security, the blanket association of terrorism with persons who appear to be Muslim or Middle Eastern has contributed to wariness about forms of dress that look "Islamic." Seven employees of Argenbright Security, Inc. were removed from their jobs at Dulles International Airport, outside of Washington, DC, in 1999, because they insisted on wearing headscarves at work.[19] As a means of avoiding a suit by the EEOC, the airport reinstated these employees to their jobs, allowed them to wear *hijab*, and awarded them lost pay and $2,500 each.[20]

Especially in the wake of September 11, however, many Muslims have reported cases of employers harassing or discriminating against women who wear *hijab*. In addition, some fellow employees and customers have muttered anti-Muslim statements, have deemed *hijab* to be inappropriate for the US context, and have demanded removal of the headscarf. Many Muslim women have reported a threatening workplace environment – due, in part, to their wearing of the scarves.[21]

Sikh men have similarly encountered a host of problems as a result of wearing turbans that make them appear, to some observers, to be Muslim. The most prominent public case involved the murder of a Sikh gas station owner in Arizona in apparent retaliation after September 11, 2001.[22] Sikh men are also obligated to wear the *kirpan*, a ritual dagger, under their clothing as a symbol of their commitment to the faith. In a highly publicized case, Sher Singh was pulled from an Amtrak train in Providence, Rhode Island, on September 12, 2001, and charged with carrying a concealed weapon – even though he acknowledged that he was carrying the *kirpan* and stated that he was doing so out of a sense of religious duty. Despite a barrage of appeals from Sikh and other religious communities, charges against him were not dropped for over a month.[23] In the workplace, Sikh men have encountered related indignities and problems. Employees have reported that their bosses have requested them to shave their

---

[19] Airport security at US commercial airports is now handled by the Transportation Security Administration.

[20] Derrill Holly, "Muslim Group Settles Religious Headgear Dispute," *Associated Press State & Local Wire*, April 28, 1999.

[21] Diane E. Lewis, "Workplace Bias Claims Jump after Sept. 11," *Boston Globe*, November 22, 2001.

[22] Kelly Ettenborough, Adam Klawonn, and Christina Leonard, "Valley Mourns Apparent Backlash Killing," *Arizona Republic*, September 17, 2001.

[23] Tom Mooney, "Charges against Sikh Dropped," *Providence Journal*, October 26, 2001.

beards and that their co-workers and clients have insulted them for their appearance.[24]

Such cases – involving Pentecostals, Jews, Muslims, and Sikhs – raise legal and ethical questions about the official actions taken by employers (for example, hiring, firing, promoting) and about wider issues of employee treatment and overall working environment. The publicity surrounding these cases typically stems from the legal matters of discrimination and/or harassment at their center. By extending the analysis of each case from a strictly legal perspective to include a moral perspective, however, it is possible to evaluate various factors, including formal rules, informal customs and practices, and the behavior and attitudes of other employees, managers, and customers.

In examples of clothing and personal appearance, the expression of faith is particularly visible. The various cases mentioned above portray religion as a *problem*. With the exception of those forms of appearance that are viewed as "normal" (for example, wearing cross-shaped pendants), religion demands "accommodation" – new understanding or even special treatment. The legal-centered analyses seem to overlook the fact that it is also possible to view these examples not only uniquely or primarily as potential causes of conflict, but also as fundamental expressions of religious identity, or as aesthetically rich cultural expressions, or as reflections of the diversity of a company's customers (or markets) as well as its employees. Some corporations have found ways to transform, or at least ameliorate, conflicts by adopting these other perspectives.[25]

Flags, buttons, posters, and artwork

The display of a button, sticker, flag, poster, or license plate by an employee usually conveys a message that the entire work force may not embrace. Indeed, a principal goal of many such displays (though not all) is to persuade co-workers to adopt the "message" of the symbol in question. I have placed "message" in quotations by way of recognizing that meanings can be polyphonic or even ambiguous – a fact that adds to the complexity of the attendant issues. These items may communicate a religious message, but the perspective may also be political, cultural, spiritual, or of another nature.

In the aftermath of the 2001 terrorist attacks, the sale of American flags soared. For many citizens, placing a flag outside their home or a magnetic

---

[24] Ralph King, "If Looks Could Kill," *Asiaweek.com*, November 30, 2001.   [25] See ch. 9 below.

flag on their automobile became a symbol of solidarity with victims and support for the national response to the tragedies. Even more than during the Gulf War, would-be critics of excessive nationalism were cautious not to criticize this strong (albeit commercialized) response. There were, however, some public debates and disagreements about the precise meaning(s) of the flag's display. Could the expression of nationalism be overstated or exaggerated to the point of discouraging one vital element of civic life, namely, critical reflection or even dissent?[26] In the workplace, the display of the American flag created controversy. Did the flag's prominent and frequent display imply that the employer was "against" foreign employees? Could non-American employees post flags of their own nation – especially if their nation was one of the sixty or more who also lost citizens in the attacks – and did these workers have to display a US flag of their own? Should multinational firms display flags for all of the countries they represented?

The NCCI Holdings company in Boca Raton, Florida, received hundreds of protests via email from critics when they insisted, during the week of September 11, 2001, that employees remove American flags from their work areas. The company was upholding its "policy against the display of any national or religious symbol that might offend other employees." Under tremendous public and employee pressure, however, the company lifted the ban and even handed out flags to its employees.[27]

More controversial have been cases of the Confederate flag – specifically, the battle flag of the armies of the Southern states in the US Civil War – when it has been displayed in US workplaces. In an extreme example, African American employees of a California company brought suit against their company's management for not prohibiting other employees from displaying Confederate flags in the workplace alongside nooses, swastikas, and pro-Ku Klux Klan graffiti. This juxtaposition suggests the Confederate flag was employed as a symbol of racism, harassment, and discrimination. The legal suit alleged a hostile workplace environment and vandalism.[28] African American employees of an Alcoa plant in North Carolina similarly brought suit against their company for allowing employees to place Confederate flags on their cars and on their clothing. They claimed that the prominent and repeated display of the symbol was contributing to racial harassment and discrimination at the aluminum plant. In response, the

---

[26] Robyn Plumner, "Don't Let Patriotism Get Out of Hand," *Milwaukee Journal Sentinel*, November 15, 2001; Martin Miller and Gina Piccalo, "For Some, an Unflagging Discomfort about Flying the Stars and Stripes," *Los Angeles Times*, September 18, 2001.

[27] "Ban on American Flags Lifted," *United Press International Wire Service*, September 17, 2001.

[28] "Workers Say Company Ignored Hate Campaign," *Los Angeles Times*, August 1, 2001.

company banned the Confederate flag entirely from its property, including its parking lots. Some white employees protested this policy as an unreasonable invasion of their right to freedom of expression.[29] From a legal framework, however, employees in the workplace do not have many rights to cultural expression.

The widespread display of the Confederate flag contributed to the production of a new flag, beginning in 1997, by a pair of African American entrepreneurs. They call it the "NuSouth" flag, and it consists of the framework of the Confederate flag, but with the colors of the African Liberation Movement: red, black, and green. The official website of this flag states that the NuSouth company "tackles the age old issue of racism between blacks and whites in America by integrating two 'opposing' symbols."[30] This flag has created controversy in public life – including an NAACP (National Association for the Advancement of Colored People) protest after a student was suspended from a school for wearing the shirt. Defenders of the Confederate flag have commented that the NuSouth design, far from creating unity, is divisive because it is a desecration of the former South's battle flag.[31] The recoloring of the Confederate flag is sure to elicit various interpretations. In any case, this flag has already generated a considerable amount of heat, lending credibility to the argument that the display of flags in the workplace can have a potentially divisive impact on employees.

T-shirts with religious slogans can also stir controversy. Businesses marketing t-shirts with the names of Christian organizations (for example, Promise Keepers) or Christian messages (for example, "What Would Jesus Do?") as well as other Christian products have boomed.[32] These shirts have stirred debate among school administrators and workplace managers alike. Can employees wear t-shirts with a religious message – or invitation – if t-shirts are generally permitted? Some workplaces have attempted to ban shirts with religious messages altogether.[33]

Likewise, difficult questions arise over the display of buttons and bumper stickers. An employee of US West Communications, Christine Wilson, wore a button on her clothing with a photo of an aborted fetus; inspired

[29] "Confederate Flag Supporters Agree to End Protest at Aluminum Plant," *Associated Press State & Local Wire*, September 15, 2000.

[30] NuSouth Apparel, http://www.nusouth.com/history.html, accessed December 5, 2001.

[31] Chris Burritt, "New Colors Unify Emblem of Division," *Atlanta Journal and Constitution*, November 26, 1997.

[32] Kristina Grish, "Christian Activewear Labels Practice What They Preach (T-Shirts with Religious Messages)," *Sporting Goods Business*, April 16, 1999; "Made in Heaven: Christian Retailing," *The Economist*, May 23, 1998.

[33] Matthew T. Miklave and A. Jonathan Trafimow, "Is There Room for Promise Keepers in the Dress Code?" *Workforce* 79/9 (2000).

by her religiously held belief that abortion is the murder of a person, she had taken a vow to wear the button at all times. Her co-workers claimed that the photo was deeply disturbing to them for reasons such as their former miscarriages or their infertility. US West reported that productivity in that unit of the company fell by 40 percent due to the rancor over the situation. The employer offered Wilson the option of wearing the button in her cubicle, covering it while at work, or wearing an alternative button with a related message but no photo. When Wilson refused these potential accommodations, her firing was upheld in court.[34] It would not have been clear, without knowing Wilson's own motivation, that she intended the an-tiabortion button to communicate a *religious* message. That is, co-workers could easily have interpreted the button as conveying, fundamentally, a moral or even a political message. More to the point, these categories – religious, moral, political – are not mutually exclusive.

Political bumper stickers, such as ones carrying the message "Anybody but Hillary" during Hillary Clinton's 2000 campaign for the US Senate, can similarly lead to division when displayed prominently by employees or managers.[35] Employees are often encouraged to wear stickers on national election day that convey the message "I voted today." The key question, then, is not whether employees are permitted to talk about participating in political activities – it is a question of which political statements should be permissible in the workplace and which should not.

Although art in the workplace can be uncontroversial in many instances, employees occasionally have strong views about what type of art should or should not be displayed in their working environment. The physical space and its decoration surely play a role in shaping a workplace culture and, literally, the working environment. Many large companies have an official curator or decorator who is responsible for the aesthetics of the office; other workplaces have less formal methods for choosing the art. In all companies, some person or group must decide about what decor should stay or be changed within the office. The selection and placement of art can raise a variety of conflicts. The issues relate to politics, gender, race, and other questions of identity.

As one example, a corporate curator in Cleveland encountered strong employee dissent over a large painting depicting African American children in what workers perceived as "racial stereotyping." The curator invited the

---

artist, who was African American, to come and explain the painting, which employees then agreed could stay.[36] In another case, women workers at Pfizer, Inc. protested about a sculpture "of a nude woman with a small head and exaggerated hips," denouncing it as degrading to women. The sculptor, a woman who insisted her work portrayed women's strength, agreed to replace the statue with one featuring women's hands.[37]

These examples are distinct from instances in which individual employees decorate their personal office space with their own artwork. The increase in such "personalizing" of one's work area is consistent with the trends in management theories and practices that encourage firms to make the workplace seem more comfortable, "like home," to employees. This, too, can be controversial. Indeed, workers who display political flags or photos of a fetus may be of the opinion that these displays add to the aesthetic decor of their workspace – in other words, they see them as art. Artwork can convey religious themes – whether it be the gentle Jesus portrayed in a popular 1950s oil painting or Mark Chagall's politicized crucifixions. In addition, crystals also decorate many offices and communicate a New Age message.[38]

As is the case with buttons and bumper stickers, employees frequently place posters in their offices or cubicles in order to convey a message and even to influence others. The messages are variously religious, spiritual, ethical, political – or all of the above. They can include words from religious scripture, or they can be more generically spiritual or "inspirational." Richard Peterson sued the Hewlett-Packard computer company after he was fired for displaying, in his cubicle, scriptural passages from the Christian Old Testament that conveyed an antihomosexual message. He acknowledged that his posting of the verses was a direct response to the firm's diversity campaign, which included a call for tolerance of homosexuals, among other groups of persons.[39]

A difficult question – and a possible analytical distinction – is whether the audience of a poster is the individual worker herself or her co-workers.

---

[36] Tanya Mohn, "Office Artwork Brings Out the Critic in Employees," *New York Times*, January 31, 2001.

[37] Ibid. Mohn notes that many managers choose to decorate offices with abstract art because it is less likely to be controversial. One art merchant sells mostly abstract art to office managers because it "can't be offensive to anyone." An interesting parallel can be drawn between this approach to choosing (or permitting) artwork for the office and a common approach to negotiating religious expression, *viz.*, rejecting "exclusive" or particular religious expressions but promoting those forms of spirituality that are not specific enough to be recognizable to most employees. See ch. 3 above.

[38] Pat McHenry Sullivan, "Workplace Thinking Has Been Altar-Ed," *San Francisco Examiner*, November 28, 1999.

[39] "Judge Asked to Rule on Complaint against Hewlett-Packard," *Associated Press State & Local Wire*, April 6, 2001.

That is, a company could allow personal messages (for instance, inside a worker's desk or locker) but not highly visible displays that are likely to convey a message to co-workers. Such a framework might be invoked, for example, in the case of messages (like that of the unborn fetus) that are likely to offend co-workers or clients. In addition to the attendant normative issues related to prohibiting or allowing the public display of posters or personal messages, pragmatic challenges remain in determining, in specific cases, what areas are appropriate and what areas are not for displaying such posters and messages. Leaders may benefit from making determinations such as *intended* and *actual* audience, but they will not solve all dilemmas simply.

These various examples of visible expression suggest that office conflict comes in a variety of forms. Religious expressions certainly can evoke deep and even visceral reactions, but a central point is that political, cultural, and aesthetic displays can also, and often do, create office tension. These examples also suggest that it is difficult, in particular cases, to determine whether an action is properly considered religious, moral, political, cultural, aesthetic, or otherwise. Even the purest "political" example noted above, the bumper sticker criticizing Hillary Clinton, could have been displayed by an employee – perhaps an antiabortion proponent – on religious grounds. The upshot is that frameworks that try to exclude religion altogether from the workplace encounter difficulties related to issues of motivation, action, and effects. If an inclusive definition of religion is employed, and then religion is excluded, the result could be a very empty workplace.

Invitation, proselytization, and/or solicitation

Another set of issues involves workplace interaction in which an employee extends an invitation to or makes a request of a co-worker. The very labels *invitation*, *proselytization*, and *solicitation* convey different kinds of inter-action and degrees of pressure. Many of the potential conflicts in this area are religiously based, but not all.

Conversations in the coffee area or hallway often involve the activities and interests of employees beyond the workplace. Sports, current events, vacations, dating, family life, and religion are part of the mix. Can a work-place policy draw a line between reporting one's interests and activities, on the one hand, and inviting others to take part in them, on the other? Such a policy would have widespread ramifications not only on religious activities but also on many other extracurricular activities as well. If employees are not allowed to invite co-workers to church or mosque, then can they also not invite them to lunch? Could they invite colleagues to a Super Bowl party? A family wedding? If we are drawing lines, does it make a difference whether a wedding is to be held in a garden or in a synagogue?

According to the results of a 2001 survey by the Society for Human Resource Management, 20 percent of employers reported instances of proselytizing of employees by a co-worker at some point during the past five years.[40] The spirituality and leadership literature tends to emphasize the extreme forms of religious proselytization in the workplace.[41] Even Mitroff and Denton acknowledge that they have created a false dichotomy between no religion and coercive, even stealthy, religion at work – yet they do not consider other alternatives.

For many people, the question of sharing their religious or spiritual convictions is not a pressing one. Indeed, arguably members of the silent majority – comprised of adherents to various faiths as well as people of no professed faith – would much prefer to live out their convictions through their actions. These individuals still face the challenge of applying their values to their daily life and actions, but usually they do not choose to invite co-workers to participate in or attend religiously based functions and events. It is important to acknowledge that, for many religious persons, however, the sharing or witnessing of their faith is a central part of their religious identity. Many Christian evangelicals doggedly adhere to this view. While some practices employ tactics that are aggressive or stealthy, those adjectives do not accurately describe the practices of many evangelicals who desire to share what they literally call *good news* with co-workers.

As suggested above, in a healthy workplace in which workers know each other well, religious faith, as well as sports, family life, and politics will be topics of discussion. If people choose to state their convictions in such a context – or even invite a co-worker to visit their religious community – are they necessarily behaving in a coercive manner? Consider Christians who bring Christmas cookies to share with colleagues, Jewish co-workers who offer Purim sweets, or Muslims who bring candies to work during Eid al-Fitr as a way of celebrating the end of Ramadan. Each of these employees

[40] Reported in Maria Mallory, "Balancing Faith at Work: Employees, Firms Must Weigh Belief Vs. Offending Others," *Atlanta Journal and Constitution*, April 8, 2001.

[41] Recall that Mitroff and Denton employ a book by Nix, *Transforming Your Workplace for Christ*, as a foil for their own argument in preference of spirituality instead of religion in the workplace. By the absence of other discussions of religious faith at work, they imply that a workplace can permit only references to spirituality (and not religion) or face the consequences of incessant proselytizing by employees. Ian I. Mitroff and Elizabeth A. Denton, *A Spiritual Audit of Corporate America: A Hard Look at Spirituality, Religion, and Values in the Workplace*, first edn., The Warren Bennis signature series (San Francisco: Jossey-Bass, 1999), 60–75; William Nix, *Transforming Your Workplace for Christ* (Nashville: Broadman and Holman, 1997).

is arguably offering, partly or wholly out of religious motivation, a "good" to fellow workers with arguably little pressure.[42] Other co-workers offer tracts, pamphlets, or even scriptural texts to co-workers. Does such an offer amount to a gracious invitation or to a coercive act? To be sure, it is difficult to answer the question once and for all; the particular aspects of the action and the context must be analyzed in each case.

The Guidelines on Religious Exercise and Religious Expression in the Federal Workplace, a 1997 document from the Clinton administration for federal government settings, recognizes the importance of a distinction between inviting a co-worker to a religious service and repeatedly pestering or threatening a co-worker. The document suggests that it is acceptable for employees – even for supervisors – to invite co-workers to religious events, as long as they are willing to accept no for an answer. Once a co-worker indicates a lack of interest or a preference not to receive such requests, the employee extending the invitation is obligated to stop.[43] As with other ground rules, this one does not solve all problems, but it does suggest a way to negotiate between religious invitation and religiously based coercion.

Religious appeals do not have exclusive claim on potentially intrusive or coercive activities. The sale of Girl Scout cookies is an interesting example. All together, fundraising through the sale of cookies, gift wrap, candy, and other items comprise a $2 billion industry. The selling of these products has increased in the workplace, for reasons including the "time bind" experienced by many workers (and their overprogrammed children), security concerns about peddling door-to-door in neighborhoods, and the heightened need for nonpublic funds to support schools and various nonprofit institutions.[44] For some co-workers, having the opportunity to purchase Girl Scout cookies in the workplace is a much anticipated and enjoyable event. Others concede that it is a reasonable way to support important charitable and civic causes. Yet many workers report that they feel a sense of pressure or even coercion when co-workers approach them with products. Workplaces have instituted policies to address this issue, but the policies vary significantly from place to place. In some offices, policies forbid employees from using company media (for example, e-mail or bulletin boards) to advertise or solicit; in others, companies designate a bulletin board

---

[42] The Council on American–Islamic Relations communicated a call on its website for Muslims to take sweets to work on Eid al-Fitr in December 2001: http://www.cair-net.org, accessed December 5, 2001.

[43] William Jefferson Clinton, "Guidelines on Religious Exercise and Religious Expression in the Federal Workplace" (Washington, DC: The White House Office of the Press Secretary, 1997).

[44] Ellen Neuborne, "Charity Begins at Work: Parents Work the Workplace as Fund-Raisers," *USA Today*, January 22, 1997.

especially for "personal" announcements and appeals. Some policies forbid solicitation of any kind; others treat the issue with "benign neglect" and leave it to local supervisors to use their judgment in particularly troubling cases.[45]

The sale of Girl Scout cookies in the workplace serves as a colorful and familiar example of a nonreligious issue of potential conflict. Like invitations to a religious service, invitations to buy cookies may seem benign to some but invasive to others. Further, they each represent different aspects of the mundane or everyday reality of workers' lives. Of course, the commitment to one's religious identity is generally much (though certainly not always) greater than the commitment to a child's identity as a Girl Scout. Whether one needs to witness to one's co-workers in order to be faithful to one's religious identity cannot be answered in a universal way. It is reasonable to assert that workplaces should have a consistent method (formal or informal) to specify ways in which religious adherents as well as workers selling items on behalf of some organization such as the Girl Scouts or a Little League baseball team may – and may not – approach their co-workers respectfully with genuine invitations.

Time for prayers, sabbath observance, and holidays

In the workplace context, questions arise over when employees will work and when they will not. How is the working schedule organized? What sense of agency or voice do employees have in determining when they work? In terms of religious observance and obligation, are employees able to observe their religious prayers, sabbaths, festivals, and holy days?

Like the discussion of religious dress, the focus on time off from work for religious observance is usually cast in terms of non-Christians – typically Muslims and Jews – who need "special" attention to their religious calendar. Once again, this portrayal frames religion – at least the "minority" kind – as a problem to be solved. In particular, it portrays employees who are observers of non-Christian traditions as particularly demanding because of their religious needs. The examples below focus on the very real problems that non-Christians face in the current working calendar. The discussion of religious minorities and their religiously based obligations should begin, however, with a critical analysis of the organization of the current calendar.

---

[45] L. M. Sixel, "To Some, Soliciting Sales at Work Is a Crummy Idea," *Houston Chronicle*, January 22, 1996; Neuborne, "Charity Begins at Work: Parents Work the Workplace as Fund-Raisers."

The American working calendar varies from industry to industry as well as from company to company, but it is fundamentally structured around Christian holidays and national holidays. As a prominent example, the Christian holy day of Christmas is the only US federal holiday whose origin is the holy day of a religious community. The only time of year when many American businesses (but often not retail or entertainment industries) slow down is the period between Christmas and New Year's Day. Christian workers seldom face problems of negotiating for Christmas Day as a day off from work, because it is a national holiday.[46]

Muslims do not enjoy the same benefits for their major holidays of Eid al-Fitr or Eid al-Adha or in the wider seasons of Ramadan and Dhu al-Hijjah, respectively. Jews face difficulties securing leave time for their "December holiday," Chanukkah, as well as the more religiously significant holy days of Rosh Hashanah, Yom Kippur, and Passover. Indeed, the Jewish high holy days (Rosh Hashanah and Yom Kippur) usually fall during the early weeks of renewed activity in the workplace – after the summer months during which families often take vacations – a most difficult time for employees to take even personal time off from work.

Even more than the American yearly calendar, the structure of the working week is highly influenced by the Christian and Jewish sabbatical structure, by which every seventh day is a day of rest.[47] To be sure, the view that each week deserves a day of rest (or two days) – and particularly the preservation of Saturday and Sunday as public, or at least commonly held, days off from work – has been eroded by increasing work hours and, in the words of Juliet Schor, the "unexpected decline of leisure time."[48] Changes

---

[46] It is important to acknowledge that some percentage of Christians do indeed have to work on Christmas. For many Christians, Easter is the more religiously significant holiday; it always falls on a Sunday. There are, admittedly, problems for Christians who want to observe Good Friday – but many companies do close on this day and some others also close on Easter Monday.

[47] The transition from the Jewish calendar, in which the sabbath is literally the seventh day of the week, to the Christian framework, in which the day of rest is Sunday, the first day of the week, is a complicated narrative. Indeed, the Seventh Day Adventists have recognized and addressed this issue in their theology and religious practice. The two biblical justifications in the Hebrew Bible or Old Testament for a sabbatical framework emphasize that humans should follow God's example of resting (Hebrew, *shabat*) on the seventh day, such as in Genesis 2:3: "So God blessed the seventh day and hallowed it, because on it God rested from all the work that he had done in creation," or they should mark the seventh day of each week by resting and giving thanks to God for freeing the Israelites from slave-labor in Egypt (Deuteronomy 5:14–15). While, liturgically, most Christians understand Sunday to be the first day of the week, some refer to it only as "the Lord's day" and leave the title of sabbath to Saturday. Other Christians have appropriated the notion of sabbath to Sunday. See R. F. Buxton, "Sunday," in *The New Westminster Dictionary of Liturgy and Worship*, ed. J. G. Davies (Philadelphia: Westminster Press, 1986). In contrast to seeing Sunday as the first day of the week, the world of business considers, de facto at least, Monday to be the first day of the week. This is consistent with the view of Saturday and Sunday as the weekend, or end of the week.

[48] Juliet Schor, *The Overworked American: The Unexpected Decline of Leisure* (New York: Basic Books, 1992).

in work style and the increasing availability of people through communications technologies have also weakened the division between work time and so-called leisure time. This latter category – meant to capture time not spent engaged in workplace endeavors – sweeps together time for familial, communal, religious, and personal pursuits, including sleep. Work has become the primary activity, and all other activities are structured around the work calendar. As described by Michael Walzer, the very notion of *free time* has shifted in the West from being free from religious (i.e., Christian) holy days in the Middle Ages to being free from working obligations in the current period.[49]

The complicated structure of the annual and weekly work schedule, influenced by Christian (and to a lesser extent, Jewish) liturgical calendars, is the context in which discussions of religious requests for accommodation from work time should take place. Although all people of faith who wish to celebrate their holy days as nonworking days face some degree of challenge and negotiation with their employer, those challenges and negotiations are not equivalent. Rather, in general terms they are increasingly difficult, respectively, for Christians, Jews, and Muslims. Some examples may illustrate the issues.

Scott Hamby was an employee at a Wal-Mart store in Missouri who requested that he not be scheduled to work on Sundays because of his Baptist beliefs that Sunday should be a day of worship and rest. When he was assigned, over his objection, a number of Sunday shifts, he resigned from the job and brought suit against Wal-Mart on the basis of religious discrimination. In 1995 Wal-Mart settled the case and, without admitting fault, agreed to institute a company-wide policy of training and education to prevent religious discrimination. That sweeping policy included additions to the employee handbook regarding discrimination, a team of corporate trainers to educate managers and supervisors on religious accommodation, and changes to scheduling policies.[50]

Jews who strictly observe their Sabbath have long encountered problems with leaving work in time to make Friday prayers or taking Saturday off

---

[49] Michael Walzer offers a fascinating account of the transition, in the Christian-dominated West, from telling time based on church holy days, to the appropriation of time for public holidays, and finally to the use of time as an input to market processes. Vacation time is the product of the Industrial Age; during earlier periods, holidays were public, while vacations are now individualized. See Michael Walzer, *Spheres of Justice: A Defense of Pluralism and Equality* (New York: Basic Books, 1983), 184–96. My framework calls for allowing religious adherents to have the ability to take time from work in order to celebrate their own religious holy days.

[50] "Wal-Mart Settles Worker's Religious Bias Suit," *St. Louis Post-Dispatch*, August 23, 1995; Janell Kurtz, Elaine Davis, and Jo Ann Asquith, "Religious Beliefs Get New Attention," *HR Focus*, July 1996.

from work. Esther Smothers and Amanda Brooks received a settlement from National Action Financial Services/SITEL in Williamsville, New York, as a result of their religious refusal as Jews to work on Saturdays. Smothers was dismissed by the company in 1999 for her requests not to work on Saturdays, and Brooks was not hired because of her expression of the same religious obligation.[51] In 2000 Sears, Roebuck, & Company settled a similar case based on its firings of Orthodox Jews who, as repair service technicians, would not work on Saturdays. Sears claimed that Saturdays were its busiest home repair days (a claim disputed by New York State attorneys) and that allowing Orthodox Jews to have Saturdays off would create an undue burden on Sears to accommodate its religious employees. The company agreed in the legal settlement, however, to pay lost wages and attorney fees, to accommodate future workers in the same situation, and to implement a training program for those involved in hiring and scheduling.[52]

The obligation to pray five times a day, the *salat*, creates distinctive challenges for Muslim workers. Two or three of these daily prayers fall during customary working hours. In early 2001, about thirty Muslims, recent immigrants from Somalia, resigned from their jobs at a chicken processing plant near Atlanta because their employer would not allow them five-minute breaks for prayer. The employer claimed that there were too many people who were taking breaks at the same time. That is, managers claimed that to accommodate the workers would have required shutting down the processing line each time Muslims needed to pray. The workers claimed that only a few workers requested a break at the same time. One of the employees told a reporter from the *Atlanta Journal and Constitution*, "[When I came to the US] I was expecting to be very happy, in a safe place where I could work freely and pray freely because this is a land of freedom. But this isn't any better than the life we left behind [in Somalia]."[53]

Muslims uphold a particular obligation to join in Friday midday prayers with members of a religious community, and not merely to pray alone as they can do more acceptably at other times. Umar ibn C. C. Cook brought suit against Cochran Electric, his Seattle employer, because supervisors would not allow him to leave work to attend Friday services. A European American, Cook argued that the company subjected him to religious discrimination because his supervisors doubted the sincerity of his

[51] Jay Rey, "Settlement Reached in Case on Religious Discrimination," *Buffalo News*, January 6, 2001.
[52] Jayson Blair, "Sears Agrees to Change Sabbath Work Policy," *New York Times*, April 5, 2000.
[53] Sandra Eckstein, "Boss, Workers in Clash over Prayer; Muslims Who Sought Five-Minute Break from College Park Assembly Line Were Refused, Left Jobs," *Atlanta Journal and Constitution*, January 26, 2001.

Muslim beliefs.[54] Around the country, Muslims have struggled to find compromises and make ad hoc arrangements with employers that would allow them to travel to a mosque or Islamic community house for prayers and then return to work.[55] Some Muslims agree to go to work early on Friday mornings, or to take shorter lunches on other weekdays, or to trade coffee breaks in order to receive a longer lunch break on Friday.[56] Blue-collar or pink-collar workers, with less flexible schedules and more supervision than white-collar employees, generally have a more difficult time making such arrangements with managers.

Religious observance and obligation account for many of the requests for personal days off work. Of course, other reasons, ranging from vacation travel to family funerals, also account for the taking of personal leave. Additionally, companies are required by law to have medical leave policies, including parental leave. Employees still have to negotiate time off for other kinds of personal needs, including medical and dental appointments, but these cases are examples of individual or familial activities – not of communal ones. Two distinctive elements of most religious observances, in contrast to personal or family needs, are that they involve an alternative calendar and that an institution, group, or community observes that calendar.[57]

The birthday of Martin Luther King, Jr., the most prominent leader of the African American civil rights movement, is an interesting case of a holiday that is celebrated by overlapping communities. His birthday was declared a US national holiday in 1986. In contrast to all federal and most state and local government workers as well as banking employees, most private-sector employees do not get the day as a paid holiday. A recent survey found that only 23 percent of firms made the day a paid vacation

---

[54] Florangela Davila, "Electrical Worker Sues for Right to Practice Religion – Growing Muslim Population Has Sparked Similar Cases," *Seattle Times*, August 15, 1998.

[55] See, for example, stories of various Muslims in Richmond, Virginia, who participate in prayers at the Islamic Society of Greater Richmond, in William Ciucci, "Muslims Finding a Place; Some in Richmond Area Content with Employer Accommodations," *Richmond Times-Dispatch*, May 30, 2001.

[56] The example of employees at the National Electric Coil company in Columbus, Ohio, is described in Lornet Turnbull, "Mixing Work, Religion Requires Flexibility by Workers," *Columbus Dispatch*, October 4, 1999.

[57] As an exception, the courts have decreed that sincerely held beliefs, even if held by a lone individual, are considered a religion and can include, for example, commitment to a sabbath day. A man who worked as a Pueblo, Colorado, air-traffic controller sued the Federal Aviation Administration for making him work on Saturdays, despite his own personal belief based on his individual reading of Genesis. A federal jury ruled that the FAA discriminated against him on account of his religion when the agency fired him, and it awarded the man over $2 million dollars in lost pay and damages. Mike McPhee, "Sabbath Observer Wins Suit on Firing Pueblan; Awarded $2.25 Million," *Denver Post*, July 18, 2001.

day for employees.[58] African Americans and other employees who wish to attend the numerous community – and church – celebrations, lectures, and parades to mark this day are not able to do so unless they take personal vacation time. Leaders from civil rights organizations have encouraged employers to include ways to acknowledge the holiday – whether it is paid time off or sponsorship of events and activities in their local community.[59] At present, despite the fact that King's birthday is significant enough to the American narrative that it is a national holiday, African American and other employees who want to observe the day face a dilemma not unlike that faced by Buddhist workers who wish to celebrate Gautama's birthday or Sikhs who wish to mark Guru Nanak's birthday.

Holiday and vacation time is a critical matter for businesses and their employees. The attendant issues raise questions of productivity for managers and questions of income, the balancing of work time and private time, and competing loyalties for workers. While management and leadership scholars address these concerns in terms of "minority" individuals who seek special accommodation because they are different, the wider structural questions include who has the power to define the working schedule, how the wider society's calendar was formed, and whether workers have the economic agency to observe their religious commitments even if it means losing (or forfeiting advantages in) their job.

CONCLUSIONS

Through a variety of examples of dress, visual displays, invitations, and holidays, I have sought to build a collage of the conflicts that can occur in the diverse contemporary workplace. Religious adherents often hold deeply rooted convictions that, in many cases, include obligations that have a fundamental effect on how they appear and act as employees – and who they are. I have tried to suggest throughout the chapter, however, that not only religious persons, but all persons, bring the basic aspects of their identity to the workplace. Their views and actions related to politics, culture, art, spirituality, religion, and even family life can be potentially divisive. None of these spheres of human activity, though, should be considered divisive in most or all cases.

In discussions of vacation time, calendars, and work schedules, I have sought to point out that the issues do not pertain only to persons of

---

[58] Marc Ballon, "For Most Firms, Business as Usual on Martin Luther King Holiday," *Los Angeles Times*, January 15, 2000.

[59] Ibid.

so-called minority traditions. Some Christians have realized that they, too, are affected by views that seek to keep religion completely out of the work-place. Evangelicals have often portrayed themselves as a minority group that is being marginalized by a hostile or secular environment. I am sym-pathetic with many of the concerns that evangelicals express on this front. Yet crucial to the larger debate is the recognition that mainstream (predom-inantly Protestant) Christianity has defined, and continues to define, much about the formal structure and the informal norms of the workplace. The Christmas holiday and the structure of the Monday-through-Friday work-week are merely indicative of wider questions concerning the workplace environment. The context of lingering Christian cultural establishment must be part of the analysis of religious diversity in the workplace.

The dominant role that Christianity plays is just one reason why treating *religion* as a category can be misleading. The examples found throughout the chapter, while not capturing all of the diversity of religious expression or conflict, nevertheless give an indication of its wide scope. Given this religious diversity, can we consider how religion in general is distinct from other kinds of potentially conflictual attitudes and actions? Analogously, it would be difficult to offer a definition of political behavior or cultural expression. In fact, the framework of respectful pluralism that I offer in the book does not require providing sharp definitions of these spheres – or drawing sharp lines between them. The rough analogies between religiously motivated buttons and political bumper stickers, between religious invita-tions and fund-raising solicitations, and between religious holidays and a civil rights holiday build support for my view that religion should not be treated as fundamentally different from other kinds of expression. I have emphasized the difficulties of even separating these aspects of identity – along with aspects of culture, race, ethnicity, nationality, and others – in the first place.

The spirituality and leadership literature often implies that conflict is an unhealthy component of a workplace. I certainly wish to acknowledge the value of human cooperation and teamwork. (Many analysts emphasize the efficiency grounds for achieving teamwork, but there are intrinsic reasons to value it as well.) Conflict can be destructive or constructive – as part of the latter, it can be instructive as well. Yet, as the examples above suggest, conflict is a part of any workplace – even the one that tirelessly purges religious expression from it.

PART II

Mapping religion and the workplace

CHAPTER 5

Being religious differently

This chapter aims to cast light on the vastly different ways in which individual leaders and followers live out their own religious commitments in the workplace. I have already discussed many kinds of conflicts that can occur from differences in employees' beliefs and practices, but I have yet to delineate the varieties of religious expression at work. For some people, being religious means they dress or act in ways that obviously set them apart from most of their co-workers. For others, it refers to their own understanding of their work as religious work or to their quiet actions to help co-workers or customers. Employees who call themselves spiritual, secular, or atheistic can also live out their deepest values and commitments in the workplace in ways that are readily compared to religious expression.

This chapter begins by drawing upon a deceptively simple distinction between individual and institutional expressions of religion. The distinction does not provide a magic key to unlock the confusion or ambiguities surrounding appropriate roles for religion and spirituality in the workplace. However, it does offer insight into the different ways – sometimes conflicting – in which scholars employ phrases like "workplace religion." Is workplace religion about the religion that individual employees bring to work or is it about the religious ethos of the organization itself? It may be both; this chapter and the following one emphasize the importance of recognizing differences between individual and institutional expressions.

It is surprising that few analysts of religion and organizational leadership have explored the individual–institutional distinction. One of the reasons for this omission, I assert, is that most approaches to religion and spirituality in the workplace underemphasize religious diversity. We have already seen that models of generically spiritual workplaces, for example, operate on the premise that particular religious beliefs are based on the same essential spiritual values. Individuals may differ in religious dogma but, in a spirituality model, it is possible for individuals to translate or apply their particular

religious beliefs into common spiritual values in a relatively straightforward and uncontroversial manner. The generic spiritual approach, then,
attaches little significance to distinguishing between individual spirituality
and official or institutional forms of spirituality.

Advocates of secular workplace views, although acknowledging the empirical reality of diversity among the workforce, try to block all religious
speech and actions from entering the office or work site. Religiously based
practices (for example, wearing a yarmulke instead of the standard workplace hat or getting release from work shifts on one's sabbath) require
accommodations on the part of the employer. Aside from the exceptional
cases, however, secular-minded employers do not consider either individual
or institutional religious expression as appropriate in the workplace.

Workplaces in which Christian beliefs and symbols hold a preferred or
established status have already addressed the institutional question, whether
wittingly or unwittingly. Quite simply, such workplaces equate Christian
values with moral values. In contrast to the secular workplace, Christian
workers in this context do not tend to perceive a void between their own
and company values. Members of minority religious traditions, in contrast,
often experience a direct tension – a religious tension – between their
personal values and official company values. As in the other frameworks,
minority-religion employees may receive accommodation, but it is clear that
their worldview is not the company worldview. As long as these employees
receive minimum accommodation, the Christian workplace view does not
see it as problematic that the CEO invokes his or her Christian tradition
when speaking for the company and its core values, or that the official
annual gathering is called a Christmas party.

Because my framework, in contrast, takes the religious diversity of employees as a given reality and a starting point, this chapter begins by
clarifying the distinction between the religious commitments and values
that individual employees bring to work and the institutional values or
commitments that companies officially endorse. I draw critically upon the
individual–institutional distinction as framed in the literature surrounding
the religion clauses of the First Amendment. The remainder of the chapter specifies various ways in which individual employees bring religion to
work with them. Few would oppose the idea that every employee brings
values and commitments (many of which are religious or spiritual in nature) to work. Not only do these various values and commitments represent
a myriad of religious, spiritual, and moral traditions, but they also affect
how individual leaders and followers understand and interpret their own
identity and their particular workplace context.

INDIVIDUAL AND INSTITUTIONAL RELIGION: LESSONS FROM FIRST AMENDMENT INTERPRETATION

The scholarly conversation about the religion clauses of the First Amendment to the US Constitution has helped define the distinction between individual and institutional expression of religion. Legal analysts, historians, political theorists, and scholars of religious studies have long debated the ways in which the clauses set the context for religious freedom in the United States, particularly in determining the appropriate ways in which deeply held and publicly contested religious commitments may – and may not – be expressed in public life. At the same time, it is important to recognize that some of the insights from this literature are not directly applicable to the focus on religion in the workplace.

The First Amendment's religion clauses are these: "Congress shall make no law respecting an establishment of religion or prohibiting the free exercise thereof." How best to interpret these clauses for an increasingly diverse population and complex society has led to arduous and sometimes tortured reasoning on the part of Supreme Court justices and the scholarly community. It is no overstatement to say that, since the founding days of the United States, determining the appropriate role for religious beliefs and commitments in public life has been a perennial challenge for the nation's leadership.[1]

In the US context, questions of the free exercise of religion and the nonestablishment of religion are conceptually and practically related to questions of religious diversity in the workplace. The legal protections afforded to the religion of individual employees, affirmed in Title VII of the 1964 Civil Rights Act, as amended, derive from the First Amendment. However, it is important to note two caveats to drawing any analogies between the state and the workplace. First, the First Amendment creates a *legal* framework for protecting each citizen's right to the free exercise of religion, while prohibiting governmental institutions from officially endorsing or legally establishing a specific religion. In contrast, I am developing a *moral*, rather than a *legal*, framework in this book. While the legal requirements of accommodation, non-harassment, and nondiscrimination relate to the

---

[1] A wide literature surrounds the interpretation of the religion clauses of the First Amendment. See, in particular, Ronald F. Thiemann, *Religion in Public Life: A Dilemma for Democracy* (Washington, DC: Georgetown University Press, 1996), chs. 2 and 3; Ronald B. Flowers, *That Godless Court?: Supreme Court Decisions on Church–State Relationships*, first edn. (Louisville, KY: Westminster John Knox Press, 1994); James Davison Hunter and Os Guinness, eds., *Articles of Faith, Articles of Peace: The Religious Liberty Clauses and the American Public Philosophy* (Washington, DC: Brookings Institution, 1990).

framework being developed, the moral argument goes beyond the legal minimums. Most aspects of the behavior recommended within respectful pluralism are not (and should not be) required by law; rather, as with most moral frameworks, the approach has the aim of convincing individual employees and institutional leaders to base their actions on what is right and good.

The second important caveat pertaining to the First Amendment concerns the difference between state institutions and private-sector institutions. Simply put, the legal discussion around the First Amendment, particularly the nonestablishment clause, addresses institutions of the government, not private-sector organizations, which are the focus of this book. The context for interpretation of the First Amendment and the wider Bill of Rights is the fundamental question of the social contract that citizens make with each other in forming a government. What powers do citizens entrust to the government, and what rights do citizens retain for themselves? What are the limits of a state's ability to coerce citizens in its governing role? What protection will persons in the minority have against majority rule? Within a social contract framework, the American founders determined that government institutions could not endorse a particular religious perspective, because it would favor adherents of that faith over other religious (and nonreligious) worldviews. As part of the fundamental commitment to an equality among citizens, then, the religion clauses aim to guarantee that no citizen's religious commitments will make him or her less than a full participant in political and civil life. In the words of Charles Taylor:

> The aim [of the religion clauses] was to prevent full citizenship [from] turning on any particular confessional allegiance, something that would infallibly have alienated a large part of the population. Confessional differences should not stand in the way of anyone's being part of the new Republic and sharing in its common values, including the religious values that were central to it.[2]

It is religious freedom that is protected equally (and thus there is no fundamental conflict in this case between freedom and equality). The religion clauses also address a third fundamental value of the American system: mutual toleration.[3]

The free expression of religion is literally the first right of citizens enumerated in the Bill of Rights. The First Amendment's guarantee of the

---

[2] Charles Taylor, "Religion in a Free Society," in *Articles of Faith, Articles of Peace*, ed. James Davison Hunter and Os Guinness (Washington, DC: Brookings Institution, 1990), 102.

[3] Thiemann's treatment of the First Amendment describes the American founders' emphasis on the three values of freedom, equality, and toleration. Thiemann, *Religion in Public Life*.

nonestablishment of religion effectively protects government from the intrusion of religious ideas or institutions on its work. Even more directly related to the free exercise of religion, however, it also assures citizens that no one religious institution or perspective holds a legally preferred status in the US. This, in turn, prevents the government or majority rule from placing unacceptable demands on citizens of divergent religious backgrounds. The genuine free exercise of religion thus necessitates that no particular religious ideas or institutions gain state endorsement or privilege.

The guarantees against undue governmental intrusion into citizens' religious life, embodied in both the free exercise and nonestablishment clauses, are intended to assure free and equal citizen participation. It is particularly important to guard against coercion – in the religious sphere or otherwise – on the part of the government.[4] Short of an exit from one's country of citizenship, a person cannot escape the binding force of laws. The state, in other words, has monopolistic power over its citizens in certain fundamental areas of life, including military, economic, and political spheres. This power should not be employed to compel citizens to support religious beliefs or institutions to which they object.

In contrast to the state's potentially dominating influence, the general assumption is that, except in rare circumstances, companies do not hold monopolistic power over their employees. Rather, in a free market economy marked by *employment-at-will* relationships, employees are seen to be able to move with relative ease from one company to another, particularly if they believe they are being treated unjustly or inhumanely.[5] The freedom of employees to choose among multiple employment alternatives, combined with the existence of many potential employers and many potential employees, would seem to guarantee that no one company (or individual employee) has undue power. Such assumptions of a free and competitive labor market are, arguably, never entirely accurate. In many cases, they fail to take into account the institutional power of large companies as well as the forces of economic necessity and the high costs associated with quitting a job and finding another one. All these factors can, and often do,

---

[4] The emphasis here is on the negative aspects of freedom. As Charles Taylor aptly points out, the concern of the founders was also to guarantee a positive, or civic, freedom – "the freedom we enjoy together to the extent that we govern ourselves as a society and do not live under tutelage or despotism." Taylor, "Religion in a Free Society," 94. Similar to Thiemann's discussion of religion and the founders, Taylor argues that the assumed religious ideas of the early American leaders would play some part in maintaining civic freedom.

[5] For contrasting views on employment at will, see Patricia H. Werhane and Tara J. Radin, "Employment at Will and Due Process," in *Ethical Theory and Business*, sixth edn., ed. Tom L. Beauchamp and Norman E. Bowie (Upper Saddle River, NJ: Prentice Hall, 2001) and Richard A. Epstein, "In Defense of the Contract at Will," in *Ethical Theory and Business*. See also ch. 8 below.

compel workers to accept suboptimal working conditions. The decline in power of labor unions – traditionally a "countervailing" force to the institutional power of companies – has contributed to the decline in relative power that many employees have experienced in recent decades vis-à-vis their employers. Thus, although workplace organizations usually do not have the same kind of coercive power as institutions of the state, they often hold tremendous sway over employees.[6]

These caveats note the significant differences between the legal framework of religion and governmental institutional power, on the one hand, and the moral framework of religion and workplace institutional power, on the other. Yet, there remains the important point that there is a rich (and hotly contested) precedent of distinguishing individual religious expression from institutional forms of religion in US public life. Two central ideas stemming from this literature contribute to understanding the individual–institutional distinction. First, the official endorsement of a specific religious framework or institution is the illegitimate use of political power, because it may have a detrimental impact on persons from other traditions or backgrounds. Closely related to this protection against religious establishment is the second idea, namely, that particular and diverse religious exercise is protected as a fundamental aspect of a free, equal, and tolerant community.

In the context of the workplace, the individual actors relate to their companies not as citizens, but as employees. Although workers are citizens of a nation (ordinarily, but not always, the nation in which they work) and many adult citizens work in the private sector, the moral status of citizens and employees is distinct, particularly vis-à-vis the institutions of the state and the company. The fact that these respective institutions are potentially and actually coercive in different ways makes an analogy between politics and the workplace incomplete. It is right, in general terms, to see greater potential coercion and actual coercion in what governments do than in what companies do. Yet it is also important to consider the ways in which companies potentially exercise coercion over their employees. To the extent that coercion is possible in turning over certain powers in the employment contract as it is in the social contract, then the concern about institutional religion and the moral aim to guarantee free religious exercise have some application in the workplace. The following chapter draws out the implications of institutional religious expression as potentially coercive of employees.

[6] See also the moral argument for respectful pluralism in ch. 8 below.

VARIETIES OF INDIVIDUAL FAITH

Once the distinction between individual and institutional religion is made, the next step is to describe the wide variety of ways in which individuals bring their faith, values, or deepest convictions to the workplace. This is a key implication of religious and spiritual diversity. Thus, it is important to delineate different ways in which individuals live out (directly and indirectly) their religious and moral beliefs at work. None of the classifications of "being religious differently" that I present in the following paragraphs should create inviolable lines between and among people. Rather, most persons in our diverse world have been influenced by beliefs from a variety of religious, spiritual, and moral traditions. In this analysis I attempt to use the labels or classifications that people use to identify themselves. Although some of the labels may implicitly convey positive or negative connotations (for example, the terms *atheist* and *Jew* are often used in derogatory ways), my intent is not to value one kind of religious expression over another in this descriptive analysis. As I have already suggested in the previous chapter, it is the substance of actions – and not their religious, spiritual, or political label or motivation – that must meet minimal criteria of prohibiting the coercion and degradation of fellow employees.[7]

Some individuals label themselves as atheists, agnostics, or non-practitioners of either religion or spirituality. Despite self-definitions in terms of what they are not, these persons surely hold moral convictions about the current realities of their world as well as beliefs about how the world, including the workplace, should operate. While these persons describe themselves as nonreligious, they nonetheless hold and draw upon one or more value systems in their daily lives, both at home and work. Some nonreligious people have explicitly thought out and articulated their value system as a comprehensive moral worldview. Others may not openly articulate their moral convictions but demonstrate them clearly in their actions.

As we have seen, another significant group of employees identifies itself as "spiritual, but not religious." Most of these people see the work of creating a moral–spiritual worldview as an individual task. Most are not part of a religious or spiritual congregation or institution. Indeed, one of the "articles of faith" of the spirituality movement is that no institution or official creed binds individuals. Yet this by no means implies that spiritual-but-not-religious employees are free from the influence of other people on their

---

[7] See chs. 8 and 9 below for a more complete version of this argument for respectful pluralism.

spiritual and moral worldview. The act of *bricolage*, or cobbling together of a worldview, is undertaken within the context of social trends and beliefs. That is, although an individual chooses not to be classified as part of a religious tradition or congregation, he or she is still open to influences, including the spirituality industry, beyond the self. Although New Age adherents seldom belong to a religious or spiritual institution, the New Age movement is itself a kind of tradition, or at least a collection of ideas with which individuals identify.

A third group includes people who identify themselves with the label of a specific religious tradition (or possibly multiple traditions). These individuals are Buddhists, Hindus, Sikhs, Jains, Wiccans, Muslims, Jews, Christians, and so on. Although some of these identifications are more exclusive than others, some individuals welcome multiple labels. Further, the boundaries of these traditions are not fixed; the traditions themselves are better described as rivers that flow and change than as territories that are bounded and fixed.[8]

It is important to acknowledge the problems that scholars face in differentiating religious traditions as distinctive categories. People within a given religious tradition do not speak about, or experience, their religion in the same way. Ninian Smart, scholar of comparative religions, offers a ten-point list of problems with classifying religions by tradition.[9] As one important example, thinking in terms of traditions – Buddhism, Christianity, Hinduism, etc. – suggests a level of common belief or practice among Buddhists, among Christians, and among Hindus that probably does not exist. Judaism can be broken down by familiar subcategories like Orthodox, Conservative, Reform, Liberal, Reconstructionist, and Secular. Buddhists follow multiple schools within Zen, Theravada, and Mahayana subtraditions. Christians fall into varieties of Orthodox, Catholic, and Protestant groups, and they can be further divided as well. For instance, Protestantism is full of broad denominations: Methodists, Baptists, Lutherans, Presbyterians, Episcopalians, Disciples of Christ, and so on. These subtraditions, in turn, have different institutional denominations – The Presbyterian Church (USA), the Reformed Church of America, the Presbyterian Church of America, and so on. As Smart notes, even naming these subtraditions only

---

[8] Many scholars use the metaphor of religious traditions as rivers. Diana Eck uses this image in a variety of interesting ways throughout her book *Encountering God: A Spiritual Journey from Bozeman to Banaras* (Boston: Beacon Press, 1993). Masao Abe uses it to describe Buddhism in Masao Abe, "Buddhism," in *Our Religions*, ed. Arvind Sharma (San Francisco: Harper San Francisco, 1993), 81.

[9] Ninian Smart, "The Pros and Cons of Thinking of Religion as Tradition," in *Teaching the Introductory Course in Religious Studies: A Sourcebook*, ed. Mark Juergensmeyer (Atlanta: Scholars Press, 1991).

captures some of the significant differences.[10] The problem of variation and disagreement is repeated at the subtradition level – i.e., a vast variety of beliefs, practices, and communities exist within every religious grouping.

A distinct problem with classification by traditions is that while these categories portend to be descriptive, in practice they tend to take on normative force. For instance, "heterodox" or "heretical" strands, say, of Buddhism, are not so easily categorized and are thus easily excluded from the classification.[11] The tendency is to focus attention on religious beliefs and practices specifically associated with a tradition's institutions and "orthodoxy." Further, the very notion of a tradition best fits those religious communities and practices that are most structured or exclusive. Hinduism, for instance – without a rigid religious dogma, no specific "founder," and an inherently pluralistic worldview – is less readily categorized as a single religious tradition than Judaism or Christianity. As scholars of Hinduism have noted, the name Hindu derives not from religious beliefs or practices but from the region of the Indus valley.[12]

Despite the pitfalls of speaking in broad terms of religious traditions, labels such as Buddhist, Christian, and Muslim manage to account for some realities of religious belief and practice that are not readily described in other ways. Smart himself notes the value of focusing on traditions – as long as no religious tradition loses it plural character and the contextual factors and interreligious complexities are noted.[13] It is important to avoid generalizations when possible and to understand persons in terms of their traditions and other kinds of characteristics.

The broad grouping of employees who identify themselves as religious adherents is more like a motley collection than a unified group. What individuals in this grouping do have in common is that, to some extent, each claims to be part of some ongoing tradition, which Alisdair MacIntyre defines as "an historically extended, socially embodied argument . . . an argument precisely in part about the goods which constitute that tradition."[14] In differing ways, each person in this category claims a relation to or an affiliation with a religious tradition which embodies or enacts some set of rituals. Consistent with the metaphor of religious traditions as rivers, the composition of a tradition itself is subject to change. To redefine or dispute

[10] Ibid., 33.   [11] Ibid., 33–34.
[12] John Stratton Hawley, "Teaching the Hindu Tradition," in *Teaching the Introductory Course in Religious Studies: A Sourcebook*, ed. Mark Juergensmeyer (Atlanta: Scholars Press, 1991), 38.
[13] Smart, "The Pros and Cons of Thinking of Religion as Tradition," 34–36.
[14] Alisdair MacIntyre, *After Virtue* (Notre Dame, IN: University of Notre Dame Press, 1981), 207.

the tradition from within, however, requires some level of acceptance of the language in which that argument is taking place.

The view of tradition as an embodied, ongoing argument squarely rejects a conception of religion as an inflexible worldview or a set of unbendable rules that adherents must follow despite their individualistic desires for autonomy. Tradition is not a set of manacles worn by religious people to stymie their freedom. Those who portray religious expression solely as the fulfillment of duties that encumber followers without permitting them a degree of choice – even in the name of positive freedom – overlook or disregard the ways in which religious traditions always involve interpretation and application to changing social contexts.[15] On the other hand, it is undeniably true that communities or traditions themselves often shape their conception of the way the world is and make demands on adherents to undertake particular actions.[16] Sometimes these calls are specific (pray five times a day, do not eat meat, or do not steal), and other times the calls are more general (honor God in all that you do, love your neighbor as yourself, avoid desire because it leads to suffering). Religious traditions themselves vary in the specificity and the nature of the commitments required; and within every tradition and subtradition there is a tremendous variety of interpretations on what the specific demands are. To return to the understanding of tradition as argument: while all arguments have room for multidirectional conversation, the degrees of structure, hierarchy, creativity, and formality differ from one tradition to another.

CHOICE AND COMMITMENTS: A TENSION?

Commitments to a religious community or tradition, with attendant requirements on behavior in all spheres of life, including work, are what tend to differentiate "religious people" from others. It is the nature of these commitments that seems to confound liberal thinkers about what place religion should play in pluralistic contemporary society. After all, Western Enlightenment philosophies have celebrated and given priority to individual autonomy – and the related value of individual choice. The view of freedom that is privileged in the liberal worldview is that of *negative*

---

[15] Michael Sandel is right to criticize liberal accounts that view all commitments as voluntarily made by "unencumbered" selves. But he goes too far in the other direction when he refuses to acknowledge that the understanding and fulfillment of religious duties do require certain kinds of choices. See Michael J. Sandel, "Freedom of Conscience or Freedom of Choice?," in *Articles of Faith, Articles of Peace*.

[16] Craig Dykstra, *Growing in the Life of Faith: Education and Christian Practices* (Louisville, KY: Geneva Press, 1999), 130–34.

freedom, by which individuals are most free when they have the least external interference into their autonomy. Religiously based commitments entail precisely the kind of *heteronomous* influences (that is, literally, the law or rule of others) that Immanuel Kant famously rejected in his classic essay "What Is Enlightenment?"[17] Obligations to an external source of morality – especially since some of these obligations can clearly work against one's self-interest – are not easily understood within a narrow view of the rational, autonomous self.[18]

Commitments to a religious tradition, however, are not the only kinds of heteronomous influences that affect people and serve to limit their choices. Although Bellah and colleagues convincingly document the decline in commitments in contemporary life, almost all people uphold commitments that have binding force on them and constrain their choices.[19] Obvious examples include the financial and moral commitments that are part of the standard marriage contract or covenant.[20] Individuals also make, and are consequently constrained by, political, civic, and moral commitments.

[17] Immanuel Kant, "An Answer to the Question: What Is Enlightenment?," in *Kant: Political Writings*, ed. Hans Reiss, Cambridge Texts in the History of Political Thought (Cambridge University Press, 1991).

[18] Amartya Sen provides an interesting analysis of how commitment and sympathy could be included within an expanded understanding of self-interest. He is critical in particular of economic theories of self-interest that lead to a conception of human beings as "rational fools." His critique could also apply to political or social anthropologies that fail to understand commitments (religious or otherwise) as part of one's well-being. See Amartya Sen, "Rational Fools: A Critique of the Behavioural Foundations of Economic Theory," *Philosophy and Public Affairs* 6 (1977) and Amartya Sen, "Goals, Commitment, and Identity," *Journal of Law, Economics, and Organization* 1/2 (1985).

[19] Robert N. Bellah, *Habits of the Heart: Individualism and Commitment in American Life* (Berkeley, CA: University of California Press, 1985); for an excellent and provocative examination of commitments from the perspective of a Catholic moral theologian, see Margaret A. Farley, *Personal Commitments: Beginning, Keeping, Changing* (San Francisco: Harper & Row, 1986).

[20] I do not assume that the moral commitments of marriage agreements made under different religious traditions are identical, though the *legal* commitments in a given state within the United States and most Western countries do not vary by the religious affiliation of the marrying couple. The institution of marriage in the United States has some peculiarities that result from the fact that either state employees or officials from religious institutions (ministers, priests, rabbis, etc.) can act on behalf of the state to solemnize marriages. (In some states other individuals can also act for the state to perform marriages.) Religious leaders who perform marriages are thus acting on behalf of their own institution and on behalf of the government, and, therefore, they can easily conflate the moral and legal obligations of marriage. In India, in contrast, this confusion is resolved, but only at the cost of other kinds of confusion. Couples can be married according to different kinds of domestic law. That is, Muslims can marry according to Muslim law, by which men, for instance, can have up to four wives. Christians and Hindus follow a different civil code. See ch. 7 below for a fuller discussion. A different kind of complexity in marriage is evident in Louisiana and several other states that have an option for couples to make a more self-binding commitment (through covenant marriage) than that found in the standard marriage contract. See Katherine Brown Rosier and Scott L. Feld, "Covenant Marriage: A New Alternative for Traditional Families," *Journal of Comparative Family Studies* 31/3 (2000); and Kaja Perina, "Covenant Marriage: A New Marital Contract," *Psychology Today* 35/2 (2002).

People often enter and uphold such commitments without regard to their own interests.[21] Many of these commitments are not as visible as religious participation, but they can be just as binding.

Admittedly, liberal theorists do not have a problem with binding commitments, as long as they are voluntary. That is, if individuals are seen to enter willingly and without coercion into a contract with another person or a community, then they preserve their autonomy. In many such contracts, individuals retain an *exit privilege* from the arrangement, such as divorce. The real issue, and the reason religious commitments tend to receive disproportionate criticism, arises when the perception is that individuals do not have a choice in the commitments they make. For many, but certainly not all, religious persons, commitments are like that: many religious persons are Muslim or Buddhist or Jewish because they were *born* that way and, therefore, they assume the religious commitments of their faith automatically. The degree of genuine exit privilege that a given person possesses varies broadly.

Michael Sandel points to the importance of the distinction between *constitutive* and *cooperative* community. Liberal political theory, Sandel asserts, can only account for "community in the cooperative sense," in which "unencumbered selves . . . are free to join in voluntary association with others, whether to advance our private ends, or to enjoy the communal sentiments that such associations often inspire."[22] But this contrasts with "community in the constitutive sense," which would entail "membership in any community bound by moral ties antecedent to choice."[23] These latter ties, more than the former, play a fundamental role in a person's identity.

I want to acknowledge in no uncertain terms that traditions or communities often have normatively undesirable characteristics. Even as I offer criticism of liberal individualist theories for their failure to take constitutive commitments seriously, I concur with liberal critics of communitarianism and traditionalism that religious practices, rituals, or rules can be (and, too often, *are*) highly oppressive. They can limit the freedom of all group members or some subgroup of members (example: a religious group requires wives to be subservient to their husbands). It should also be noted that religiously based actions contribute to the oppression of outsiders as well (example: a Christian religious group teaches that homosexuality is

---

[21] Sen, "Goals, Commitment, and Identity."

[22] Michael J. Sandel, *Liberalism and the Limits of Justice* (Cambridge University Press, 1982), 76.

[23] Ibid.; see also Sandel, "Freedom of Conscience or Freedom of Choice?" and Thiemann, *Religion in Public Life*, 99–102.

sinful and lobbies government to deny civil rights to gay and lesbian persons, some of whom may well be "closeted" members of that group).

Religious duties, like other deeply held commitments, should be viewed as neither wholly negative nor as wholly positive in the abstract. They simply are a part of the worldview and practices of many people. In this sense, I am making a descriptive claim. At the same time, I seek to employ this descriptive claim within a normative framework that recognizes and respects religious commitments in the sphere of work. The workplace need not welcome any and all commitments; the workplace should be free to shun commitments that are coercive and degrading to other people. Yet, religious and other commitments deserve a presumption of legitimacy, although some way to exclude clearly degrading or coercive forms should be determined and put into practice.

Usually commitments are neither fully voluntary nor fully constitutive. Even choices freely undertaken are made within certain constraints (for example, a person chooses to join a particular political party or a religious community, not out of complete or unencumbered choice, but within the context of the available options and in light of her own worldview shaped by her family and social history). Conversely, many, if not most, religious communities include some sort of ritual process by which young adults confirm their intention to be part of the religious community. Most commitments, then, involve some, but not unlimited, choice.

Thus, persons of all persuasions – atheists, agnostics, spiritual adherents, and religious people – are affected to some degree by external influences. Religious participants may be more willing than others to acknowledge those influences and consequent duties. However, as noted previously, Wade Clark Roof's research documents the tremendous importance of the language of choice amongst religious "seekers" and "shoppers."[24] When employees enter the workplace, no one enters commitment-free or value-free; conversely, few employees enter the workplace so confined by their religion that they lack any genuine freedom to act as agents.

WORDS OF INVITATION – OR OFFENSE

Within each of the categories discussed above – nonreligious people, spiritual adherents, and religious practitioners from a variety of traditions – individuals vary according to the extent that they choose to express their

---

[24] Wade Clark Roof, *A Generation of Seekers: The Spiritual Journey of the Baby Boom Generation* (San Francisco: Harper San Francisco, 1993).

beliefs and commitments in the workplace. Some Muslims understand their tradition to impose a strict dress code, especially upon women. Other Muslim women have chosen to adopt a more "Western" form of dress and thus have opted, for instance, not to wear *hijab* at work. This particular example, however, raises the question of voluntariness of behavior. Some Muslim women report fearfulness about wearing a scarf at work, particularly in light of the post-9/11 backlash against Muslims, and they have thus chosen to forgo wearing *hijab*, despite their religious convictions. If they deemed it safe to wear a headscarf, many more would probably do so. Thus, especially for members of minority or marginalized traditions, it is overly simplistic to equate observed behavior with genuine preference; a more respectful workplace environment could result in different behaviors.[25]

Nonetheless, in this and other cases, people of similar or related religious traditions interpret their obligations differently and, frequently, they translate these obligations into distinct actions in the workplace. For example, within the Christian tradition, many individuals (and the religious institutions to which they belong) understand their call to Christian discipleship to involve *evangelizing* (literally, sharing the good news) by inviting non-Christians to become Christians. This effort is variously termed "witnessing," "testifying to Christ," "bringing people to Christ," and "sharing Christ." For many people who undertake or desire to undertake workplace evangelism, such actions are not merely about doing what their religion requires. Evangelizing in the workplace and elsewhere, in some Christians' view, is about offering people the way to eternal salvation.

It would be unfair to the Christians who actively practice workplace evangelism not to recognize that many or most of them undertake their efforts with positive, loving intentions for their co-workers. At the same time, people of other religious traditions, no religious tradition, and even the Christian tradition itself often do not interpret co-workers' acts of evangelism in this benign light. Indeed, evangelistic words and actions might be interpreted, not as an invitation, but as proselytism or intrusion. And it is too simple to say that the critics of workplace evangelism merely misunderstand the motives or the message of their evangelizing co-workers. Rather, more often than not, these critics do not wish to have a conversation

---

[25] Conversely, critics could state that some women who wear *hijab* do not do so in a fully voluntary way. Rather, in such a view, they are coerced (perhaps to the point that their own will is deformed) by men in their tradition, or by the tradition itself, in terms of what they should wear and in other senses. Such a contention, vis-à-vis any number of practices in various religious traditions, is an important one. Moral evaluation of specific religious commitments themselves is simply beyond the scope of this book.

about religion or to change their own beliefs or actions. Some co-workers – whether atheists, agnostics, spiritual people, Christians, Jews, or others – do not mind being approached. They may be happy to engage in religious and spiritual discussions or even debates without ever feeling threatened, pestered, or coerced. The key question should not be whether religion or spirituality is discussed at work, but rather how those conversations take place.

In the US context, Christian evangelicals are undoubtedly the group of employees and bosses who are most often accused of trying to discuss their faith at work in an effort to convince co-workers to adopt their commitments. This is not surprising, given not only the numerical majority of Christians in the US, but also the historically privileged status of Christians in US society. In contrast, cases of Muslims, Hindus, Buddhists, or Jews who are accused of proselytizing are rare in this country. This is due in part to the different nature of these traditions and in part to the smaller numerical and societal influence of these traditions.

For instance, Jews generally do not have the same conception of religious conversion that Christians do. People can convert, to be sure, into the Jewish community, but, as Nicolas De Lange suggests, "Since in [Jews'] minds the religion is somehow secondary to Jewish identity, it is not conversion to Judaism that is the issue. In the relatively rare cases where a non-Jew does opt to become a Jew, this is probably seen more in terms of joining a people than subscribing to a faith."[26] Non-Jews most often convert to Judaism because they are marrying a Jew. Jewish employees have little theological or cultural imperative to convert their co-workers.

Hindus also tend to be uninterested in converting people to their religion. This has to do with the very notion of Hinduism as a tradition. Hinduism itself is an amalgam of various practices and beliefs, almost all of which are inclusive and flexible. Pluralism is built into the very philosophical–theological conceptions of Hinduism.[27] It is generally not hard for Hindus to accept Jesus, for example, as a manifestation of the Divine, because the Divine for Hindus is present in many forms, in many people, and indeed, in many gods. Neither the concept of monotheism nor that of polytheism fully describes Hinduism; the Divine may be present in many forms and manifestations. This view makes Hindus more likely to celebrate different forms of religious action or idea as another expression of the Divine than, say, Christians or Jews who hold more exclusivist conceptions of

[26] Nicholas De Lange, *An Introduction to Judaism* (Cambridge University Press, 2000), 1–2.
[27] Arvind Sharma, "Hinduism," in *Our Religions*, ed. Arvind Sharma (San Francisco: Harper San Francisco, 1993), 4–5.

God. Arvind Sharma states that "[p]ushed to its logical extreme, a Hindu can claim that one is most a Hindu when least a Hindu, that is, when one has dissolved one's Hindu particularity in Hinduism's all-embracing inclusiveness."[28] Such a view makes conversion much less urgent to Hindus.

Some question whether Buddhism is a *religious* tradition, because in general terms the tradition is not theistic. That is, much of Buddhist tradition does not include the belief in a God or gods. (There are figures, though, most notably in Mahayana traditions, who receive a deified status as *celestial Bodhisattvas* and *celestial Buddhas*.[29]) The paradoxical nature of Buddhist ideas – including the central notion of discovering oneself by realizing that there is "no self" (*anatta*) or the view that the "ultimate reality . . . is not God, or Being, or Substance [but] *Sunyata*, which is often translated as 'Emptiness' "[30] – has long confounded thinkers influenced by theistic and rationalistic traditions. Buddhist practitioners are willing and sometimes eager to share practices and concepts with others, but these are not always seen by Buddhists to conflict directly with Christianity, Judaism, or other traditions. Many maintain, then, that it is possible to remain a Christian or a Jew and to practice Buddhist techniques or rituals. Some people do convert, in fact, to Buddhism; European American converts to Buddhism now pepper the various Buddhist communities in the US.[31]

Most often, however, Buddhists and Hindus invite co-workers to join in some of their practices – particularly yoga or meditation – without believing that it requires a renunciation of their (other) religious convictions. Indeed, on the organizational level, employers have sometimes sought to bring techniques like meditation into official company practice, with the claim that meditation is not religious. They assert that it is either a secular or a broadly spiritual activity. Some employees from other religious traditions

---

[28] Ibid., 4.

[29] Richard H. Robinson and Willard L. Johnson, *The Buddhist Tradition: A Historical Introduction*, third edn., The Religious Life of Man series. (Belmont, CA: Wadsworth, 1982), 78–90; see also Abe, "Buddhism," 105.

[30] Abe, "Buddhism," 114. Abe also states an additional level of paradox in contrasting Buddhism and Christianity: "In Buddhism, Emptiness as ultimate reality must be emptied. However important Emptiness may be, if it is represented and we attach ourselves to it as 'emptiness,' it is not true Emptiness" (p. 120).

[31] Abe suggests, interestingly, that Buddhism, along with Islam and Christianity, is a missionary religion. But he goes on, by "developing a hint provided by Max Weber," to assert that Buddhism is an "emissary" religion, by which he means it involves "establishing a presence and minimizing the differences between one's own religion and the religion one encounters while retaining one's commitment to one's own tradition." He sees Christianity (as "promissory") and Islam (as "commissary") as placing greater emphasis than Buddhism does on religious uniqueness, and hence to having a stronger conversion impulse. Ibid., 129. See also the chapter on American Buddhism in Diana L. Eck, *A New Religious America: How a "Christian Country" Has Now Become the World's Most Religiously Diverse Nation* (San Francisco: Harper San Francisco, 2001).

(for example, Christians or Jews) have protested this claim and have called attempts to bring "Eastern techniques" into official company life an affront to their religious convictions.

Islam may be most akin to Christianity in terms of the emphasis on inviting non-adherents to join a community and tradition in order to worship their God (in Arabic, *Allah*) in an exclusive way. Muslims mark their conversion by "making *shahadah*," that is, by professing that "there is no God but one and Mohammed is the prophet of God."[32] In the United States, conversion to Islam has gained the most public attention among the African American community; indeed, a good deal of media attention has focused on conversion of African Americans through Islamic prison outreach programs.[33] While there is a theological imperative toward conversion in Islam as well as in Christianity, the different social and numerical realities of the two religious communities keep Muslims' proselytizing from being a significant component of the religion-and-the-workplace discussion. Indeed, for most Muslims, the question of their basic acceptance in the workplace is a more pressing one than the question of converting Christians or other co-workers to Islam.

Adherents of generic or general spirituality may also try to convince co-workers that some spiritual beliefs or practices could be valuable to them. Spiritual employees extend invitations, in other words, to religious, agnostic, or atheistic co-workers, but these invitations are sometimes seen as bothersome or insulting efforts at proselytism. Recall that, at the institutional level, some of the complaints brought against companies for imposing religious practices actually involved New Age or generically spiritual practices. Spiritual proselytism, however, is somewhat distinct from instances in which Christians seek to evangelize. Christians who actively evangelize typically claim that their religious teachings are distinctive and exclusive and that a radical conversion is needed in order for non-Christian co-workers to become Christians. They are often aware that others might see their actions as bothersome, but they may be prepared to be despised in order that they might bring a salvific message to co-workers. In contrast, spiritual adherents de-emphasize the distinctive or exclusive elements of their message, claiming instead that everyone can practice what they are practicing, regardless of their religious affiliation. For this reason, they may

[32] Ibid.; Seyyed Hossein Nasr, "Islam," in *Our Religions*, ed. Arvind Sharma (San Francisco: Harper San Francisco, 1993), 428.
[33] Dan Freedman, "Terror Suspects Place Islam under New Lens; Some Say Prisons Are Fertile Ground for Radical Muslims," *Milwaukee Journal Sentinel*, July 7, 2002; "Jailers Are Studying Islam as Ranks of Inmate Converts Grow; Faith Encourages Less Violence, One Muslim Says," *St. Louis Post-Dispatch*, April 12, 1999.

be less able to understand why their invitations are not welcomed. What, they wonder, could be offensive about a crystal, or a sunrise, or a book about angels?

Atheists can also offer invitations that co-workers perceive as offensive or inappropriate. Indeed, atheism can take a strong stance on matters religious – viz., it entails a worldview that God or gods do not exist. (Agnosticism is typically a less strident position, since the uncertainty of knowing suggests the lack of definite conviction.) Just as some Hindus and Christians do not openly promote their religion, so many atheists also prefer to keep their values and commitments private. Other atheists, though, wish to share their convictions. Indeed, if a "Jesus Saves" t-shirt is likely to find its way into a highly pluralistic workplace, so, too, is a t-shirt claiming that "God Is Dead."

One's atheism need not be stated in negative terms (notwithstanding the etymology of the term itself). Indeed, many persons who do not practice religion or spirituality are eager to state their values in positive terms. They try to share those values (for example, human rights, secular humanism, libertarianism) with co-workers and, in some cases, convince co-workers that all people should hold these values; and, as is often true with religious and spiritual examples considered above, co-workers may view such attempts to share values as bothersome or offensive.

The issue in each of these cases is not necessarily that one person or group of persons has bad *motivations* in seeking to promote their religion or in preferring not to be approached about religious matters. Rather, diverse employees hold disparate and, often, competing *worldviews*. Individuals vary not only in their spiritual, religious, or moral worldviews, but also in whether or not and to what extent they choose to express their convictions in the workplace. They also vary in how and how much they would like their co-workers, bosses, and subordinates to express theirs. The reality of diversity in the workplace creates a situation in which many – but by no means all – employees will seek to share their deepest convictions with one another. Sometimes co-workers will welcome hearing other perspectives (whether or not they are convinced), and other times co-workers will be annoyed or offended at being approached.

ACTIONS OVER WORDS

In the attempt to understand religion in the workplace, it is easy to focus on the flashy or divisive cases. The legal cases are fascinating and offer plenty of issues to debate. Employees who attempt to convince co-workers to adopt their religious views receive the lion's share of attention in the discussion on religious speech at work. Although the controversial cases and actions are important, a quiet (and diverse) majority are engaged in a phenomenon that is, arguably, just as worthy of attention: applying their own religious understandings without fanfare to how they perform their work and treat their co-workers and customers.

I have already argued that all employees bring some set of values and some wider worldview with them when they enter the workplace. For some employees that worldview is explicitly religious, for others it is generically spiritual, and for others it is atheistic or humanistic. Regardless of their worldview, employees differ in their degree of conscious and critical reflection upon their values. Some employees understand that their work is an integral part of their religious life: Christians may articulate that vision in terms of vocation, or discipleship, or grateful response to God's gifts.[34] Many Muslims articulate duty in terms of *al-din*, or the belief that one is so indebted to Allah that one should devote one's entire life to serving Him. In Nasr's words, "In the Islamic perspective, religion is not seen as a part of life or a special kind of activity along with art, thought, commerce, social discourse, politics, and the like. Rather, it is the matrix and worldview within which these and all other human activities, efforts, creations, and thoughts take place or should take place."[35]

Individuals from different religious traditions will vary in the extent to which they can keep their religious motivations and ideas to themselves. To be sure, all persons can have religious and other kinds of thoughts without articulating them, but some traditions may allow adherents to undertake actions quietly in ways that are distinct from the actions of other traditions. For example, Gregory Pierce suggests in his book *Spirituality@Work* (which is cast in a combination of Christian and more inclusive or general spiritual language) that, if employees choose to practice spiritual disciplines at work, they should try not to call their co-workers' attention to it.[36] They should not be performing religious practice, in other words, in order that others can see that they are religious or spiritual. Yet this suggestion by Pierce

---

[34] Willliam Diehl employs language of discipleship and calling in his account. William E. Diehl, "Sharing Personal Faith at Work," in *Faith in Leadership: How Leaders Live Out Their Faith in Their Work – and Why It Matters*, ed. Robert J. Banks and Kimberly Powell (San Francisco: Jossey-Bass, 2000). Nicholas Wolterstorrf offers a Reformed Christian vision of world-transformative Christianity, based upon grateful response to God's grace. Nicholas Wolterstorff, *Until Justice and Peace Embrace* (Grand Rapids, MI: Eerdmans, 1983).

[35] Nasr, "Islam," 439.

[36] Gregory F. Pierce, *Spirituality@Work: 10 Ways to Balance Your Life on-the-Job* (Chicago: Loyola Press, 2001), 32.

overlooks the problem that Muslims, for example, face when their religious obligations to wear *hijab* or to observe *salat* make them conspicuous.

These highly visible obligations notwithstanding, individuals' application of their religious, spiritual, or moral commitments – whether articulated or not – are a significant way in which religion in diverse forms affects the workplace. Will an employee decide to undertake a morally ambiguous action? Why or why not? When an employee decides to take a particular job, does she believe that she will be able to do good in the position – or even to do God's will? Does a leader or follower at work treat others according to the moral dicta of his religious or spiritual tradition?

The relationship between religion and ethics is by no means straightforward or uniform. It is not clear that various religious faiths essentially share the same "core" values. Initiatives such as the interreligious statement "Towards a Global Ethic," spearheaded by Hans Kung at the 1993 World's Parliament of Religions, are fascinating and potentially significant efforts at ethical understanding across religious boundaries, but they do not strive to resolve the genuine differences among the traditions.[37] Even if, in a broad sense, "love" or "justice" is seen to be a central value within every identifiable religious tradition, the level of generality would preclude simple and practical application of the principle.[38] That is, the more general the principle (religious or moral), the less straightforward it is to apply in practice.

Even putting the question of "quiet actions" in terms of the application of religious and moral principles can be problematic. Do employees (whether formal leaders or not) often think explicitly in terms of the dictates that are part of their religious, moral, or spiritual worldview and then seek to enact those principles when they face a difficult situation? I suggest that the process is rarely so linear. It is more likely that employees reflect morally, religiously, or spiritually on their workplace in a less direct way. Here the virtue ethicists are right – living a moral life has as much to do with moral formation and character as it does with stating and then enacting a set of principles in a given situation.[39]

It is not even necessary to be conscious of the ways in which religious or moral perspectives affect persons' actions in order for them to play a role. In

---

[37] Hans Kung and Karl-Josef Kuschel, eds., *A Global Ethic: The Declaration of the Parliament of the World's Religions* (New York: Continuum, 1993).

[38] For an effort to distill the "common values" of world leaders across cultures, see Rushworth M. Kidder, *Shared Values for a Troubled World: Conversations with Men and Women of Conscience* (San Francisco: Jossey-Bass, 1994).

[39] MacIntyre, *After Virtue*; Stanley Hauerwas, *A Community of Character: Toward a Constructive Christian Social Ethic* (University of Notre Dame Press, 1981).

this sense, persons' quiet actions can be more religious or otherwise value-centered than employees themselves recognize. Other employees, even if they are aware of their moral, religious, or spiritual motivations, are intentional about *not* stating those motivations. In both cases, employees do not make a point of stressing the religious motivation behind their actions to their co-workers.

Finally, an employee might understand co-workers' actions as being religious in some sense or another – whether or not the actor herself thinks in those terms. For example, a Christian employee might see God at work in the extra compassion shown by his boss (whatever the boss's actual background or motivation) at a difficult time. A Buddhist might see the Buddha nature in acts of generosity of her Jewish and Wiccan co-workers. The understanding of a colleague's action is separate from the actor's own reasons for acting. Astute leaders who recognize the religious, spiritual, and moral diversity of their team members will realize that each employee may understand the actions of their co-workers in distinct ways.

INDIVIDUAL VIEWS OF INSTITUTIONAL ARRANGEMENTS

Classifying employees in a variety of religious and nonreligious traditions and then exploring how those employees express their beliefs differently in terms of words and actions help to describe the variety of ways in which different individuals bring their religious, spiritual, and moral commitments into the workplace. An additional way to differentiate how individuals interact with religion or spirituality in the workplace is to specify their respective views about what *institutional* arrangement for religious expression would be best in the workplace. As I noted, an atheist may enjoy discussing her moral or political values in the workplace more than a given Christian enjoys talking about his deepest convictions. While the atheist might prefer a generic spirituality framework or a value-centered variation of it,[40] the Christian in this example might well prefer a wholly secular workplace instead of either a generic spirituality environment or a Christianized one. It may (or may not) be empirically true that atheists, more than religious practitioners, tend to prefer that religion be kept out of the

---

[40] See the categories to describe different ways of being a spiritual workplace in Ian I. Mitroff and Elizabeth A. Denton, *A Spiritual Audit of Corporate America: A Hard Look at Spirituality, Religion, and Values in the Workplace*, first edn., The Warren Bennis signature series (San Francisco: Jossey-Bass 1999). Mitroff and Denton describe the "values-based organization" (pp. 143–63) as just one of the five "models for fostering spirituality."

workplace, but individual atheists and religious adherents will differ on the subject.

People who consider themselves spiritual, but not religious, may often enjoy a spiritual workplace instead of a workplace that is either wholly secular or representative of effective Christian establishment. But some spiritual people may prefer that everyone restrict visible forms of spirituality to their lives outside of work, thereby ensuring a secular workplace. Other spiritual people might hold a view of Christian culture as a comfortable environment for them, even if they do not call themselves Christians, and thus they would have no problems with a culturally established Christian workplace.

Within the Christian community, people differ in terms of whether their own tradition should enjoy a kind of special status in the workplace. Christians hold various opinions about the historical linkages between Christianity and American history and the demographic fact that Christians comprise a majority in many US workplaces. Liberal mainline Protestantism has embraced a privatization of religious expression – though without acknowledging that much of Christian culture, like the calendar and workweek, is embedded in the environment. Evangelicals and conservatives, in contrast, tend to prefer more explicit references to Christian symbols in the workplace. Thus, there are multiple "Christian" perspectives on how individuals should be allowed to bring their faith to work; the culturally established Christian workplace represents only one such perspective.

It is not clear how employees from religious traditions other than Christianity would choose among the secular, spiritual, and Christianized workplaces. The secular option at least places them on a supposed equal footing with other employees, but it may prove the most hostile to their religious expressions and to all religious adherents. The spiritual workplace might welcome their religious expression, or it might create environmental pressures against any particularistic practices. A workplace that officially or de facto endorses Christianity could be either hostile or relatively welcoming of other traditions.

Finally, many workers from various religious and nonreligious traditions may well prefer something like the position of respectful pluralism that is detailed in Part III of this book. Whether atheistic, agnostic, spiritual, Jewish, Hindu, or Christian, employees may favor a framework in which the company itself does not endorse any particular religious or spiritual tradition but, rather, creates the space for individuals of various backgrounds to live out their own particular, deeply held, complex, and sometimes conflict-producing commitments in the workplace.

CONCLUSIONS

This chapter has named multiple ways in which religion is present in the workplace. A key element of the argument is that religion is present in disparate forms. This chapter began with one critical distinction – individual employees' expressions of their religion and institutional expressions of religion. My critical overview of the scholarly debates over the First Amendment suggests the value of distinguishing individual from institutional religion. When religious diversity is taken with full seriousness, institutional forms of religion inevitably, if not intentionally, favor some persons' religious beliefs over those of other people. Institutional frameworks may or may not create a context in which all persons (whether citizens vis-à-vis the state or employees vis-à-vis the corporation) have an equal capability to live out their religious beliefs.

At the same time, my discussion has acknowledged the limitations in drawing analogies between the *legal* interpretation of issues involving religion (both individual and institutional) and *government* institutions, on the one hand, and the *moral* evaluation of the relationship between religion (both individual and institutional) and *private-sector* institutions, on the other. The concern about state coercion is well developed in social-contract thought; the potential coercion of employees by private-sector companies, often overlooked, also deserves careful consideration.

Once the distinction between institutional religious expression and individual religious expression is made, it becomes possible and necessary to focus upon variations of each. This chapter has focused on different ways in which individuals express their religious commitments at work. I have delineated many ways – but certainly have omitted other important ways – to understand differences of religious expression at work. Employees may identify themselves as atheistic, agnostic, humanistic, or "spiritual, but not religious." Many others are religious, though some such people will claim *not* to be religious in a general sense but profess to be aligned with a particular religious tradition (for example, Christianity, Buddhism, Judaism). I stress that all of these categorizations are problematic, and a given person may reject all of them or claim to fit into multiple ones.

Criss-crossing those categorizations is the issue of how explicit an employee is in expressing his or her religious, spiritual, or moral system to fellow employees. Christians disagree amongst themselves about the meaning and obligations of evangelizing. Muslims disagree about which religious practices are obligations in predominantly non-Muslim workplace environments. Atheists disagree about how vocal to be in their beliefs. One thing is certain, however: there are many ways to express one's faith at work.

Finally, individuals from all of these groupings hold different views about what institutional arrangements would create the most morally or religiously acceptable workplace environment. No necessary linkage exists between atheists and a preference for a secular (godless?) workplace; between spiritual people and a preference for a generically spiritual workplace; or between Christians and a culturally established Christian organization. On the contrary, acceptance or rejection of these institutional viewpoints varies by person.

All of these issues are further complicated by the fact that many people choose not to acknowledge (even if they recognize them) the religious, spiritual, or moral influences on their actions at work. For disparate reasons, they prefer to be quiet about the motivating influences behind their actions. Without claiming that every action in the workplace is religiously, spiritually, or morally based, this discussion does suggest that the influence of religion in the workplace should be understood in a much larger context than just those well-publicized cases in which explicitly religious speech, or action, or dress creates conflict.

Factors of societal and organizational environment certainly affect employees' decisions about religious expression in the workplace – recall the female Muslim employees who choose not to fulfill what they understand to be religious obligations out of a perceived fear of backlash. Other persons, believing that management and co-workers expect and accept the display of religious expression in the workplace, parade their religiosity. The following chapter considers questions of the institutional context and how, in turn, that context influences the kinds of individual religious, spiritual, and moral expressions we have just considered.

CHAPTER 6

Religions of the workplace

Religion and spirituality *in* the workplace often refer to a religion or spirituality *of* the workplace. I have suggested that a critical distinction can be made between the beliefs and practices of individual employees, on the one hand, and the rituals and ethos of the organization, on the other. The wider question of organizational culture has received significant attention in the leadership and management literature.[1] Some scholars have noted, in descriptive–analytical terms, the ways in which an organization's culture can be religious, quasi-religious, or spiritual.[2] Other scholars have actually played a direct role in contributing to, or even promoting, the religion or spirituality of corporations, accepting the view that business leaders should serve as "spiritual guides" and that firms should develop their own "organizational spirituality."[3]

That some scholars have encouraged companies to become more explicitly religious or spiritual – whether via de facto Christian establishment or via a generic spirituality – has created significant controversy and criticism.[4] Why would a business get involved in promoting spirituality or a specific religion among its employees? Do the company leaders take proper consideration of the religious, spiritual, and moral diversity of their employees?

---

[1] See ch. 9 below for a discussion and references.
[2] One analyst has gone so far as to assert that management studies and leadership studies have themselves taken on religious forms, through their taken-for-granted worldview or their accepted "articles of faith." Stephen Pattison, *The Faith of the Managers: When Management Becomes Religion* (London: Cassell, 1997); Stephen Pattison, "Recognizing Leaders' Hidden Beliefs," in *Faith in Leadership: How Leaders Live Out Their Faith in Their Work – and Why It Matters*, ed. Robert J. Banks and Kimberly Powell (San Francisco: Jossey-Bass, 2000).
[3] Gregory N. P. Konz and Frances X. Ryan, "Maintaining an Organizational Spirituality: No Easy Task," *Journal of Organizational Change Management* 12/3 (1999).
[4] Heather Hopfl, "The Making of the Corporate Acolyte: Some Thoughts on Charismatic Leadership and the Reality of Organizational Commitment," *Journal of Management Studies* 29/1 (1992); Dennis Tourish and Ashly Pinnington, "Transformational Leadership, Corporate Cultism, and the Spirituality Paradigm: An Unholy Trinity in the Workplace?," *Human Relations* 55/2 (2002). See also Chris Lee and Ron Zemke, "The Search for Spirit in the Workplace," *Training* 30/6 (1993).

Advocates of both the Christian workplace and the generically spiritual workplace are in agreement – and are correct – on one point: Workplaces that promote a fully secularist position (i.e., keeping all religious and spiritual expressions outside the workplace) are also imposing a values-based worldview on their employees. That is, secular workplaces, too, reflect an organizational culture with a specific view toward religion and spirituality – namely, that they are not welcome. A culture that frowns upon all religious and spiritual expression communicates a certain set of values to its employees and to its other constituents or stakeholders. All workplaces have some sort of organizational culture, even if management did not make explicit efforts to create that culture. It is simply impossible to avoid taking a values-laden position vis-à-vis the diverse religious and spiritual (and cultural and political) commitments that employees and managers bring with them to work.

Thus, I concur with the proponents of the Christian workplace and the proponents of the generically spiritual workplace in arguing that a fully secularist approach to religion and spirituality is unduly and unrealistically restrictive on employees. This is, in part, a pragmatic claim – based on the problems of asking employees to compartmentalize their lives. More fundamentally, I am making a moral argument that asserts, in brief, that workers should not be asked to divorce their religious expression from their workplace identity.[5]

My concurrence in rejecting the fully secularist position, however, does not mean that I endorse either the Christian workplace or the generically spiritual workplace. To the contrary, I believe that each of these positions pays inadequate attention to the religious, spiritual, and moral diversity of employees and, in this omission, each of these institutional approaches fails to respect equally the beliefs and practices of employees.

This chapter explores the ways in which workplace organizations themselves embody or reflect a religious or spiritual environment. It focuses on the Christian workplace and the generically spiritual workplace and offers a critical perspective on their respective benefits and problems. Insights from religious studies on establishment religion and civil religion can add analytical precision and fresh perspective to an examination of religion and spirituality in the workplace. I thus draw on the more developed literature on religion and politics to understand the institutional use of religion and spirituality in the workplace. By applying these concepts to organizational contexts, the chapter exposes the problems with each perspective – the generic spiritual framework and the Christian framework.

---

[5] See ch. 8 below.

CIVIL RELIGION AND WORKPLACE SPIRITUALITY

The concept of civil religion came into modern Western political thought via the concluding chapter of Jean-Jacques Rousseau's classic work, *On the Social Contract*. Within his account of the social contract, Rousseau struggles with the appropriate role for religious beliefs and commitments in a democratic political order. His treatment is clear in describing the potential conflicts between religious obligations and political duties. His chief concern in the chapter on civil religion is how a political state can maintain the loyalty of religious citizens.

Christians, in particular, pose a problem for the state. According to Rousseau's abbreviated history, the Roman Empire permitted an unprecedented interrelationship of religious and political identity. Unlike the henotheism practiced in earlier civilizations in which all people in one nation worshiped that nation's god (or gods) but each nation worshiped a different god (or gods), Rome granted legal standing to the national and local deities of all its conquered subjects. Roman subjects, in other words, could worship their particular gods as long as they honored the emperor. Rousseau suggests that, in this context, "Jesus came to establish a spiritual kingdom on earth. By separating the theological system from the political system, this brought about the end of the unity of the State, and caused the internal divisions that never ceased to stir up Christian peoples."[6] Rousseau names the potential conflict of loyalties that Christians (and by suggestion, other religious persons) can suffer between their religious and political obligations.

Rousseau's account of Christianity is shaped by his view that "true Christians" would only be interested in other-worldly realities. "Christianity is a totally spiritual religion, uniquely concerned with heavenly matters."[7] Their lack of attention to this-worldly matters (such as political and military concerns of the nation) makes them suspicious citizens. As a prime example, Rousseau argues that Christians make lukewarm and, therefore, poor soldiers:

What if a foreign war breaks out? The [Christian] citizens march readily to combat: none among them thinks of fleeing; they do their duty, but without passion for victory. They know how to die rather than to win. What does it matter if they are victors or vanquished? Doesn't providence know better than they what is good for them? Imagine how a proud, impetuous, passionate enemy can take advantage of their stoicism.[8]

---

[6] Jean-Jacques Rousseau, *The Social Contract*, ed. Roger D. Masters, trans. Judith R. Masters (New York: St. Martin's Press, 1978), IV:viii, 126.
[7] Ibid., IV:viii, 129.   [8] Ibid.

Rousseau emphasizes that religion plays an important role in maintaining social order, asserting that "a State has never been founded without religion serving as its base."[9] In his view, Christianity is particularly problematic in providing this base.

Rousseau's discussion of civil religion, then, results from his suspicion that Christians and other religious people are not sufficiently devoted citizens. He is realistic about the differing religious beliefs of the citizens of his own day, and he has enough respect for the freedom to pursue "true religion" that he rejects any state-imposed theocracy or a single god of the state. Yet he insists upon the need to harness religion in order to maintain citizen loyalty and keep religious differences from interfering with the social contract. Thus he proposes his own solution: a *civil religion* that all citizens, regardless of their religious background, must uphold.

> The dogmas of the civil religion ought to be simple, few in number, stated with precision, without explanation or commentaries. The existence of a powerful, intelligent, beneficent, foresighted, and providential divinity; the afterlife; the happiness of the just; the punishment of the wicked; the sanctity of the social contract and the laws. These are the positive dogmas. As for the negative ones, I limit them to a single one: intolerance. It belongs with the cults we have excluded.[10]

Ideally, all citizens would be required to accept these tenets. Indeed, in his earlier draft known as the *Geneva Manuscript*, Rousseau goes so far as to say that every citizen should reaffirm these articles every year in order to remain a citizen.[11] The key point is clear: the religious beliefs of all citizens must be directed to support the basic elements of the social contract.

Rousseau's civil religion is thus an instrument of the state. He makes no apologies for it. Rousseau offers a way to make religious people loyal citizens; within that constraint, he is a protector of any religious beliefs and practices. But that constraint is no small matter. As his concern about Christian soldiers reveals, the civil religion requires a certain level of loyalty to the state that does not permit substantial dissent. Religious persons are permitted to be citizens, in effect, as long as they uncritically serve the state.

The idea of civil religion came to dominate the discussion of religion and society in the United States with the publication of Robert Bellah's 1967 article, "Civil Religion in America."[12] Although Bellah makes more room in civil religion for "prophetic" stances to political life, like Rousseau he is interested in understanding how religious ideas and religious citizens can be part of a democratic society. Bellah offers a fascinating analysis to support

---

[9] Ibid., IV:viii, 127.   [10] Ibid.   [11] Ibid., 199–200.
[12] Robert N. Bellah, "Civil Religion in America," *Daedalus* 96 (1967).

his claim that "there exists alongside of and rather clearly differentiated from the churches an elaborate and well-institutionalized civil religion in America."[13] The US type of civil religion draws deeply upon Christian symbols (some of which are also part of the Jewish tradition), but it is a distinct institutional phenomenon: "Though much is selectively derived from Christianity, this [civil] religion is clearly not itself Christianity."[14]

Within the US context, the high priest of the civil religion is the president. The holy days are the national holidays, particularly Memorial Day, Independence Day, and Thanksgiving Day. Bellah approvingly cites Rousseau's list of "the simple dogmas of the civil religion" (those noted above).[15] Central themes of American civil religion include divine providence, the covenant between God and America, and the sacrifice that Americans are called to make for their country. In the civil religion, America is a chosen nation – the new Israel – and with that identity comes the obligation to be a city set upon a hill. Each of these themes addresses the identity that individual persons hold, not as Christians, or Jews, or humanists, but as Americans.

In his analysis of civil religion as articulated in presidential addresses, Bellah considers the objection that many references to civil religion are merely symbolic, with "only a ceremonial significance."[16] Bellah replies convincingly that it is precisely the symbolism and ritual of civil religion that gives it its power. Civil religion helps shape the national ethos around specific themes and toward particular goals. It contributes to the way in which Americans view their identity. Echoing insights of scholarship on organizational culture, Bellah emphasizes that "[w]hat people say on solemn occasions need not be taken at face value, but it is often indicative of deep-seated values and commitments that are not made explicit in the course of everyday life."[17]

Bellah, more than Rousseau, is motivated to show that a mature civil religion can include dissenting, critical, or prophetic elements. (Martin Marty suggests there are priestly and prophetic forms of civil religion.[18]) As an important example, Bellah asserts that Abraham Lincoln "certainly represents civil religion at its best," because he was willing to call America to judgment; as Lincoln put it in his second inaugural address, America stood under God's judgment.[19] When writing in 1967, Bellah stated his hope that American civil religion would be able to offer resources to address not only racial injustices in the US but also the international challenges of the day,

---

[13] Ibid., 1.   [14] Ibid., 7.   [15] Ibid., 5.   [16] Ibid., 2.   [17] Ibid.
[18] Martin E. Marty, "Two Kinds of Two Kinds of Civil Religion," in *American Civil Religion*, ed. Russell E. Richey and Donald G. Jones (New York: Harper & Row, 1974).
[19] Bellah, "Civil Religion in America," 12.

including the Vietnam War. Bellah had an optimistic view of American civil religion's capability to offer prophetic perspectives upon American public life.[20]

Bellah's point that civil religion offers resources for critical national reflection and positive social change is surely correct. Yet the force of the civil religion tradition is located in Rousseau's concern for shaping loyal citizens. In the American context, that point is most succinctly – and cynically – made in Dwight Eisenhower's dictum (which Bellah notes) that "[o]ur government makes no sense unless it is founded in a deeply felt religious faith – and I don't care what it is."[21] Eisenhower is even more direct than Rousseau in naming the *instrumental* nature of the interest of the state in individual citizens' religious faith.

This aspect of civil religion illuminates what I view to be principal concerns about not only the instrumental use and abuse of religion in politics but also the instrumental employment of religion in the workplace as *corporate religion*, or *workplace spirituality*. (I employ these two terms interchangeably here; the former is a closer parallel to the term civil religion, but workplace spirituality is arguably used more frequently.) Consider these similarities: civil religion is employed in order to help form loyal, committed American citizens; workplace spirituality is often used in order to create loyal, productive workers. Civil religion draws central tenets and symbols from the Christian tradition but seeks to reach all citizens in common denominator fashion; workplace spirituality draws from Christian tenets and symbols (with elements borrowed from more "exotic" Eastern traditions) but seeks to be inclusive, in common denominator fashion, of all workers. The *high priest* of the civil religion is not a member of the clergy but, rather, the president; the *spiritual guide* of workplace spirituality is not a member of the clergy but, rather, the enlightened company executive. Given civil religion's principal aim of creating loyal citizens, it offers little room for views that dissent from government policy, especially in time of national crisis; given workplace spirituality's aim of creating loyal, productive workers, it offers little room for views that dissent from company policy, especially in times of tough market competition.

Civil religion and corporate religion thus have certain parallels. They are also interrelated in at least one significant way. Civil religion creates

---

[20] Indeed, he later states his fatigue in "arguing against those for whom civil religion means the idolatrous worship of the state, still the commonest meaning of the term." Robert N. Bellah, "Comment [on Robert Mathisen's Essay, "Twenty Years after Bellah: Whatever Happened to Civil Religion?" *Sociological Analysis* 50/2 (1989): 129–146]," *Sociological Analysis* 50/2 (1989): 147.

[21] Will Herberg, *Protestant–Catholic–Jew: An Essay in American Religious Sociology* (Garden City, NY: Doubleday & Company, 1960), 84; Bellah, "Civil Religion in America," 3.

loyal, committed citizens by lifting up the virtues of democracy. Workplace spirituality aims at creating loyal, productive employees by emphasizing the virtues of the free-market system. The market virtues are often couched in terms of freedom, equality, and respect for consumer choice. The free-market system is sometimes exalted in ways that give it a quasi-religious feel; a number of scholars have offered powerful critiques of the religious faith placed in the market itself.[22] The *interrelationship* of civil religion and workplace spirituality occurs when market virtues are portrayed as closely related to democratic virtues. In other words, celebrating the market system in workplace spirituality often overlaps with celebrating the virtues of American democracy. Corporate religion often entails civil religion and the expression of national pride, as has been particularly evident in post-9/11 responses.

Rousseau's and Bellah's respective analyses of the idea of civil religion clarify that specific religious beliefs and commitments of individuals are not necessarily synonymous with the tenets and symbols of the civil religion. In a parallel fashion, we can say that the specific beliefs of individual employees are distinct from the tenets and symbols of workplace spirituality. Indeed, as both Rousseau and Bellah acknowledge in different ways, citizens (employees) face conflicting internal and external demands in terms of their own identity and their own loyalties. As long as civil religion "borrow[s] selectively from the religious tradition [e.g., Christianity] in such a way that the average American [sees] no conflict,"[23] then it is not problematic to view oneself as a faithful adherent of a religious tradition, of the civil religion, and of workplace spirituality – all at the same time. But when difficult situations arise (for example, should my country be engaging in this war at this time? Or, can I support my company when we are falsifying our accounting records?), these multiple loyalties are not so easy to uphold.

Heather Hopfl offers a complementary critique of the religious or quasi-religious dimension of workplace culture. Her article in the *Journal of Management Studies* focuses on what she calls "the corporate acolytes," those middle managers "who are rewarded according to their role performance and who are called to serve and reinforce the corporate culture."[24] Hopfl notes that, in the current workplace, managers are expected to help create

---

[22] Harvey Cox, "The Market as God: Living in the New Dispensation," *The Atlantic Monthly* 283/3 (1999); Franz J. Hinkelammert, *The Ideological Weapons of Death: A Theological Critique of Capitalism*, trans. Phillip Berryman (Maryknoll, NY: Orbis Books, 1986).
[23] Bellah, "Civil Religion in America," 13.
[24] Hopfl, "The Making of the Corporate Acolyte," 25.

and manage meaning for their employees.[25] She notes the danger associated with giving too much power to leaders, reinforced by the emphasis in some leadership theories on charismatic figures who "control and manipulate the ways in which their followers make sense of their world."[26] In this system, followers accept their leader's control over them and offer their (uncritical) commitment to the workplace. Hopfl may speak in hyperbole with the following assertion: "[W]hen employees are exhorted to greater commitment to the organization, they are effectively required to pledge more of themselves to the company than they would normally be required to commit to a marriage."[27] Yet she is surely correct in suggesting that the firm's effort to form loyal, productive workers can lead to levels of time commitment that impinge on other important spheres of life, including one's personal, familial, civic, and religious involvements.

Compare Bellah's account of civil religion to this colorful description of a typical training session by Hopfl:

> [What] . . . is about to unfold is not unfamiliar to those who attend management training courses with large organizations. What is about to take place is the reading of the corporate gospel, the 'Hear, O Israel,' the *sursum corda*. What we are about to hear is how much the company loves, cherishes and needs these poor unworthy servants; how, if they will only give their heart, soul and mind to the company, they can take their place with the chosen ones, the elect. The language is thick with quasi-religious imagery, eclectic and all-embracing. It speaks to the Humanist, to the Christian, to the Jew, to the Muslim. It is all-purpose, higher order, well practised . . . No reasonable person could object to these platitudes. If the company be for us, who can be against us?[28]

Hopfl captures the juxtaposition of traditional religious symbolism with various kinds of spiritual and value-laden symbolism that comprise much of corporate culture and workplace spirituality. Like civil religion, this combination is crafted in order not to offend anyone, but rather to appeal to all and to gain their loyalty to the company. The training session seeks to earn the dedication of the middle managers, who will then become the "acolytes" responsible for bringing the corporate gospel to their staff.

Unlike the instances of *established* corporate religion discussed next, this kind of workplace spirituality does not claim to be religious in a particularistic way. If there are references to God, or a higher power, or spirituality, they are worded in such a way as to seem uncontroversial to as many employees

---

[25] Contrast Hopfl's critical perspective on this enterprise with Konz and Ryan's approving position on it. Konz and Ryan, "Maintaining an Organizational Spirituality: No Easy Task."
[26] Hopfl, "The Making of the Corporate Acolyte," 26.
[27] Ibid., 27.   [28] Ibid., 23.

as possible. (Note that Hopfl's own analysis emphasizes the religious or quasi-religious imagery in order to illuminate its presence.) Civil religion and workplace spirituality are distinct enough that they can legitimately be seen as separate from Christianity and other traditions. Like established forms of religion, however, they may well privilege Christian employees because of the closer relation of civil or corporate symbols to Christianity than to any other tradition.

Civil religion and workplace spirituality each shift the institutional *locus* of religious expression from the church, synagogue, or mosque to another public institution – the state or the company, respectively. The presence of these different institutions raises the important question of identity and possibly competing loyalties. Both civil religion and workplace spirituality de-emphasize the possible conflicts and difficulties often faced by employees who are also religious practitioners. Jews, Christians, or Muslims who are employees of a company may well have reason to question the practices of their company on religio-moral grounds. Institutionally sponsored workplace spirituality does not recognize such potential conflicts. Robert T. Handy makes this point in relation to his own criticism of civil religion:

Troubled over what [scholars] may discern as idolatrous overtones in public religion, they may too readily slap a negative label on individuals and groups within the church and synagogue life who are legitimately, in terms of their own religious principles, expressing and acting out concerns for the nation and its people.[29]

In parallel fashion, institutionally expressing workplace spirituality is clearly not synonymous with allowing individual employees to express their own beliefs and practices at work. This critical view of workplace spirituality should not be understood, then, as a criticism of individuals who seek to live out their specific religious or spiritual worldview at work. On the contrary, it lays the groundwork for the creation of a level playing field for religious and spiritual expression among employees of all backgrounds.

ESTABLISHED RELIGION AND THE CHRISTIAN WORKPLACE

Let us turn from civil religion and generic workplace spirituality to examine the relationship of established religion and workplaces that endorse or favor some understanding of Christianity. In First Amendment discussions, a religion is *established* if individuals or organizations of that religion receive preferred status or special advantages from the government over individuals

---

[29] Robert T. Handy, "A Decisive Turn in the Civil Religion Debate," *Theology Today* 37/3 (1980): 349.

or organizations of other religious traditions or of no religion. The analogies between the state and the workplace are not complete, but it is potentially fruitful to examine situations in which a particular religion receives de facto established status in a workplace. In the US context, the religion receiving preferential status is most often Christianity. Establishment in the workplace sometimes has to do with the formal status of Christianity in the company (for example, when mission and vision statements explicitly refer to serving Jesus Christ or offer a Christian approach to business). More often, however, the establishment takes the form of cultural advantages for Christianity, such as the effective preference given to Christian symbols, ideas, and holidays in the organizational culture.[30]

Recall that during the post-World War II boom of faith in the workplace, religion and spirituality almost always referred to Protestant Christianity.[31] The present-day spirituality movement combines both generic workplace spirituality and Christian faith at work. Both sub-movements embrace the term *spirituality*. A significant number of the works on Christianity and workplace leadership downplay the distinctive Christian focus or foundation of their approach, and they tend to assume that a Christian approach to spirituality could readily be applied to organizations. In so doing, they assume a Christian approach pertains to the workplace as a whole – and to its employees, whether or not they are adherents of another religion or none.

One example of this perspective is a recent volume edited by Robert Banks and Kimberly Powell, *Faith in Leadership: How Leaders Live Out Their Faith in Their Work – and Why It Matters*, which features Christian authors exclusively. Some contributors use very little Christian theological language. Other authors directly employ Christian themes and ideas while making occasional reference to religious diversity; nevertheless, there is a comfortable equation of *religious* faith and *Christian* faith. One result of this is that, in the application of Christian principles, there is little distinction between an *individual leader's* work and an *institution's* overall mission or culture. For instance, Benjamin D. Williams is able to state that in a company "[p]ersonal and organizational vision enables us to achieve a local incarnation of the vision of the Kingdom of God."[32] The unnamed

---

[30] For a related discussion about changes in religion's role in US civic life, see Ronald F. Thiemann, *Religion in Public Life: A Dilemma for Democracy* (Washington, DC: Georgetown University Press, 1996), 32–37.

[31] See ch. 1 above.

[32] Benjamin D. Williams, "Humility and Vision in the Life of the Effective Leader," in *Faith in Leadership: How Leaders Live Out Their Faith in Their Work – and Why It Matters*, ed. Robert J. Banks and Kimberly Powell (San Francisco: Jossey-Bass, 2000), 75.

assumption seems to be that if a leader is Christian, the organization's vision should also be understood in Christian terms. Williams notes the importance of consensus and consent in developing an organizational vision;[33] yet he does not acknowledge the possibility that employees from non-Christian religious traditions (or no religion) might have a problem with stating a corporation's vision in relation to the Kingdom of God.

In her widely read book *Believers in Business*, Laura Nash documents the different approaches that Christian business executives take in drawing upon their faith in their work.[34] Some, she writes, are explicit in employing Christian language in their communications with employees and outside stakeholders. They believe that inherent in their leadership positions is the responsibility to evangelize. The majority of her interviewees, however, prefer a more deliberate tension between Christian language, on the one hand, and the secular or pluralistic (she employs these words almost interchangeably) reality of the business world, on the other. These CEOs and managers search for different ways to translate or apply their Christian ideas into language that others will understand. Although more complex than cases in which executives directly adopt Christian language and symbols for their workplace, the effects of faith-based actions of CEOs employing this approach are not always merely individual but, rather, are frequently institutional. For example, one founder adopted a four-leaf flame shaped like a cross as the company logo. While the religious imagery is not obvious to all observers, it is intended to refer to the Christian cross.[35] This example illuminates the use of a Christian symbol as an official company logo – an example of establishment Christianity – but one that does not appear blatantly Christian. Imagine how much more controversial the imagery would be in the US context if the logo were in some form of a Jewish star or an Islamic crescent. Surely, in those cases, the official endorsement of a particular religion would be more jarring to many US observers and employees.

I have offered these examples of thoughtful efforts to apply Christian ideas to workplace leadership in ways that tend to make only subtle references to Christian particularity. I assert that, unless these efforts take care not to assume a Christian paradigm, they too easily lend support to an effective Christian establishment in the workplace. Clearly, the preferences and advantages that Christians receive can range from the egregious treatment of non-Christians to less offensive messages that the Christian

[33] Ibid., 69–71.
[34] Laura L. Nash, *Believers in Business* (Nashville, TN: Thomas Nelson Publishers, 1994).
[35] Ibid., 256.

faith, not other spiritual, religious, or moral perspectives, is the best fit with organizational culture.

A prime example of effective Christian advantage – whether or not work-place leaders or employees discuss it – concerns the working calendar and the significance of holidays. One aspect of this issue is what happens at prominent Christian holidays – especially Christmas. The very suggestion that Santa Claus and the Christmas tree are no longer religious, but "just part of the culture," is evidence to the prominent role of Christianity in American social and workplace culture.[36] The converse question concerns whether holidays of other religions receive equivalent attention in the work-place environment.[37] While holiday-related practices (and omissions) may not be intended to support effective Christian establishment, they never-theless often have that effect. I suggest that many Americans, especially Christians, take much about Christian establishment practices for granted.

In contrast to the above-mentioned situations that often unintentionally reinforce de facto establishment, other cases provide examples of explicit and intentionally established Christian workplaces. In these instances, lead-ers label their companies as "Christian based" or "Christ centered." Unlike organizations that subtly or unwittingly give preference to Christian sym-bols and advantages to Christian employees, these firms make no apologies for establishing some understanding of Christianity within their company. Although many acknowledge that applying Christian faith is no simple task, they also see no fundamental problems in being Christian based. One study in the *Journal of Business Ethics* makes the following statement about these firms:

Self-described "Christian" firms assert that it is possible to function in the world of business according to Christian values with a master image from the Bible, i.e., there is no conflict over the interface between corporate and religious values . . . Not only is there no inherent conflict . . . but any material success is perceived to be due to the organization's belief in, and active application of, biblical principles.[38]

For many leaders of these businesses, institutionalizing Christian principles within the company is a way of living out the imperatives of the Gospel. One website that caters to Christians who are business leaders invites them to sign a simply stated "Christian Business Covenant": "I shall operate/manage

---

[36] See Douglas A. Hicks, "Workplace Understanding without 'Secret Santa,'" *Providence Journal*, December 18, 2001.

[37] These issues are discussed in ch. 4 above.

[38] Nabil A. Ibrahim et al., "Characteristics and Practices of 'Christian-Based' Companies," *Journal of Business Ethics* 10 (1991): 124.

my business in a manner consistent with the teachings of Jesus Christ."[39] It is not clear from this website whether or not the leader intends to act as a Christian individual in leadership or to make his or her business into a Christian business; indeed, the inattention to potential tensions between individual and institutional religion in such a short covenant is the issue at hand.

A number of organizations have formed in recent years to bring together leaders who are trying to express Christian values in business leadership. The Christian Chamber of Commerce, the International Christian Chamber of Commerce, and the Fellowship of Companies for Christ International each have active websites which offer individuals membership to their respective organizations and access to articles, announcements, and web discussions about Christian business leadership.[40] Two of these sites list company members, thereby providing networking opportunities to Christian firms.[41] In addition, "Christian yellow pages" are available in many cities as a way to advertise and locate such businesses.[42]

These networks of Christian companies pay little attention in their published and web-based literature to the religious diversity of their employees. The emphasis is on the need to combat present-day secular and unethical business practices and to share the word of Christ in all realms of life, especially in business. Such a conversation simply does not focus on creating the space or guaranteeing the opportunities for employees from other traditions to express their faith.[43] Even more problematic is the unquestioned assumption that Christian leaders can act simply on behalf of their entire company and declare it a Christian-based business or make it a member of a network of Christian companies. It is important to ask, of course, what kinds of companies designate themselves as "Christian." Certainly,

---

[39] The Christian Chamber of Commerce, "Christian Business Covenant." http://www.christianchamber.com/mission.html, accessed August 15, 2002.

[40] The Christian Chamber of Commerce, http://www.christianchamber.com; The International Christian Chamber of Commerce, http://www.icci.net/home; and the Fellowship of Companies for Christ International, http://www.Christianity.com/fcci, all accessed August 15, 2002.

[41] As of August 15, 2002, the Christian Chamber of Commerce listed over 30 companies; the International Christian Chamber of Commerce listed about 550 businesses. The Fellowship of Companies for Christ International does not include a list of members accessible to the public.

[42] For example, the Champion Christian Yellow Pages in Dallas, Texas (http://www.championchristian.com, accessed August 15, 2002), boasts that it "has been providing a highly targeted and efficient channel through which companies can maximize their advertising dollars, thereby prospering and growing in their community."

[43] This does not necessarily imply that none of the leaders of these Christian enterprises believe people of other traditions should live out their faith at work. They do not, however, pay attention to the issue in their publications.

there are "numerous 'mom-and-pop' businesses" in these networks.[44] Small, individual- or family-owned businesses may justifiably have less pragmatic and moral concern about employee diversity than major corporations. More interesting, and morally significant, is whether large companies can manage to address diversity while maintaining an intentionally Christian mission.

Many of the examples above suggest that Christian business leaders uncritically conflate their own individual religious values with organizational religious values. That is, Christian leaders speak in Christian terms on behalf of their companies, as if they are speaking for the organization as a whole. In many workplaces, the founder or the CEO has declared the firm to be Christian. In these cases, leaders and scholars alike implicitly accept a "great man" approach to leadership and a top-down view of organizational culture. Companies are Christian because a courageous leader has declared them so. In such a view of leadership, why should it be a problem that a leader wants to build the company in terms of his Christian values – which are assumed to be basically universal values?

Much of the literature on Christian workplace leadership not only emphasizes the view that the real movers and shakers in leadership are those with positional authority, but it also reinforces the belief that these figures can almost single-handedly shape the organizational culture. In their article on "Christian-based" companies, Nabil A. Ibrahim and colleagues make this statement about organizational culture and leadership:

> The chief executive or the "founding father" has a vision which has an impact on all organizational members. Employees observe management's behavior and listen to and read management's pronouncements. Over time, norms that filter down through the organization are established.[45]

This quite literal top-down understanding of organizational culture tends to subvert potential issues raised by a diverse workforce. Such a great-man view promotes the notion that it is fitting for the leader to create a "strong culture,"[46] and it should not matter that the environment is strongly Christian. If we understand organizational culture in a more complex fashion, however, and take the religious diversity of employees seriously, the simple assumption that the presence of a Christian CEO will automatically result in a Christian-based company cannot be made.

---

[44] Ibrahim et al., "Characteristics and Practices of 'Christian-Based' Companies," 125. At the level of family-owned businesses in the US, there are Jewish-owned firms, Muslim-owned firms, and the like.

[45] Ibid.; Ibrahim and colleagues cite S. Davis, *Managing Corporate Culture* (Cambridge, MA: Ballinger, Inc., 1986) in this discussion.

[46] Terrence E. Deal and Allan A. Kennedy, *Corporate Cultures* (Boston: Addison-Wesley, 1982).

WORKPLACE CHAPLAINS: ESTABLISHED OR
CORPORATE RELIGION?

The implications of this focus on civil religion, established religion, and the workplace can be drawn out by exploring a particular case of institutionally sponsored religious action in the workplace. Specifically, let us examine the issue of "corporate chaplains," individuals who are contracted or hired by companies to minister to the spiritual needs of employees through pastoral services, such as crisis counseling, voluntary prayer, and stress management. This phenomenon occurs relatively frequently among corporations. At a minimum, a number of organizations flourish as providers of these corporate chaplains. Although the practice is not fully documented, estimates place the number of business chaplains between 2,000 and 4,000.[47]

Corporate chaplains are either contracted through an organization by which they are employed or they are retained directly by a company to provide pastoral services. In either case, a company pays to have chaplaincy services provided in its workplace.[48] One of the largest chaplain provider organizations is Marketplace Ministries, Inc., which reports that it employs over 1,000 chaplains and "car[es] for more than a quarter of a million employees and their family members."[49] Like programs in either generic spirituality or low-key establishment Christianity, the front pages of the Marketplace Ministries website do not include Christian language. Rather, Marketplace Ministries advertises itself as a "faith-based employee assistance program." Yet, when one delves further into the site, especially on pages designed to inform and recruit prospective chaplains, it becomes clear that this program is "Christian ministry," through which "[m]en and women chaplains are bringing God's care and concern to the marketplace in companies across our country. They are taking the gospel of Jesus Christ to the frontier of Christian ministry: the modern marketplace."[50]

[47] See Donald Coolidge, "A Demanding Time for Chaplains Who Give at the Office," *Christian Science Monitor*, January 2, 2002; Corporate Chaplains of America website http://www.inneractiveministries.org/, accessed August 16, 2002.

[48] There are examples of church, para-church, and other religious organizations that send people to provide religious "outreach" to employees. I have not directly discussed these unpaid outreach programs here. Consider the Full Gospel Businessman's Fellowship International's "SWAT" program. This organization is reported to have an evangelizing presence in 160 countries. The SWATs, or Spiritual Warfare Attack Teams, offer to go into workplaces to minister to and pray for owners and employees (Brett Hoffman, "Spirituality at Work: Employers Finding Ways to Integrate Religion into the Workplace," *Fort Worth Star Telegram* [June 30, 2001]). I go on to contrast contracted chaplains with clergy who serve their own members in the workplace, below.

[49] Marketplace Ministries, http://www.marketplaceministries.com, accessed August 16, 2002.

[50] Marketplace Ministries, http://www.marketplaceministries.com/chaplainmain.html, accessed December 1, 2001.

Different pages of the same website offer varying perspectives on the chaplaincy through the use of two different kinds of language. In this sense the website's approach is similar to the Christian establishment approach of many of the businesses considered above. On pages targeted to would-be chaplains, the language is clearly Christian and theological, noting the importance of "be[ing] a dedicated, mature Christian who has victoriously walked with Christ for many years," "be[ing] an active witness for Jesus Christ," and "adher[ing] to the Marketplace Ministries Statement of Faith."[51] In contrast, the pages addressing potential business clients employ market-based language. At the head of its "invitation to [business] leaders," one page states:

"Caring" is the one word that best describes the Employee Assistance Program (EAP) provided by MARKETPLACE MINISTRIES INC. Our appeal is to those corporate leaders who genuinely care about their employees and family members, realizing they are the primary asset of any business.[52]

By virtue of the fact that Marketplace Ministries claims both to be a fully Christian organization and to meet the needs of all of its employees, its practice represents a form of Christian establishment. As the website explains, the principal chaplain in a company is Christian. Marketplace Ministries does pledge to make arrangements for spiritual counseling for "Catholics, Protestants (cross-denominational) and Jews, along with representatives of other faith groups . . . when needed, without additional charge to employees or the client company."[53]

Some corporate chaplains, by invitation of the client company or its leaders, hold voluntary prayer services on the worksite – particularly in response to personal crises (for example, the death of an employee or employee's family member) or a public crisis (for example, September 11, 2001). If the contracted employees are Christian (as are all chaplains employed directly by firms such as Marketplace Ministries and Corporate Chaplains of America), then those services are likely to be framed as Christian, with perhaps some attempt to be inclusive. Some firms also have chapels built in the workplace in which persons can pray – if the CEO is Christian, the symbols of that chapel are also likely to be predominantly Christian.[54]

---

[51] Marketplace Ministries, http://www.marketplaceministries.com/qualifications.html, accessed December 1, 2001.
[52] Marketplace Ministries, http://www.marketplaceministries.com/invitationtoleaders.html, accessed December 1, 2001.
[53] Marketplace Ministries, http://www.marketplaceministries.com/worksiterelationships.html, accessed December 1, 2001.
[54] Consider the example of the Leaman Container company, which has "a 10-by-20-foot chapel that contains a Bible, Christian books, and a prayer rail. It was constructed 15 years ago by company

These practices highlight the problems associated with effective Christian establishment.

Other dimensions of corporate chaplaincy resemble not Christian establishment, but corporate religion. For instance, recall that corporate religion is the religion of a company, not of a church or a synagogue. The congregants are not Christians or Jews or all spiritual people, but, rather, all employees. The institutional locus, that is, for chaplains is not an explicitly religious community but the workforce itself. Indeed, this is the point; as the Corporate Chaplains of America website notes,

[a] large percentage of people today do not have any relationship with a church or organized religious groups. Often rushed for time, their beliefs and personal needs take a back seat to the meetings, deadlines and agendas of the workplace.[55]

Because workers are too busy to attend church, synagogue, or mosque, the chaplains come to them. (To the extent that the chaplains are, in most cases, "sharing Christ" in the workplace is a reflection of Christian establishment and not merely corporate religion.) In a word, the workplace becomes the religious congregation. Chaplains can do almost everything that a congregational clergy member does: visit the sick, grieving, and imprisoned; provide confidential listening and counseling; and conduct weddings and funerals.[56] For their part, Marketplace Ministries and Corporate Chaplains of America state that they want denominational certification from their chaplains in order to give them some credibility with religious congregations.[57] The linking of chaplain credibility to a relationship with a Christian denomination clearly highlights the problem of Christian establishment in the workplace. Yet, the pay-for-service arrangement demonstrates that the institutional locus of this relationship is officially the company and not the chaplain's religious denomination.

A related issue of the corporate-religion aspect of chaplaincy is the instrumental treatment of religion. The Marketplace Ministries website makes

owner Don Leaman and opened for employees to use before and after work and during break time" (Hoffman, "Spirituality at Work").

[55] Corporate Chaplains of America, http://www.inneractiveministries.org/, accessed August 16, 2002.

[56] It is important to acknowledge that other institutions, particularly the US military and hospitals, employ chaplains. Business organizations, that is, are not alone in this practice. This fact does not change the substance of my critique of corporate chaplains, although the critique would suggest the need to consider potential problems with the chaplaincy in those other institutions as well. It would be important to note the contextual factors in each of those institutions (e.g., for many military, being part of a local congregation is not a possibility; some hospitals have carefully struggled with inclusiveness in their chaplaincy staffs and have developed extensive relationships with clergy from many religious traditions in their area).

[57] Marketplace Ministries, http://www.marketplaceministries.com/qualifications.html, accessed December 1, 2001; www.inneractiveministries.org/whofaq.htm, accessed August 16, 2002.

the instrumental roles of workplace chaplains quite clear in its "benefits of service" page. Four of the eleven listed benefits for the company are:

- Employees express a more loyal spirit toward the providing organization when an atmosphere of caring is established by company leadership, through and with the help of chaplains . . .
- Many times productivity increases when employees' personal problems are dealt with by an outside third party chaplain . . .
- Personnel tend to stay on the job, lowering turnover rates, when a caring spirit is exemplified by management and company leadership . . .
- Lawsuits have been prevented (and/or dropped) when MARKETPLACE MINISTRIES' chaplains have been involved in working with forced employee retirements and/or employee firings and layoffs.[58]

In one sense, it is not very surprising that employers, wishing to see positive benefits to their economic performance, would make a contract with a chaplain or chaplain provider to pay for services. Indeed, in many cases these business leaders need to justify such action to stockholders, managers, or other stakeholders in terms of the financial benefits of the arrangement. Yet that bottom-line reality raises the fundamental issue: What conflicts of identity and loyalty are raised by corporate chaplaincy when the practice must be justified economically? It is hard to imagine that a chaplain (or chaplain provider) who raises serious questions about essential business practice will be long employed. The corporate chaplaincy requires a domesticated stance toward the corporate mission.

Marketplace Ministries, Inc., makes clear the requirement for chaplains, in cases of possible conflict, to stand, not with employees, but with the company. One of the "pastoral care ministries" duties is described in this way:

Provide post-termination pastoral care for laid-off or fired employees, in order to foster smooth transition to another work environment, and prevent potential retaliation toward the Company management or other employees.[59]

Following this task as it is framed in the job description, how could a corporate chaplain respond according to the dictates of personal conscience if he or she felt the employee was unjustly terminated? It is difficult to take a prophetic stance toward corporate actions when one is on its payroll.

---

[58] Marketplace Ministries, http://www.marketplaceministries.com/benefitsofservices.html, accessed December 1, 2001.
[59] Marketplace Ministries, http://www.marketplaceministries.com/pastoralcare.html, accessed December 1, 2001.

A possible objection to my critique could run as follows: surely corporate chaplaincy can do some good in the lives of individual employees and in the life of the corporation. Given the highly competitive and stressful workplace, any pastoral care that chaplains can provide will help humanize the workplace. In the contemporary world, workers do not have sufficient time to balance home life and work life and still manage to fit in participation in a religious congregation.

There is merit in the contention that chaplains can and do accomplish many valuable acts of service and compassion in their work. I do not mean to suggest that chaplains on the payroll of a corporation can never maintain their personal or professional integrity. At the same time, I want to suggest that the arrangement under which they are paid by corporations puts them in a morally difficult situation, one in which they may need to reject aspects of their job description in order to maintain their integrity. It is not, therefore, the integrity or the work of individual chaplains that should be at issue; it is, rather, the nature of the arrangement of work-for-pay chaplains of the corporations.

The fact that employees are stressed out and that many "overworked Americans" lack time for family life or religious participation should not, in my view, be accepted as an unalterable state of affairs. Rather, this is part of the context that is under critique. Perhaps the solution to over-worked employees is not to hire in chaplains, but to lessen work hours or at least to arrange work hours for Christians, Muslims, Jews, and others in a way that accommodates their religious and civic participation. Besides permitting employees free sabbath or holy days, this could also mean making allowances for church, synagogue, or community meetings, for prayer time, or for vacation time flexibility to allow people to attend religious activities.

In addition, it is important to acknowledge the difference between paid corporate chaplains and clergy from religious congregations who care for their own members in the workplace. Laura Nash and Scotty McClennan argue that many Christian clergy do not understand the struggles that their laypeople who work in the marketplace face in integrating their faith and their work.[60] Clergy and others entrusted with the pastoral care of members of their religious congregation should not have to see a dividing line between their members' working lives and their spiritual lives. For their

---

[60] Laura L. Nash and Scotty McClennan, *Church on Sunday, Work on Monday: The Challenge of Fusing Christian Values with Business Life* (San Francisco: Jossey-Bass, 2001).

part, employers can place legitimate limits on the presence of clergy at their worksites, but they also can be open to allowing the clergy of all employees, on an equal basis, to have some presence at the worksite as they minister to their own members. The workplace can and should also place strong prohibitions on attempts at proselytizing by clergy who are invited by their own members.

Allowing clergy to offer pastoral care to members of their congregation at their place of work does not address the religious, pastoral, or spiritual needs of employees who do not identify as religious. Is it possible that corporate chaplains could fill in the gap to help meet these people's spiritual needs? The question still remains of whether it is appropriate for companies to be sites of religious care provided by chaplains paid by the company. Nor does such an arrangement in support of chaplains address the question of the efficacy of having a person with a clearly defined religious perspective minister to a person with an intentionally secular perspective. There is clearly no simple solution to the issues raised by the current reality of many overworked, religiously unaffiliated employees. This section has aimed to show, at a minimum, that the practice of institutionally endorsed and funded pastoral providers is not the simple solution that its promoters portray it to be.

CONCLUSIONS

This chapter has uncovered various problems associated with institutional forms of religion and spirituality in the workplace. When religion *in* the workplace becomes religion *of* the workplace, questions arise about the particular or general stance of the official company religion. If all people were either (a) nonreligious or (b) similarly spiritual/religious, then the problems of institutional workplace religion would not be as difficult as they actually are. The issue of why companies would promote religion at all, however, would remain.

If all expressions of spirituality and religion are not the same, then it is not possible to offer an uncontroversial and unifying institutional corporate spirituality. The corporate leader cannot be the spiritual guide or guru to his or her workforce. The undertaking of company-wide and company-sponsored spiritual rituals will surely offend some religious, spiritual, and/or humanistic employees. Further, when a company officially sponsors or promotes some kind of spirituality, its motives can and should be called into question. A corporate spirituality with a strongly prophetic edge is an oxymoron.

The problems of Christian establishment also turn on the religious, spiritual, and moral diversity of the workforce. In subtle and explicit ways, Christian leaders apply their individual beliefs and practices to the institution as a whole. The wider cultural context in the US, in which Christianity's stories, symbols, and holidays enjoy culturally advantaged positions, makes it difficult to discern many instances of Christian establishment in the workplace. Much of the scholarly and popular literature of organizational culture exalts charismatic leaders who shape or reshape corporate culture, thereby reinforcing the ability of Christian CEOs to impose their own beliefs and practices on their company.

The concerns I have raised about institutional expressions of spirituality or religion depend upon the normative claim that every employee should be treated as a moral equal in the workforce. When a company takes on or communicates particular spiritual or religious ideas, then employees from all other perspectives will understand that their beliefs, commitments, and practices are not the officially accepted ones. It may be easy for Christians (this author included) to downplay the significance, for example, of subtle messages in the workplace that convey the privileged status enjoyed by Christian symbols, ideas, or holidays, but for Jewish, Muslim, and atheistic co-workers these messages are overtly present and reinforce their experience of marginalization.

CHAPTER 7

Comparative contexts: India and Singapore

Which dimensions of negotiating religion are specific to the US workplace and which are common to companies in any diverse society? Is it possible to gain constructive insights by viewing other societies' struggles with religious diversity? Conversely, can we also avoid pitfalls by studying governmental or organizational policies in other nations? As with most contextual analyses, the examination of US workplaces will be sharpened by the comparative examinations of other national contexts.

This chapter analyzes the implications of religious diversity and governmental policies toward religion for workplaces in India and Singapore. These strikingly dissimilar countries have national policies and ongoing public discourse about the role of religion in public life, including its roles at work. Although vastly different in terms of population statistics and religious and ethnic composition, India and Singapore are similar in the sense that both have cultivated a long-standing, intentional, and, at times, creative public effort to understand religious diversity among the population. In distinct ways, each nation has designed official approaches to managing religious and spiritual diversity. At the same time, significant practical and moral problems plague both countries' official efforts. These two comparative examples, not typically cited as models for US public policies or workplace institutions, include both highly problematic features of addressing religious diversity as well as some positive components.[1]

India confronts the reality of religiously influenced violence. The current ruling party of India, the Bharatiya Janata Party (BJP), has campaigned and promoted policies to "Hinduize" Indian public life and to marginalize Muslims and other minority religious groups. In February of 2002, Hindu

---

[1] Not only does it make sense to compare diverse organizations in the United States with those of other countries, but it is also important to understand the extent to which workplaces in many parts of the world – the developed world, at least – are becoming global workplaces. As just one example, the World Trade Center housed some of the most international and religiously diverse workplaces in the globalizing world. See ch. 1 above.

134

rioting against Muslims in Ahmadabad, in the state of Gujarat, led to the death of scores of Hindus and hundreds of Muslims.[2] In September of that year, Islamic militants attacked hundreds of worshipers and killed dozens in the Hindu temple in the city of Gandhinagar, also in Gujarat.[3] Violence with religious, political, and ethnic dimensions continues to threaten not only the stability of the contested region of Jammu and Kashmir but also that of all of India and Pakistan. For its part, Singapore has become one of the leading fronts in the "war on terrorism," and Singapore's jails now house scores of alleged al-Queda supporters. As a result of terrorist activities perpetrated by a few Islamic militants, almost the entire minority Malay population – almost all are Muslims and already experience marginalization in various forms – has come under increased suspicion. Both India and Singapore face challenges of religious pluralism, in workplaces and in society at large, that are at least as complex as those confronted by US society.

THE PROBLEMS AND PROSPECTS OF COMPARISON

It is essential to acknowledge the major demographic, economic, political, and cultural differences among India, Singapore, and the USA; nevertheless, the disparity of contexts can also help spark discussion about alternative approaches to addressing religious diversity. Before examining India and Singapore, it is important to focus on the difficulties of comparing very different national contexts.

In his book *Mencius and Aquinas: Theories of Virtue and Conceptions of Courage*, Lee Yearley seeks to compare the ethical writings of two towering figures from radically different times and places.[4] Yearley argues that, by employing his "analogical imagination," he can make a fruitful comparison between Mencius and Aquinas. He realizes that critics question whether any meaningful comparison can be made between a fourth century BCE Confucian philosopher and a thirteenth century CE Christian philosopher–theologian. Any attempt at comparison requires justification and specificity. Toward that end, Yearley offers a method that seeks to forge "similarities within differences" and "differences within similarities." This method is instructive for this chapter's comparison as well.

---

[2] Celia Dugger, "More Than 200 Die in 3 Days of Riots in Western India," *New York Times*, March 2, 2002.

[3] Amy Waldman, "Gunmen Raid Hindu Temple Complex in India, Killing 29," *New York Times*, September 25, 2002.

[4] Lee H. Yearley, *Mencius and Aquinas: Theories of Virtue and Conceptions of Courage* (Albany, NY: State University of New York Press, 1990).

Yearley disavows two different views on the comparative enterprise. The first view rejects altogether the comparison of distinct cultures and world-views. Yearley defines this position as "radical diversity." In this view, there is no objective position (for example, a neutral bystander position) from which to make a comparison, and thus the biases of the observer and the power relations of the respective worldviews will predetermine the outcome of the exercise. In contrast, the second view – which Yearley calls "univocality" – holds that it is a relatively simple matter to compare any two worldviews and that no epistemological or contextual differences provide insurmountable obstacles.[5]

In an effort to steer between these two contradictory positions, Yearley enlists the concept of the analogical imagination as a way to compare two things that are, at first glance, dissimilar. The enterprise of finding difference in similarity and similarity in difference depends, of course, on who is undertaking the comparison. Yearley acknowledges that no "comparer" can claim an objective ground. On the contrary, the scholar is a vital third party in the process. The process of comparison via the analogical imagination requires constructing a terrain on which the two items demonstrate some similarity and some difference. "[T]he locus of comparison must exist in the scholar's mind and not in the objects studied. That fact, the reasons for it, and implications of it must be accepted."[6] The scholar's role is not merely to evaluate and compare two distinct entities but to engage in a constructive, imaginative process that will be of service either to the comparative study of religion or to another cross-cultural enterprise.

The analogical imagination calls for an ad hoc approach to the comparative endeavor, and it suggests that the analyst doing the comparison must acknowledge his or her creative role in the process. Applied to this project, this means that the comparisons I shall make between the USA and India and between the USA and Singapore are constructions that are shaped by my own perspective. There is no objective position from which to compare the American, Indian, and Singaporean realities.

Yearley's framework also notes that the "comparer" must choose which dimensions of a worldview or culture to examine.[7] With that in mind, I will not even attempt to analyze all of the many elements of religious diversity and responses to it in India and Singapore in this chapter; indeed, I acknowledge that I am not an expert in either Indian or Singaporean religion and society. Yet, despite such real limitations, Yearley's framework

[5] Ibid., 195–96.   [6] Ibid., 198.
[7] For his part, Yearley chooses a locus of comparison that he calls "practical theory" and does not compare, for instance, the philosophical and metaphysical tenets of Mencius and Aquinas. Ibid., 7.

suggests that it is possible to gain insights into respectful pluralism in the USA by examining these other contexts.

INDIA: NON-WESTERN MEANINGS OF COMMUNALISM AND SECULARISM

Conflict and poverty

With a population greater than 1 billion people, India is the second largest country in the world. The religious composition of the population varies tremendously from state to state. According to the 1991 Indian census, within India as a whole, Hindus comprise 82 percent of the population; Muslims, 12 percent; Christians, 2.3 percent; Sikhs, 1.9 percent; and Jains, Buddhists, and others, the remaining part.[8] India is often described – albeit inaccurately – as a "Hindu nation"; Hindu fundamentalists, including in the ruling BJP, and their political parties would like to perpetuate this understanding of Indian nationhood. Scholars point out that, with over 120 million Muslims, "India is the third largest Muslim country in the world."[9]

It is impossible to speak of religious diversity in India without understanding the context of the Hindu–Muslim tensions, the 1947 partition of Pakistan and India, and the continuing struggles to eliminate religious–ethnic violence between Hindus and Muslims. Much of the public and scholarly debate about religious diversity in India in the past decade has had at its root the December 1992 destruction of the Babri Masjid (a four-hundred-year-old mosque in Ayodhya) by Hindu zealots who claimed that it was located on an earlier temple dedicated to the deity Rama. The violence surrounding that act claimed over 2 thousand lives, and every year scores of smaller religiously based riots between Hindu and Muslim communities occur in different parts of India.

It is also important to note, even briefly, the diverse understandings of the term *workplace* in India. In a country where economic development ranges from rural poverty to the high-tech corridors surrounding Bangalore, and from urban shantytowns to the highly modernized sectors of Mumbai

---

[8] The Census of India, http://www.censusindia.net/religion.html, accessed February 20, 2003. Alternative figures to the official Indian census are these: Hindus, 75 percent; Muslims, 12 percent; Christians, 6 percent; Sikhs, 2 percent; and Jains, Buddhists, Bahais, and others, the remaining 5 percent. David B. Barrett, George T. Kurian, and Todd M. Johnson, *World Christian Encyclopedia: A Comparative Survey of Churches and Religions in the Modern World*, second edn., 2 vols. (New York: Oxford University Press, 2001), 1:360.

[9] Amartya Sen, "The Threats to Secular India," *New York Review of Books* (1993): 26.

(Bombay), the notion of work itself varies immensely. If it is possible to generalize about a labor market and the institutions of workplace organizations in the USA and even in Singapore, it is much more difficult to do so in the case of India. Indeed, for many urban Indians and almost all Indian villagers, there is no such thing as a formal workplace or labor market. In one example discussed later in the chapter, the workplace is an urban street corner where a cobbler plies his trade. At the same time, this chapter's discussion of the Indian banking holidays points to the more institutionalized sectors of the economy.

Indian religious diversity and communalism

Long before its independence from Great Britain in 1947, religious diversity played a key role in India's self-understanding. Hinduism originated in the third millennium BCE in the Indus Valley civilization and developed with the influx of the Aryan civilizations into the South Asian subcontinent in the second millennium BCE.[10] Buddhism, Jainism, and Sikhism also originated on Indian soil; Arvind Sharma suggests that Hindus readily accept all three of those traditions as expressions of Hinduism, although he acknowledges that "the Buddhists, Jainas, and Sikhs may demur" about such a classification.[11] St. Thomas may have brought Christianity to India in the first century CE, and by all accounts, it had some presence by the fourth century CE.[12] Islam arrived with invaders as early as the eighth century CE, and larger Muslim expeditions into the Punjab began at the turn of the eleventh century. By 1556, the Islamic Mughal Empire dominated the political landscape of India. Although it is largely beyond the scope of this book, it is difficult to understand the contemporary reality of religious diversity in India without acknowledging the tremendous, enduring influence of Islam on the philosophical, cultural, and political history of India. And, to be sure, the centuries of political struggle between Hindus and Muslims provide a backdrop, not only for British colonial rule, the Raj, but also for the partition of India and Pakistan in 1947.

Although religious and political tension accounted for much of the fragmentation of India before British rule, scholars point out that the Raj

---

[10] Thomas J. Hopkins, *The Hindu Religious Tradition*, ed. Frederick J. Streng, *The Religious Life of Man Series* (Belmont, CA: Wadsworth, 1971), 3–16.
[11] Arvind Sharma, "Hinduism," in *Our Religions*, ed. Arvind Sharma (San Francisco: Harper San Francisco, 1993), 4.
[12] Stanley Wolpert, *A New History of India*, sixth edn. (New York: Oxford University Press, 2000), 73, 84.

contributed to the forging of religious *communalism*, or the division of Indian subjects according to their religious community. That is, British administrators exacerbated the conflicts of Indian people by classifying persons according to religious identity.[13] In the Indian context, the notion of communalism connotes sectarian strife or a kind of balkanization among peoples according to their religious identity. An index entry in a leading history of India sums it up: "Religious separatism – see Communalism."[14] The potential fragmentation of India by sectarian strife set the context for the formation of a secular Indian government after the Partition – in intentional contrast to Pakistan's formation of an Islamic Republic.[15]

The Indian Constitution of 1950 was written to guarantee religious freedom of expression by its citizens. Articles 25 and 26 of the constitution allow for the "freedom of conscience and the right freely to profess, practice and propagate religion" within the limits of "public order, morality and health."[16] The constitution also acknowledges the reality of diverse and divided religious communities – particularly Hindu and Muslim ones, but also Christian, Sikh, Buddhist, Parsee, Jain, and others – and their different traditional laws and practices. Because of the profound degree of communal strife and different religious practices, the constitution did not impose a universal civil law to govern domestic matters upon all of its citizens; rather, it included the process-oriented directive principle that "the state shall endeavor to secure for its citizens a uniform civil code throughout the territory of India."[17] Up to the present moment, there is no single civil code. Rather, Indian citizens, depending upon their religious identity, are held accountable to different marriage, divorce, and inheritance laws. As an important example, neither Hindu nor Christian men are permitted to have more than one wife, but Muslim men are legally permitted to have as many as four wives.

An important paradox of Indian law that bears directly on religious identity and diversity is the question of the caste system. The Indian Constitution outlawed discrimination on the basis of caste. Yet, in the constitution, and in subsequent amendments, the government has followed a policy of "compensatory discrimination" toward the "backward" classes – those

---

[13] Joseph Tharamangalam, "Religious Pluralism and the Theory and Practice of Secularism: Reflections on the Indian Experience," *Journal of Asian and African Studies* 24/3–4 (1989): 205–06.

[14] Wolpert, *A New History of India*, 507.   [15] Sen, "The Threats to Secular India," 26.

[16] Indian Constitution, Part III, Art. 25 and Art. 26; see discussion in Thomas Pantham, "Indian Secularism and Its Critics: Some Reflections," *Review of Politics* 59/3 (1997): 526–27.

[17] See discussion in Ralph Buultjens, "India: Religion, Political Legitimacy, and the Secular State," *The Annals of the American Academy of PSS* 483 (1986): 108.

of lower castes and the untouchables.[18] The law stipulates that a certain proportion of spaces for public university matriculation and government positions be "scheduled" or reserved for members of lower castes and the untouchables. This system receives its share of criticism but constitutional amendments have regularly extended it. In order for this government policy to remain in practice, of course, the government must recognize the enduring reality of caste-based identity.[19]

The compensatory or remedial advantages offered to members of the scheduled classes may well reflect the Indian government's good intentions for marginalized Indian citizens. But one problem of this policy, in addition to the paradox that it reinforces the notion of caste, is that the advantages have only been extended to Hindus, Sikhs, and Buddhists of the scheduled classes.[20] That is, if an untouchable converts to Christianity, he or she effectively loses the compensatory benefits extended to the scheduled classes.

One test case of this reality – related to the Indian sphere of work – reached the Indian Supreme Court in 1985. The case of Soosai the cobbler is narrated by religion scholar William J. Everett:

Soosai had belonged to the Adi-Dravida caste of cobblers in Madras before his conversion to Christianity. As a leather-worker, he was deemed untouchable by the caste Hindus. His caste . . . was listed as a scheduled caste in the Presidential Order of 1950. Soosai exercised his craft at a hot and dusty street corner in Madras. While possessing a few basic tools he had virtually no place he could call his own. As part of its general program of uplift for this caste, the Tamil Nadu Khadi and Village Industries Board allotted free bunks to some members of this cobbler caste in 1982, but they excluded Soosai because he was not a Hindu or Sikh.[21]

The Indian Supreme Court denied Soosai's claim that this action discriminated against him on the basis of his religion. The court asserted that Soosai did not suffer discrimination *within the Christian community* because of his (Hindu-originated) caste and, therefore, he did not have a legitimate claim.

[18] Indian Constitution, Part IV, Art. 46. The term "compensatory discrimination" was coined by Marc Galanter in *Competing Equalities: Law and the Backward Classes in India* (Delhi: Oxford University Press, 1984) as cited in William Johnson Everett, "Religion and Federal Republicanism: Cases from India's Struggle," *Journal of Church and State* 37 (1995): 64. See also Buultjens, "India: Religion, Political Legitimacy, and the Secular State," 103.

[19] In Buultjens's words: the policy of caste-based reservations "provides official recognition only to the Hindu religion. No reserved seats were given to Muslims or other minority religions, and caste, after all, is based on Hindu social divisions. Any special caste representation enables those divisions to endure and become constitutionally entrenched." Buultjens, "India: Religion, Political Legitimacy, and the Secular State," 104.

[20] Everett, "Religion and Federal Republicanism: Cases from India's Struggle," 65.

[21] Ibid., 66.

That is, rather than viewing the impact of caste on Soosai's life *within the society and economy* of Indian life, it focused on his communal identity inside the Christian community.

That Soosai suffered discrimination in his public work as a cobbler did not gain the attention of the court. Everett makes the following insightful observation from this case:

The [Indian] Constitution addresses people as citizens – individuals who have the capacity to reason, to express themselves in public, and to secure their claims through due legal process within a fundamental constitutional order. The categories of traditional Indian culture, however, consider people as members of all-encompassing communities. "Religion" does not really attach to an individual but to a "community" which embraces economic, familial, social, and cultural aspects of life.[22]

By focusing on Soosai's treatment within the Christian community alone, the Supreme Court followed the communal, and not the societal, understanding of religion in this case.

It is this fundamental aspect of religion in Indian public life that is so distinct from religion in American public life. Although the Indian Constitution guarantees freedom of religious expression, the predominant understanding of religion in that context is communal and not individual. Indeed, in complex cases of political and religious conflict, such as with Soosai the cobbler, citizen identity can be preempted by religious communal identity. In this case, as in many others, the same law applies differently to persons according to their religious tradition. In other cases, including domestic law, the government literally applies a different set of laws to persons according to their religious community.

In the instance of Soosai, the legal decision based upon religious communal identity offers a clear socioeconomic advantage to Hindu cobblers over a cobbler who converted to Christianity, in this case a minority tradition. Various analysts of Indian religion and society note the ways in which religious communalism directly or indirectly privileges Hindus over members of minority religions in social and economic life.[23] In effect, if not in principle, political, social, and economic aspects of public life in India disadvantage minority religious adherents who are not part of the majority Hindu community, which is too easily equated with Indian society. Such a reality undermines the Indian Constitution's guarantee of the fundamental

---

[22] Ibid., 66–67.
[23] Buultjens, "India: Religion, Political Legitimacy, and the Secular State," 103–04; Tharamangalam, "Religious Pluralism and the Theory and Practice of Secularism," 201; Everett, "Religion and Federal Republicanism: Cases from India's Struggle," 67; Sen, "The Threats to Secular India," 28.

equality and, therefore, the equal treatment of all citizens regardless of their religion.

Indian secularism

In the Indian context, secularism has various meanings. In 1973, the Indian Supreme Court ruled "that 'secularism' is a constitutive feature of the basic structure of the constitution."[24] Three years later secularism became an explicit part of the national constitution through an amendment. Few scholars or politicians use the term *secularism* to denote the absence of religion from the public sphere altogether.[25] Many Hindus argue that secularism refers to the universality of religions. The nationalists then suppose that Hinduism is the paradigm within which minority religious can easily fit.[26] In other words, such a view suggests that, if different religions broadly communicate the same truths, persons from minority religious communities should not be bothered when leaders who "just happen" to be Hindu embody those values in public life. Such de facto preferential treatment for Hinduism enables Hindu practices and rituals to define much of India's public life. The aforementioned case of advantages afforded to Hindu cobblers is just one example.

The echoes of US debates about the relationship between religion and the state are evident in Indian discussions of secularism. Some of the positions familiar to US analysts, such as strict separationism and symbolic accommodation of the majority tradition, are present in Indian debates as well. The US context and the Indian context differ in at least two clearly defined ways, however. First, in India, proponents of many different perspectives employ the word *secular*, albeit in different ways. (In the US context, only the separationists – and not all of them – would label themselves as secularists in calling for government to be free of religious entanglement and for the more broadly understood public sphere to be free of religious symbols and language.) Most positions in the Indian context embrace Indian secularism but hold to their particular interpretation of it. For many scholars, secularism refers only to the equality of free religious expression that is guaranteed

---

[24] Pantham, "Indian Secularism and Its Critics," 525–26.
[25] Tharamangalam argues that few scholars or leaders are promoting the process of moving toward such a reality: "Secularization in the western sense, of rationalization of culture and the withdrawal of religion into the private sphere has had only a minor impact on Indian society, and is not promoted either in theory or in practice by the state. It has influenced only a small group of westernized intelligentsia." Tharamangalam, "Religious Pluralism and the Theory and Practice of Secularism," 210.
[26] Ibid.: 202–04; see also Pantham, "Indian Secularism and Its Critics," 528–30.

in constitutional articles 25 and 26 – and this provision does not require strict separation. In this view of Indian religion and public life, secularism is wholly compatible with religious pluralism. Amartya Sen summarizes the friendly relationship between secularism and pluralism within the Indian context:

> [S]ecularism is, in fact, a part of a more comprehensive idea – that of India as an integrally pluralist country, made up of different religious beliefs, distinct language groups, divergent social practices. Secularism is one aspect – a very important one – of the recognition of that larger idea of heterogeneous identity.[27]

In keeping with Sen's analysis, the Indian government has attempted to put into practice the appreciation for religious heterogeneity.

A second, and closely related, difference between the contemporary US and Indian contexts is that, in India, secularism is defined in opposition to the sectarian strife and violence of communalism. This was also the case in the rise of the modern West, as secularism arose as a rejection of the violence across Europe, violence that was often triggered by religious differences. Currently, though, the specter of widespread violence based on religious identity is not a reality in the USA in the same way that it is in India. Indian secularists range from those who adhere to a strict separation of religion and the state, to those who advocate pluralistic public expression of religion, and even multiple legal systems. However, they all stand united in opposition to the very real possibility of religiously based violence. Stanley Wolpert emphasizes that the widespread backlash against Hindu fundamentalists following Mohandas Gandhi's 1948 assassination at the hands of a member of the Hindu Rashtriya Svayamsevak Sangh (RSS – National Volunteer Association) led to the Indian Constitution's guarantee of religious freedom for all persons and the founding of a secular state free of Hindu establishment.[28] Indian secularism does not generally mean the absence of religion from public life; on the contrary, secularism-as-pluralism calls for a kind of religious tolerance in public life or, at a minimum, the absence of violence motivated by religion.

Indian holidays

One manifestation of how the secularism-as-pluralism outlook affects the Indian workplace involves the observation of religious holidays. If Indian secularism allows for the plural expression of the religious identity of its

---

[27] Sen, "The Threats to Secular India," 26.   [28] Wolpert, *A New History of India*, 355–56.

citizens, then the holidays of those religions should gain some recognition in public life. India has fourteen federal holidays known as central holidays – these are the days on which banks and national government offices (including the post office) are closed. Many private businesses also follow this central holiday schedule. It is crucial to emphasize here, however, that this policy affects a small minority of Indian workers, since the formal private sector is limited. Unlike the United States, where only one national holiday (Christmas) has a religious origin, eleven of these fourteen Indian holidays are rooted in religious traditions. The *diversity* of the religions represented is remarkable: Hinduism, two (Dussehra and Diwali); Sikhism, one (Guru Nanak's birthday); Jainism, one (Mahavir's birthday); Buddhism, one (the Buddha's birthday); Islam, four (Eid al-Adha, Muharram, Muhammad's birthday, and Eid al-Fitr); and Christianity, two (Good Friday and Christmas).[29]

Each state in India observes its own list of holidays whereby all government offices and many private-sector businesses close. The interregional variation, like India's religious and cultural diversity among states, leads to disparate lists of holidays across those states. The holidays are negotiated within each context as an important, and often contested, communal issue. For example, in the state of Maharahstra, but not in other states, the Parsee New Year is a holiday.[30] In this way, states seek to adapt to the religious diversity of their particular population, but it is seldom without protest. There are frequent debates, sometimes quite fiery, over which holidays should gain recognition.[31]

In addition to closed holidays, government and some private-sector offices determine their own list of restricted or optional holidays, from which each employee (whether in government or private-sector employment) may choose a set number of additional – usually two or three – holidays. One Indian scholar commented, "Curiously, however, nothing in the policy prevents a Hindu from taking a restricted holiday on Eid-ul-Fitr [or Eid al-Fitr] and vice versa [i.e., a Muslim from taking a Hindu holiday]. That's Indian Secularism – I cannot think [of] any Western democracy where this is the case."[32] The list is lengthy and varies by state. Almost all of these additional holidays are religious in nature. Many, but by no means all, of them are Hindu.

The reality of religious variety in many Indian companies and government agencies is not as diverse as this discussion might portray. Particular

---

[29] Indiapost, http://www.indiapost.org/Holidays.html, accessed October 20, 2002.
[30] Asghar Ali Engineer, personal e-mail correspondence, December 11, 2001.
[31] Devesh Kapur, personal e-mail correspondence, December 10, 2001.   [32] Ibid.

workplaces often employ only members of one caste or subcaste, thus excluding Muslims and Christians, among others. Yet, in a society marked by a great tension between religious communities, the degree of religious pluralism reflected in these holiday policies is significant, even as a symbolic ideal of pluralism toward which to strive. The national policy of secularism does not deny that religious holidays are worthy of being national holidays; on the contrary, the government of India has developed a policy that respects the major festivals of its most significant religious traditions. The additional policy of restricted holidays allows employees of all religious communities (and none) to observe, if they choose, additional festivals of their own tradition.

The effects of religious diversity in India are distinct from those in the United States in many ways. The idea that government policy could encourage the observance of holidays from six major religious traditions is possible, perhaps, only in India's version of secularism. Despite efforts such as these, India's history of religiously and politically based conflict continues to fuel religious and political conflict in the present. The notion that a person's religious community determines his or her very identity as a citizen baffles many Western observers. As the case of Soosai demonstrates, legal rulings based on communalism can have the effect of socioeconomically disadvantaging members of minority religions. The ruling BJP would seek to build a Hindu-dominated national identity that further marginalizes non-Hindus. Despite these problematic features of Indian communalism, however, the federal and state governments continue the struggle to forge a secular, pluralistic India. The handling of public holiday observances is just one example of such efforts. Other expressions of religious pluralism abound in the colorful and striking contrasts between traditional Hindu, traditional Muslim, and Western forms of dress in the Indian workplace and marketplace. For better *and* for worse, religious pluralism more deeply pervades the framework of Indian life than it does US public life.

SINGAPORE

Diversity at the level of a city-state

The disparity in the sheer number of citizens represents one fundamental difference between India and Singapore. In contrast to India's population that is one-sixth of the earth's inhabitants, Singapore is a city–state with under four million citizens, or less than one-half of 1 percent of India's population. Known as one of the mini-dragons of the Asian economy, however, Singapore enjoys international prominence disproportionate to its relatively tiny population. Like India, it is a former British colony, having become an East India Company trading post in 1819, a British possession in 1824, and a formal British crown colony in 1857.[33] Since its founding, Singapore has been a center for international migrants and traders and, thus, has been a remarkably diverse and cosmopolitan site.

Singapore is undeniably religiously complex. Of approximately 3.6 million Singaporeans, about 55 percent are adherents of Chinese folk religions, Taoism, or Buddhism; 15–18 percent are Muslims (most are ethnic Malay, with much smaller groups of Indian, Pakistani, and Chinese Muslims); 12–14 percent are Christians; and about 5 percent are Hindus. Sikhs, Bahais, Jews, "non-religious" persons, and others comprise the remainder of the population.[34]

Even more discussed and contested than religious identity in the present-day public life of Singapore is ethnic identity. Oft-quoted figures of the government refer to the population as 77 percent ethnic Chinese, 15 percent Malay, 7 percent Indian, and 1 percent other (including European). Ethnic and religious identities are interrelated but distinguishable from one another. Religious identity within the ethnic Chinese grouping is arguably the most complex of these interrelationships; as scholars of religion have shown, the notion of "religious tradition" does not readily fit the intersection of Chinese rituals, practices, or beliefs. Many persons in this grouping would not call their rituals religious at all. Few persons call themselves Taoists or, in a religious sense, Confucians. Further, the government's attempts in recent decades to draw consciously and energetically upon a version of Confucian ethics as a national ethos or shared culture has further complicated the question of Confucianism in Singapore. For some Singaporeans, Buddhist practices intersect seamlessly with these other kinds of Chinese religions; other ethnic Chinese identify themselves more exclusively as Buddhists. In addition, some ethnic Chinese (at least 10 percent[35]) have converted to Christianity, and a smaller proportion have adopted Islam. The closest overlap between ethnicity and religion occurs between Malays and Muslims. Indeed, Singaporean public discourse usually fails to distinguish between

---

[33] Beng Huat Chua and Kian-Woon Kwok, "Social Pluralism in Singapore," in *The Politics of Multiculturalism: Pluralism and Citizenship in Malaysia, Singapore, and Indonesia*, ed. Robert W. Hefner (Honolulu: University of Hawai'i Press, 2001), 87; Barrett, Kurian, and Johnson, *World Christian Encyclopedia*, 1:661.

[34] Estimates are taken from Country Table 1 – Religious Adherents in Singapore, AD 1900–2025. Barrett, Kurian, and Johnson, *World Christian Encyclopedia*, 1:661; see the notes to the table for a discussion of methodology.

[35] See ibid., 11:200.

these two categories. A very small percentage (less than 1 percent) of Malays are non-Muslims. As noted above, however, not all Muslims are Malays. Most Indians are Hindus, but some are Muslims, Sikhs, and Christians. In Singapore both ethnicity and religion figure prominently in public conversations about identity and multiculturalism, but they should not be juxtaposed too readily.

A modern authoritarian state and efforts to forge a national identity

Singapore ceased to be a British colony in 1959 and, after attempting a federation, split from Malaysia in 1965. Ethnic Malays comprise the majority population in Malaysia as a whole but currently make up only about 15 percent of the population of Singapore. For the past four decades, the People's Action Party (PAP) has governed Singapore; the city–state experiences the longest-enduring noncommunist, one-party system in the world. Under the strong-armed leadership of Lee Kuan Yew, prime minister from 1965 until 1990, Singapore sought to build a stable political order and a highly efficient economy. Since the late 1950s, ethnic and religious identities have been central to the debate over what kind of nation Singapore would be. Singapore separated from Malaysia largely out of concern for the rights of the non-Malay (and mostly non-Muslim) population in Singapore. In particular, the majority population of ethnic Chinese in Singapore refused to be part of a nation in which ethnic Malays enjoyed privileged status and in which Islamic understandings of society were codified into law.

The constitution of 1966 established Singapore as a secular state and mandates that "[i]t shall be the responsibility of the government constantly to care for the interests of the racial and religious minorities in Singapore."[36] In comparison to the constitutions of the United States and India, Singapore's constitution includes a stronger caveat on its protection of religious liberty: "This article [guaranteeing freedom of religion] does not authorize any act contrary to any general law relating to public order, public health or morality."[37] Indeed, as time passed, it became very clear that Singapore's government would not tolerate any religion (or other ideology or institution) that challenges the "public order." The Jehovah's Witnesses were declared illegal in 1971;[38] at present, various religious organizations, including the Jehovah's Witnesses, the Divine Light Mission, and the Unification

---

[36] Singapore Constitution, Part XIII, Art. 152. See Barrett, Kurian, and Johnson, *World Christian Encyclopedia*, 1:663.
[37] Singapore Constitution, Part IV, Art. 15.
[38] Barrett, Kurian, and Johnson, *World Christian Encyclopedia*, 1:663.

Church, are outlawed on the grounds that they are a threat to the order and harmony of Singapore.[39] Concerns about potential conflicts between political identity and religious identity discussed in the US and Indian contexts are even more apparent in Singapore. In this latter context, the government simply declares that some religions are not legal because they represent a threat to public order and political stability.

Since the 1960s, the Singaporean government has attempted to implement a national ideology that would bind together an ethnically and religiously diverse population around some set of shared values. Toward that end, Prime Minister Lee developed a vision of "shared values" or "right values" that Singaporeans should hold.[40] The government relies on an understanding of Confucianism to support those common values; namely, it embraces a civic perspective defined in terms of the five relationships described by Mencius (father–son, ruler–subject, husband–wife, old–young, and friend–friend[41]) that would support a highly ordered political system stressing loyalty to the state. The government has also appropriated Confucianism as an ideological support for the hard work, sacrifice, and discipline that have successfully transformed Singapore into a highly economically developed nation-state.[42]

On this latter point, politicians in the PAP as well as a number of scholars have sought to demonstrate that the Confucian ethic is a functional equivalent of, or even a superior alternative to, the Protestant ethic in fostering the spirit of capitalism in the West.[43] Representatives of the Singaporean government have argued that a "Confucian ethic" has helped Singapore (and the other mini-dragons – South Korea, Taiwan, and Hong Kong) to embrace a form of modernization that is as productive as Western capitalism but free of its individualistic roots. Some scholars have defended the importance of more democratic understandings of Confucian ethics, and critics of the government's efforts have maintained that Singapore's use of Confucian ideas is a politically and economically expedient misreading of the tradition.[44]

---

[39] Joseph B. Tamney, "Conservative Government and Support for the Religious Institution in Singapore: An Uneasy Alliance," *Sociological Analysis* 53/2 (1992): 205.

[40] Joseph B. Tamney, "Religion and the State in Singapore," *Journal of Church and State* 30 (1988): 111.

[41] Tu Wei-ming, "Confucianism," in *Our Religions*, ed. Arvind Sharma (San Francisco: Harper San Francisco, 1993), 186–93.

[42] Robert W. Hefner, "Introduction: Multiculturalism and Citizenship in Malaysia, Singapore, and Indonesia," in *The Politics of Multiculturalism: Pluralism and Citizenship in Malaysia, Singapore, and Indonesia*, ed. Robert W. Hefner (Honolulu: University of Hawai'i Press, 2001), 40–41.

[43] Terence Chong, "Asian Values and Confucian Ethics: Malay Singaporeans' Dilemma," *Journal of Contemporary Asia* 32/3 (2002): 394. See also Tamney, "Religion and the State in Singapore," 116–17.

[44] Chong, "Asian Values and Confucian Ethics."

For the purposes of this book's exploration of religion and the workplace, Singapore's attempt to appropriate Confucian ethics for economic productivity is particularly significant. The government's interest in Confucianism is clearly and unabashedly grounded in the desire to create efficient, profitable enterprise in Singapore. Confucianism – as interpreted by the government – serves as a combined civil and corporate religion. Political and workplace policies pay some attention to minority religious expression, but the national emphasis on Confucian values as common values contributing to economic development is the dominant, and little-disguised, ideology. The overriding theme is one of a national ethos of hard work and social obligations.[45] These obligations apply to one's citizenship and to one's work duties. The Confucian philosophy thus supports obedience not only to the state but also to the workplace organization. Good citizens are perceived to be good workers, and vice versa.

Policies of religious and cultural pluralism

The national emphasis on shared values, informed by the authoritarian understanding of Confucianism, does not result in a complete denial of religious difference on the part of its citizens. In fact, Singapore's de facto civil religion is generally framed as *cultural* and not as *religious*. At a minimum, the government asserts that the shared values are not contradictory to the beliefs of Muslims, Christians, Hindus, Sikhs, and Buddhists. This presumed compatibility leaves room, but clearly not unlimited room, for expression of religious identity in various spheres of public life. However, the Singaporean ideology of shared values necessitates even greater constraints upon dissent than does US civil religion.[46]

Before examining policies aimed at religious pluralism in the workplace, it will be illuminating to consider efforts in the sphere of public education. The Singaporean government has long understood the important role of civic and moral education in its schools. Prime Minister Lee commissioned his lieutenant Goh Keng Swee in 1978 to undertake a study of the Ministry of Education that would include an examination of the effectiveness of its civic and moral education initiatives. The resulting Goh Report led to a new curriculum on moral education. When the program began in 1984, it included a "religious knowledge" program for the last two years of secondary education. Students could choose from among the following subjects (note that they did not have to take a course from their own

---

[45] Tamney, "Religion and the State in Singapore," 116.   [46] See ch. 6 above.

tradition or practice): Bible knowledge (Roman Catholic), Bible knowledge (Protestant), Buddhist studies, Confucian ethics, Hindu studies, Islamic religious knowledge, Sikhism, or world religions. Religious organizations prepared the curriculum for their respective traditions, with one exception: the government itself prepared the Confucian ethics curriculum.[47] The prime minister and other officials stressed that the purpose of this program was to help students further cultivate, in scholar Joseph B. Tamney's words, a "common moral code, which would express the state ideology."[48] When introducing the religious knowledge curriculum, the government made it clear that its mission was to inculcate shared moral values in its citizens.

The religious knowledge program lasted only six years. In 1989 the government voted to replace it with a "Civics/Moral Education Program," which took an even more direct approach to indoctrinating students in the shared national values of Singapore.[49] Tamney suggests that the government abruptly canceled the earlier program for at least three reasons. First, and perhaps most important, the Confucian ethics course did not prove to be a popular option for students. Less than 18 percent of all students enrolled in the Confucian curriculum. The other two reasons involved the more popular options: 44 percent of students enrolled in the Buddhist curriculum, and 21 percent enrolled in either the Catholic or Protestant Bible curricula.[50] The government had expected that many ethnic Chinese students would take the Confucian ethics program; instead, many chose the Buddhist program. It became apparent that the Confucian ethics curriculum was, therefore, not even helping to shape the ethnic Chinese citizens. The concern about Christianity was perhaps even greater. Tamney notes that in the 1980s the government viewed with suspicion both the liberation theology espoused by more progressive Christians and the more traditional evangelization from Christian conservatives.[51] Christians posed a threat in the eyes of the government because, unlike Muslims and Hindus, they were very interested and engaged in converting ethnic Chinese and other citizens. While the government did not think it necessary to outlaw mainstream Christian organizations as it had the Jehovah's Witnesses in 1971, it did not wish to fuel their efforts by funding and supporting Christian

---

[47] Tamney, "Religion and the State in Singapore," 114–15.   [48] Ibid., 113.
[49] Tamney, "Conservative Government and Support for the Religious Institution in Singapore," 204.
[50] Ibid., 210; Chong, "Asian Values and Confucian Ethics," 402–03.
[51] Tamney, "Conservative Government and Support for the Religious Institution in Singapore," 206–08; Hefner, "Multiculturalism and Citizenship," 39; Khun, writing from a more sympathetic position to the government, emphasizes the need for concern over Christian proselytism. Khun Eng Kuah, "Maintaining an Ethno-Religious Harmony in Singapore," *Journal of Contemporary Asia* 28/1 (1998), 108–09, 111–13.

education in its secondary schools. The national effort to create shared values and loyal citizens through the Religious Knowledge curriculum was not working, so the government terminated it.

The attempts to combine a strong national identity with respect for different religious communities, beliefs, and practices continued into the 1990s. The government released a White Paper on Shared Values in 1991 and the Religious Harmony Act the following year. In his sympathetic analysis of Singapore's policies, Khun Eng Kuah explains that the Religious Harmony Act seeks to assure that no religious organization will disrupt the public stability of Singapore's diverse peoples. The act also addresses Singapore's concern about "aggressive proselytization and conversion." Kuah notes that the act "allows the government to take action against the various religious groups which violate the act, i.e., to serve restraining orders on leaders and members of a religion who threaten Singapore's religious harmony by their words or actions, and those who conduct political and subversive activities under the guise of religion."[52] This statement fits within the Singaporean legal context that does not permit freedom of the press and which requires a police permit for public gatherings of five or more people.

Within (and only within) this constrained atmosphere for religious and political expression, the government attempts to understand the particular needs of various minority religious communities. Notably, the government has established a Presidential Council for Religious Harmony in the Ministry of Home Affairs. In addition, the government has Hindu and Sikh "advisory boards." The Majlis Ugama Islam Singapura (MUIS, or the Islamic Religious Council of Singapore) is a government organization with a mission statement "to lead in Islamic matters and to guide in the building of a Muslim Community of Excellence serving for the well-being of the community and the nation."[53] This organization has four units: a mosque division, religious development and research, finance, and corporate affairs. One of the defined purposes of the corporate division is "[t]o develop a pool of committed, competent and knowledge-driven MUIS' work[ers], who strive for excellence in their work, in their personal development, and in serving the general public and/or MUIS' clients, thus gain[ing] acceptance and respect from both the Muslims and non-Muslims."[54] The state organization unapologetically and unabashedly declares that it helps Muslim Singaporeans become more loyal citizens and better workers.

---

[52] Khun, "Maintaining an Ethno-Religious Harmony in Singapore," 107.
[53] Majlis Ugama Islam Singapura, http://www1.muis.gov.sg/about/index.asp, accessed November 2, 2002.
[54] Majlis Ugama Islam Singapura, www1.muis.gov.sg/about/index.asp, accessed November 2, 2002.

The government has also promoted religious pluralism in public-sector and private-sector workplaces through its national holiday policy. Like India, the national calendar includes holidays representing multiple religious traditions. Of the ten public holidays, three are clearly secular (New Year's Day, Labour Day, and National Day), but the other seven reflect religious (or religious–cultural) observances: two are Christian (Good Friday and Christmas), two are Muslim (Hari Raya Haji [or Dhu al-Hijjah] and Hari Raya Puasa [or Eid al-Fitr]), one is Buddhist (Vesak Day), one is Hindu (Deepavali [or Diwali]), and one is related to Chinese religions (Chinese New Year).[55] All government employees receive all of these holidays as paid vacation days. Adherents of the particular religious tradition that is celebrating a day as a religious holiday often receive a half-day of vacation on the day prior to the national holiday. Many of the private-sector businesses follow the same holiday schedule as the government agencies and give these days as paid vacation days. To augment the holiday policy, the government funds public displays of holiday-related decorations for the various celebrations – Christmas, Chinese New Year, Deepavali, and so on.

The present-day challenges of religious pluralism

Recently, much like India and the United States, Singapore's attention to religious diversity has been tinted by a concern for global terrorism. Singapore's response is distinctively colored by its strong government policies focused on maintenance of order. In October 2002, Prime Minister Goh Chok Tong proposed a draft "code of interaction" for religious harmony.[56] This code was to be in the form of a pledge that all Singaporeans would be expected to recite:

We, the citizens of Singapore, acknowledging that we are a secular society; enjoying the freedom to practise our own religions; and recognizing that religious harmony is a cornerstone of our peace, progress and prosperity; hereby resolve to practise our religions in a manner that: promotes the cohesion and integration of our society; expands the common space of Singaporeans; encourages mutual tolerance, understanding, respect, confidence and trust; fosters stronger bonds across religious communities; and prevents religion from ever being a source of conflict.[57]

---

[55] National University of Singapore, http://www.nus.edu.sg/registrar/calendar20022003.html, accessed November 2, 2002.

[56] Alicia Yeo, Arlina Arshad, and Sue-Ann Chia, "Religious Code Goes Beyond Keeping Peace," *The Straits Times*, October 16, 2002.

[57] Quoted in Chua Lee Hoong, "Code Red? Code Green? Code Orange!," *The Straits Times*, October 16, 2002.

Statements by public officials make it clear that this most recent attempt to strengthen the national commitment of citizens of all religions is aimed in particular at the Muslim community, in light of the fears about the Islamic terrorist group Jemaah Islamiah (JI), which has active cells in Singapore.

Also, in recent months, Muslims in the workplace have sought to address potential cases of discrimination that Muslim, Malay employees could face in light of public suspicion of Islamic terrorists. Labor unions have been working with employers to establish a code of conduct and a panel to guarantee against anti-Muslim discrimination in the hiring process or in the workplace itself.[58] At present, Muslims and other minority religion employees do not have anti-discrimination protections such as those provided in the US context in Title VII of the Civil Rights Act.

Given the current environment Singapore faces significant challenges regarding religious pluralism in public life, in general, and in the workplace, in particular. The recent crackdown to preempt terrorism does not bode well for Muslims' civil rights, already limited by a strong government more interested in public order and economic productivity than in individual rights, but recent public discussion of Muslims' rights and the discourse about mutual toleration provide some hope for interreligious respect. The policy on religious and national holidays at least acknowledges the importance of various religions' biggest celebrations. Yet Singapore's government severely limits the bounds of religious pluralism through its excessive emphasis on order, stability, and harmony. The final phrase of the recently proposed code and pledge of interaction makes plain the fundamental challenge for pluralism in Singapore: citizens are to practice their religions in a fashion that "prevents religion from ever being a source of conflict." Genuine respect for religious difference requires not denying the possibility of conflict but finding ways to resolve conflicts constructively.

CONCLUSIONS

These examinations of religious pluralism in India and Singapore suggest that the United States is certainly not alone in confronting the realities of diversity. Indeed, the religious complexity in both India and Singapore strike at the heart of those nations' respective identities: India's secularism-as-pluralism offers an alternative to the model of an Islamic republic, such

---

[58] "Unions Act to Allay Fears of Anti-Muslim Bias," *The Straits Times*, September 26, 2002; "Unions Push for Panel to Prevent Discrimination against Moslems," *Deutsche Presse-Agentur*, October 12, 2002.

as that found in Pakistan, and Singapore's shared-values model similarly rejects the adoption of an Islamic state, such as that found in Malaysia. One principal insight of this comparative chapter concerns the prior legal and societal conditions in which religious diversity in the workplace must operate. That is, the issues associated with negotiating religion and other forms of diversity in the workplace must be viewed within the wider contexts of governmental structure and societal norms and values.

The United States, India, and Singapore all experience a wide diversity of religious traditions in their respective populaces; but in each there is a predominant, or majority, tradition. In the USA, Christianity is the "religious preference" of over four-fifths of the population. Over three-fourths of Indians are Hindus. Singapore's majority population is ethnic Chinese, although it is more difficult to classify the array of Chinese religious and philosophical traditions as *religious*. Indeed, Singapore's government has targeted ethnic (not religious) Chinese as its principal base for shared values, and it has emphasized, somewhat expediently, that Confucian values are not religious values. Nonetheless, institutions and leaders in all three nations face the challenge of guaranteeing that adherents of the majority tradition do not receive unfair preference in public life. Leaders in politics and in workplace organizations in each of the three countries have a mixed record on this front.

This comparative examination highlights the fact that my analysis of religion and the workplace in the United States assumes that all citizens are subject to the same legal code – and that, in the workplace and other spheres of public life, religious identity does not trump citizen identity.[59] The Indian case of the Christian cobbler suggests that the similar legal treatment of citizens regardless of religion is not universal practice. The Indian Supreme Court ruled that Soosai's religious identity precluded him from partaking in government-sponsored initiatives designed to benefit his caste. If pluralism translates into fundamentally different treatment of citizens – such as different application of laws or even different laws according to religious community – then pluralism can go too far. The quest for a framework of respectful pluralism in the workplace is for a moral, not a legal, framework, but it does assume a legal framework of equality under the law that should apply to all citizens.

---

[59] A well-functioning state, to be sure, allows for significant accommodation of religious belief and practice when they conflict with government-sanctioned practices; legal protections allow, for example, for conscientious objection and for reasonable accommodation of religious dress and practices as protected by the US Civil Rights Act Title VII.

In Singapore, the government has developed and communicated a civil religion in order to shape citizen identity and loyalty to the nation. I have offered some criticism of the excesses of a similar practice in the United States in the previous chapter. The analysis of Singapore reveals, in a way more explicit than the US case, the dangers of coercion when the state makes it national policy to propagate a civil religion. In Singapore, the efforts to justify an authoritarian regime by public appeal to Confucian values has led to an instrumental use of religious concepts for controlling the political order as well as for motivating loyal and efficient employees in the workplace.

On a related note, the Singaporean government has been more severe than either India or the USA in declaring illegal any religious traditions that appear to threaten political stability. All three nations, the USA, India, and Singapore, face terrorist threats and, in all three, public discourse includes a too-simple equation of Islam and terrorism. Within the context of the wider public challenge to show respect for the vast majority of Muslims who have no involvement in terrorism, workplace organizations in all three countries face the particular issue of guarding against anti-Muslim discrimination at work. Public efforts in all three nations to educate fellow employees about potential anti-Muslim bias are positive steps.

The holiday policies of India and Singapore also offer promise of acceptance and tolerance in religiously diverse societies. Each nation has gone so far as to recognize multiple religious holy days as national holidays. (I note here that I am not suggesting that such an approach be appropriated in the US context.) This practice originated, arguably, as a political necessity in each country, as people with deeply divided religious loyalties struggled to come together as a nation. Such major concessions were imperative in order to obtain a workable consensus on the government by adherents of all major religious traditions. (India had to go even further with its compromise on civil codes.) In addition to the religious holidays policies, both nations have other practices that allow for religious difference. In India, employees can choose additional holy days as their own vacation days. Singaporeans who observe a given holy day often receive part of the prior day off from work as well. Notwithstanding the legal, moral, and practical issues raised with the wider national approaches, such practices are fascinating examples of negotiation and compromise in religiously diverse workplaces.

The recently proposed "code of interaction" in Singapore suggests that religion should never be allowed to be a source of conflict. Whether in Singapore, India, or the USA, it is wrongheaded to frame the challenges of religious diversity in such a manner. As I have shown in this and earlier chapters, religious difference and other kinds of difference in diverse workplaces often create the potential for division. The Singaporean policy of repressing religious difference and denying the possibility of conflict is an unacceptable approach. India's adjudication of generally applicable laws by religious–communal identity (and its multiple civil codes) may have been politically necessary for that context, but it is not a model for treating all citizens and employees as moral equals. As I will argue in the remaining chapters, a model of respectful pluralism for workplaces in the US context (and probably all others) requires that a prior, more fundamental civil right of religious freedom be guaranteed to all citizens within a single legal system. Neither India nor Singapore provides a satisfactory model for negotiating religious diversity in US public life, particularly the workplace. There are some interesting insights, nonetheless, in the attempts at mutual respect for, observance of, and even education about multiple religious traditions through public recognition of their respective holy days. How best to appropriate the positive lessons within a framework of respectful pluralism in the US context is a topic for the remaining chapters.

PART III

Constructing respectful pluralism

CHAPTER 8

Respectful pluralism at work

The analysis thus far has critically engaged with disparate approaches to addressing religious diversity, such as keeping religion and spirituality out of the workplace altogether, translating or reducing diverse religious beliefs and practices to a so-called common spirituality, or maintaining an era of Christian establishment. Building upon these earlier arguments, the remaining chapters construct an alternative perspective on how workplace leaders and followers can most adequately negotiate religion, in its various forms, in their organizations.

The central aim of this chapter is to provide a defensible and convincing explanation of and moral justification for respectful pluralism. I argue that this framework allows employees to express, within constraints to be outlined, their religious as well as political, cultural, spiritual, and other commitments within the workplace. In addition, no religious tradition should receive undue institutional preference or priority. In order to explain the constructive framework, the first section outlines the descriptive realities of the contemporary workplace in which respectful pluralism would operate and to which it would respond. It also describes the nature of the moral argument I am making and how it can contribute to ongoing debate about religion and the workplace. The subsequent sections present the moral argument for respectful pluralism, including a concise statement of the framework's guiding principle and limiting norms. Finally, the framework is examined in practice vis-à-vis a number of real-life dilemmas that workplace managers and employees face. As a whole, the chapter offers a vision of how putting respectful pluralism into practice can help leaders – and religious adherents – to address religious diversity as well as other kinds of diversity at work.

CIRCUMSTANCES OF THE CONTEMPORARY WORKPLACE

The framework begins by identifying those descriptive factors – *circumstances* – that contribute to the context in which workplace organizations must navigate the myriad forms of religion.[1] These circumstances are not normative visions of how the workplace or society should be; rather, they account for the most relevant factors that workplaces currently confront. In that sense, these are not value-based claims. Of course, they do reflect certain values in the sense that all descriptive exercises reflect some *framing* of reality.[2] For example, compared to approaches advocating a generic spirituality at work, my account of the circumstances of the workplace places more emphasis on religious diversity. Each of the circumstances included here, then, depends upon a prior evaluation of which factors are significant in the current context.

The first circumstance of the contemporary workplace has received significant attention throughout the book: *a broad and increasing religious diversity among employees within organizations.* Diversities of various kinds (beliefs, traditions, practices, dress, speech) are fundamental elements that contribute to the need for a complex approach to religion and the workplace. If everyone in an organization held the same beliefs and engaged in the same practices, an institutional establishment of a specific religious or spiritual system of beliefs and practices would not be as morally or practically troubling as it is under the condition of diversity. (Even if such a situation did not exist, however, the institutional establishment of a particular religion in a workplace would still raise moral concerns.[3])

The second circumstance of the contemporary workplace is the descriptive understanding of *non-compartmentalization.* Stated in the framework of Hickman and other theorists of organizations, this simply refers to the phenomenon that, like it or not, employees bring their own identity, problems, and beliefs to work.[4] For many employees, religious or spiritual beliefs and

---

[1] This approach to understanding and responding to descriptive circumstances is parallel to John Rawls's attention (drawing upon David Hume) to the "circumstances of justice" as those conditions that necessitate a theory of justice. John Rawls, *A Theory of Justice* (Cambridge, MA: Harvard University Press, 1971), 126–30.

[2] See Amartya Sen, "Description as Choice," *Oxford Economic Papers* 32 (1980).

[3] Three kinds of problems would remain in that case, however. First, there would still be concern about potential coercion, viz., whether individuals are allowed to practice their religion on their own terms. Second, we would have to ask, why are adherents of other religious, spiritual, or moral backgrounds not included in the company? – and, will an employee from a different background who joins the company be respected? Third, there would still remain the issue of whether the workplace, through establishment, was inappropriately becoming, in itself, a *religious* institution. See ch. 6 above for a fuller discussion of this latter point.

[4] See chs. 2 and 3 above.

practices are an essential and inseparable part of their life. Even in so-called secular workplaces, workers do not and cannot fully leave them behind. Hickman and others assert that workplaces that accommodate this fact are able to address the needs of their employees more efficiently and humanely.[5] The descriptive circumstance of non-compartmentalization has implications for various aspects of human resource management, including work–family policies and sick leave. It also pertains to how and how much religious and other "personal" expression should be permitted at work. Many workplaces forbid explicitly religious speech or actions, but they cannot force employees not to think about, or to be influenced by, their religious commitments.

The third circumstance understands *workplaces as increasingly public sites in American society*.[6] Citing increased working hours and new technology that make workers available around the clock, social scientists assert that work has taken on a larger role in persons' lives in recent decades.[7] Employees spend more of their time and conduct more of their everyday lives in the workplace. Indeed, much of the current interest in spirituality and leadership can be attributed to this phenomenon, which often restricts people's involvement in traditional communities of faith.[8] In addition, through a process of transformation in the size and nature of firms, companies themselves have taken on an increasingly important role in American public life. Corporations hold a great deal of influence in terms of public policy, public opinion, and the shaping of civil society.[9] Moses L. Pava argues for calling corporations "quasi-public institutions," because they exercise a certain degree of power over employees, customers, and other citizens and they

---

[5] Note that non-compartmentalization can also be a normative claim – asserting that, since people should live integrated lives, they should be allowed to express themselves religiously and in other ways at work and elsewhere. Respectful pluralism makes such a moral argument. But it is based, in part, on the descriptive fact that it is difficult if not impossible for employees to keep the workplace free of personal "encumbrances" like religious commitment.

[6] The term "private sector" is a misnomer; the business sector is only private in the sense of being non-governmental.

[7] Juliet Schor, *The Overworked American: The Unexpected Decline of Leisure* (New York: Basic Books, 1992); Robert D. Putnam, *Bowling Alone: The Collapse and Revival of American Community* (New York: Simon & Schuster, 2000). In Arlie Hochschild's language, managers have sought to make work more like home, even as home-life has become more like work. Arlie Hochschild, *The Time Bind: When Work Becomes Home and Home Becomes Work* (New York: Metropolitan Books, 1997).

[8] See ch. 2 above.

[9] Patricia Werhane and Tara Radin, acknowledging the tremendous size and political and social power of corporations, suggest that corporate employees should receive due process rights in order to protect themselves from the potentially coercive influence of corporations – influence that is not recognized explicitly in standard views of work as "employment at will." Patricia H. Werhane and Tara J. Radin, "Employment at Will and Due Process," in *Ethical Theory and Business*, ed. Tom L. Beauchamp and Norman E. Bowie, sixth edn. (Upper Saddle River, NJ: Prentice Hall, 2001).

have a large public role in society.[10] In contemporary America, the work-place is one of the principal places in which people encounter religious and other forms of difference.[11] The ways in which employees from diverse religious backgrounds are either included or excluded in the corporate en-vironment convey messages about who counts in public life. The public or quasi-public role of corporations also suggests that the workplace is a site in which employees might learn from one another.

The fourth circumstance that affects the contemporary workplace is *the complex and contested role of religion in public life*. This factor captures many roles that religion plays in American society. Scholarly and public discourse about the role of religion in the workplace does not occur in a vacuum but, rather, is informed by debates over the lingering Christian cultural establishment in public life, the realities of Christianity as the "religious preference" of a majority of Americans, the tradition of avowed secularism in the market sphere, and the recent interest in "spiritual leadership."[12] The first two of these elements serve as a reminder that any approach, including respectful pluralism, does not address a context in which adherents of all religious, spiritual, and other backgrounds have the same experience of expressing their religion at work and in public life; many employees who are Christians have received or do receive preferential treatment at work and in society. The current discussions of generic spirituality can marginalize atheists and some adherents of many religious backgrounds. At the same time, the secular understanding of modern society has pressured people of various religious and spiritual backgrounds to divorce some or all of their commitments from all aspects of their public lives.

The fifth and final circumstance considered here is the *for-profit nature of companies*. Workplace organizations in the so-called private sector are not (and should not be) religious institutions, and it bears restating that it is not their central purpose to serve as the principal religious site for employees.[13]

---

[10] Moses L. Pava, "Religious Business Ethics and Political Liberalism: An Integrative Approach," *Journal of Business Ethics* 17 (1998). In particular, Pava notes that corporations: "A – create and sustain monopolistic markets, B – impose costs or externalities on non-contracting third parties, and C – lobby governmental official[s] for personal and corporate gain" (p. 1637). Pava chooses not to call corporations fully public because he notes, rightly, that the degree of coercion that a corporation can have on an employee is still not as great as that which a government can have on a citizen.

[11] For one description of contemporary workplaces as a context for interreligious encounter, see Diana L. Eck, *A New Religious America: How a "Christian Country" Has Now Become the World's Most Religiously Diverse Nation* (San Francisco: Harper San Francisco, 2001), 316–20.

[12] For a helpful framework for analyzing the multiple kinds and levels of context, see J. Thomas Wren and Marc J. Swatez, "The Historical and Contemporary Contexts of Leadership: A Conceptual Model," in *The Leader's Companion: Insights on Leadership through the Ages*, ed. J. Thomas Wren (New York: Free Press, 1995).

[13] See ch. 6 above.

My analysis assumes that, within the bounds of legality and morality, companies have the legitimate right to seek profits and to pursue the financial interests of the company. The Nobel laureate in economics Milton Friedman asserts that "the one and only social responsibility of business [is] to use its resources and engage in activities designed to increase its profits so long as it stays within the rules of the game."[14] It is not necessary to embrace Friedman's unconditional view in order to recognize the very important point that, within appropriate constraints, companies have a worthy and legitimate (instrumental) goal of profitability. Practical concerns require that, while moral concerns about employees and managers are fundamental, companies need to be profitable in order to exist as workplaces over the long term.

THE NATURE OF MORAL ARGUMENT IN A PLURALISTIC CONTEXT

An argument for constructing respectful pluralism in the workplace should acknowledge that the reality of moral, philosophical, and religious disagreement among diverse perspectives applies not only to employees but to scholars as well. This section discusses the method and language used to construct that framework in subsequent pages.

Drawing upon Thiemann's "conditions of publicity,"[15] my book *Inequality and Christian Ethics* offers an extended account of how and why a variety of religiously based and other moral arguments should be allowed in public debates about contemporary economic issues.[16] I argue against a strict political liberalism that advocates a very narrow public sphere in which citizens can speak to one another only in terms of values reportedly held by all members of a society. Political liberals argue against welcoming appeals by some citizens to doctrines and worldviews that other citizens do not support and that they may not understand. Although these theorists' commitment to uphold equal respect of citizens is correct, their position unnecessarily impoverishes moral discourse, because it precludes citizens from drawing upon morally rich and imaginative perspectives. John Rawls, in his account of "public reason," offers one of the most articulate defenses of such liberal positions, though it is interesting to note that he substantially loosened

---

[14] Milton Friedman, *Capitalism and Freedom* (University of Chicago Press, 1962), 133.
[15] Ronald F. Thiemann, *Religion in Public Life: A Dilemma for Democracy* (Washington, DC: Georgetown University Press, 1996), 135–41.
[16] Douglas A. Hicks, *Inequality and Christian Ethics*, New Studies in Christian Ethics 16 (Cambridge University Press, 2000), 85–113. In that work I construct a Christian ethical approach to well-being and socioeconomic inequality.

the constraints he advocated for religious speech during the last ten years of his life.[17] In his argument for the use of public reason, Rawls rightly emphasizes that citizens have a duty to act with civility and should uphold the virtue of mutual respect toward fellow citizens. This helps guarantee that any power yielded by citizens to the state is justifiable to all citizens in language they understand. For Rawls, civility and respect can best be guaranteed when citizens speak to one another in terms that everyone holds in common. This position is problematic for a number of reasons, including the high level of confidence Rawls places on people's ability to concur on what values are commonly held as part of public reason. Further, his position does not adequately capture the importance of religion, and the difficulty of compartmentalizing it, in many citizens' lives.[18]

Rawls states that his argument for public reason applies only within the public political sphere, when citizens are deliberating matters of basic justice in a society. Rawls is not as concerned about the potential for coercion in institutions such as the workplace as he is when the state is involved. Pava, however, builds upon Rawls's framework and suggests that Rawls's account of public reason provides a helpful analogue for the workplace context as well. Managers should show respect toward their co-workers and subordinates by using language they can comprehend; however, "under appropriate and limited circumstances, [managers] may invoke and rely upon a religious, albeit private, worldview."[19] Employees, and especially corporations as institutions, have a moral obligation to justify their actions in terms that are as publicly accessible as possible.

My argument for how respectful pluralism should operate in the workplace attempts to broaden the liberal framework while upholding its concern that citizens (and employees) communicate to each other in ways that respect other citizens (and co-workers). I support Pava's contention that the corporation has tremendous public power and the capacity to influence employees' lives. After all, because corporations are major institutions of American public life, the explicit or implicit messages that companies send can strike at employees' overall sense of identity.

[17] Rawls's basic position is laid out in John Rawls, *Political Liberalism*, The John Dewey Essays in Philosophy No. 4 (New York: Columbia University Press, 1993), Lecture VI, pp. 212–54. He widened his perspective significantly in John Rawls, "The Idea of Public Reason Revisited," *University of Chicago Law Review* 64 (1997); specifically, he allowed for persons to appeal to religious reasons or to any other "reasonable comprehensive doctrine," as long as they also provided "proper political reasons" (for example, commonly held public political values) alongside the reasons of the more particular worldview (pp. 783–84). For a fuller discussion, see Hicks, *Inequality and Christian Ethics*, 93–101.
[18] Hicks, *Inequality and Christian Ethics*, 97–101; this point relates to the second circumstance of the workplace, discussed above.
[19] Pava, "Religious Business Ethics and Political Liberalism: An Integrative Approach," 1635.

The political liberal position does not adequately recognize that people can communicate – on their own terms – across religious, spiritual, and moral divides. That is, I contend that workers can uphold mutual respect toward their co-workers even as they practice their particularistic religious commitments in the workplace. Does this mean that workers will constantly communicate with one another in religiously particularistic language as they go about the normal routines of their work? I do not believe so.[20] But I do mean to assert that employees should have the freedom to draw upon their religiously based ideas and symbols as they work; they should feel free to explain their beliefs to their co-workers and how their beliefs affect the way they approach their work. Like Pava's and Rawls's perspectives, however, the framework does contain a strong presumption against institutional use of religious language and symbols because of its potential to coerce or degrade employees from differing or minority backgrounds.

One factor influencing this pluralistic approach to moral conversation is my belief that there is no single "complete" language or set of values that is held in common by all citizens.[21] Otherwise stated, if citizens do hold in common a few values, such as freedom, equality, and toleration, these values are not "thick" enough to provide the resources to settle morally challenging leadership questions such as what role religion should play in the contemporary workplace. Attempts to translate religiously particular values into common spiritual or secular values are reductionistic at best and inaccurate at worst.[22] The framework also suggests, however, that citizens in the public sphere should welcome open discussion and debate of multiple perspectives in order that some level of agreement might be attained.

It is appropriate to specify more fully the kind of language I am employing to make the moral argument for respectful pluralism. While the aim of the argument is to suggest that organizations should allow religious, spiritual, and other forms of expression in the workplace, the moral argument of this book is not framed in the language of a particular religious or theological tradition.[23] The framework presented herein draws upon less comprehensive moral language, language that is typically, but not always, employed in leadership studies, religious studies, and business ethics.

[20] Note that much of the expression of religious commitment (dress, symbols in one's work area, taking time off for prayers or holy days) is not about direct communication with co-workers at all.
[21] Rawls employs the language of "completeness" in his analysis of public reason, asserting that public reason is complete when its "values alone give a reasonable public answer to all, or to nearly all, questions involving the constitutional essentials and basic questions of justice," in Rawls, *Political Liberalism*, 225.
[22] See ch. 3 above.
[23] Surely my own perspective and training in Christian ethics, as I noted in the introduction, has influenced my argument in various ways.

As one possible objection to this part of my method, some scholars might argue that this position – like leadership ethics more broadly – lacks a coherent foundation, is not part of a community of discourse, or is an attempt to universalize values that are not universally held. Despite my own constructive critique of political liberalism, significant elements of that perspective inform respectful pluralism, and thus my framework is undoubtedly subject to some of the same criticisms directed against political liberalism.[24] I do *not* intend to claim that my perspective offers all of the moral resources for solving workplace dilemmas or that it should replace religious, philosophical, or other traditions of moral reasoning in the workplace or elsewhere. On the contrary, I am constructing an argument precisely in order to encourage pluralistic debate and the inclusion of multiple perspectives. I reject generically spiritual frameworks that have the effect of reducing more substantive resources of religious traditions to common denominator beliefs. Respectful pluralism is an "incomplete" framework for settling issues in any given setting.

The framework of respectful pluralism is not, however, a purely procedural one, devoid of substantive claims. In order to construct respectful pluralism, I must appeal to substantive views concerning human dignity, equal respect, noncoercion, nondegradation, etc., that are not universally held. In Rawlsian language, an "overlapping consensus"[25] may or may not be reached on the substantive as well as procedural features of the approach. I offer the framework of respectful pluralism in the hope that some or many readers will find it convincing and that those who disagree will offer a superior approach that addresses the circumstances of the contemporary workplace.

THE MORAL FEATURES OF RESPECTFUL PLURALISM

Dignity and equal respect

It is now possible to specify the moral features of respectful pluralism in organizations. This section views the circumstances of the contemporary workplace, discussed above, as the challenge to which respectful pluralism is a proposed response.

Constructing the framework begins not with the nature of the workplace, but with a series of basic assertions about the employee as a *human person*. The specific concerns and contextual factors of the workplace should fit

---

[24] I consider some of these criticisms in *Inequality and Christian Ethics*, ch. 5, esp. pp. 93–113. See also Thiemann, *Religion in Public Life*.
[25] See Rawls, *Political Liberalism*, Lecture IV, pp. 133–72.

within the general moral understanding of the human being. The most fundamental claim of the framework is that all persons possess an inviolable *human dignity*. There are many ways to ground such a basic assertion about dignity – that all humans are vulnerable or suffer pain, that they are all created by God, that all are in some sense sacred, etc. The debate about this justification of dignity is beyond the scope of this book.[26] Scholars and practitioners of various religious and other moral traditions will have different ways in which to ground the claim.

If the assumption that each person possesses human dignity is granted, the next claim is that every human being deserves to be accorded *respect*. It will be necessary, of course, to debate precisely what obligations people and institutions (including companies) owe to each human being based on that respect.[27] These fundamental assertions do not differentiate among human beings in terms of any feature that individuals possess that make them merit respectful treatment. Persons simply have dignity and deserve to be accorded respect because they are human.[28]

The third assertion is that all human beings possess *equal* dignity and thus deserve *equal* respect. Since the concept of human dignity is not based on human merit, or distinctive features of some people and not others, there is no justifiable reason to differentiate in the degree of respectful treatment due each person. Given that excluding any person would constitute a differentiation among persons, the scope of equality must extend to include all people. Some philosophers posit that equality (and the prior assertions) should be accepted as self-evident.[29] As Amartya Sen has argued, few if any

---

[26] I have treated related questions in Hicks, *Inequality and Christian Ethics*, 20–23. In that work I go on to develop a Christian account of equality, based on human dignity and the claim that humans are created as equals by God.

[27] It is important to note that this claim, that persons be treated with respect, pertains to the speech and actions that individuals and organizations should make toward persons. It does not, and cannot, require people to have moral respect, in a deeper (passive) sense, for individuals whose actions or beliefs do not accord with their own moral conception of the world. Indeed, to attempt to require people to hold an interior feeling or moral evaluation of respect for all other persons would be coercive. It is, rather, reasonable to ask persons to act with respect toward all persons because they are human beings, with dignity. It is possible for a workplace to fire an employee, or for the state to convict a criminal, by following laws and procedures that respect the person in that process. My framework makes substantive claims about what respectful speech and actions are required in the diverse workplace. I am grateful to Jonathan Wight for discussions on this point.

[28] Some scholars seek to ground dignity in the capacity to reason; but then persons with impaired reasoning or severe related disabilities may not be seen as having dignity. Such grounding cannot justify the fundamental assertion of human dignity of *all* persons and would thus be a *competing* moral conception to the ones based on that fundamental assumption.

[29] For his part, Thomas Jefferson makes precisely this claim in the Declaration of Independence – "We hold these truths to be self-evident, that all men are created equal." Most modern scholars would agree with Jefferson's claim if the interpretation of the word "men" were broadened to include females as well as males and slaves as well as free persons.

contemporary moral philosophers (or citizens) debate whether moral equality exists among humans; they generally concur on that point. Rather, a central and contested moral question is, *Equality of what?*[30] In other words, while they agree that equal respect should be accorded to each human being, ethicists argue over precisely how moral equality should be guaranteed and what it demands. Respectful pluralism accepts the assertions regarding human dignity and equal respect outlined above and seeks to show what they require of companies and co-workers, given the circumstances of the workplace.

The comparative, critical analysis of religion in public life in India and Singapore suggests that some basic political and civil rights are owed to citizens prior to their entry into the workplace. Specifically, the framework of respectful pluralism takes as given, regardless of their workplace, that all employees (as citizens[31]) enjoy the basic freedoms of religious exercise, speech, assembly, press, and government petition that are guaranteed in the First Amendment to the US Constitution. Even as we debate how or if we can legitimately balance these rights within the instrumental market relationship, it must be assumed that these rights are part of the political structure in which employment occurs.

Respect, voluntariness, and coercion

Having identified these fundamental claims of human dignity and equal respect and some relevant political and civil rights, we can turn to consider the workplace. What conditions must be operative in the workplace relationship in order to guarantee equal respect for all employees and employers?

A just society morally precedes and constrains the economic system. It should be seen as a precondition for the efficient operation of markets. Adam Smith, moral philosopher and founder of classical economics, states that "justice . . . is the main pillar that upholds the whole edifice" of society.[32]

---

[30] This was the title of Sen's 1979 Tanner Lectures on Human Values. Amartya Sen, "Equality of What?" In *The Tanner Lectures on Human Values*, ed. S. McMurrin (Salt Lake City: Utah University Press and Cambridge University Press, 1980). See my discussion in Hicks, *Inequality and Christian Ethics*, 23–24.

[31] It is vitally important to note that the assumption that all employees are citizens of the nation in which they work does not address directly the issue of the rights of migrant workers or immigrants – whether legal or illegal. For this moral argument, I am assuming that the civil and political rights of all persons, regardless of nationality, should be protected equally and that all persons are deserving of equal respect.

[32] Adam Smith, *The Theory of Moral Sentiments*, trans. D. D. Raphael and A. L. Macfie, Glasgow Edition of the Works and Correspondence of Adam Smith (New York: Oxford University Press, 1976), II.ii.3.4, 86.

No relationship in the market sphere or any other sphere of life can justifiably violate the equal respect owed to each person. The basic human dignity of both employees and employers, by virtue of their status as human persons, constrains the profit-seeking activities of firms. As part of the fundamental moral guarantee to all persons undergirding economic relations, workers must be treated humanely and fairly. The specific conditions that guarantee humane and fair treatment, of course, must be determined in any given context. At a minimum, they must have commutative justice; the employment transaction (labor for salary) must be just.

For many ethicists, the essential justice of the transaction is seen in the *voluntariness* of both parties. People who enter into a market relationship of employment enter into a contract with a company. There is general agreement that deception or coercion should not be present in the labor contract. What other conditions ensure the voluntariness of such a contract? Under what conditions does a person give his or her genuine consent? The fact that a person accepts or enters into a work-for-pay relationship does not necessarily prove that that person has done so voluntarily. If there is no other reasonable choice – as in a monopolistic labor market – or if there is no reasonable option in which minimum dignity could be guaranteed and therefore laborers must accept an oppressive job over starvation, then it is difficult to say that the decision is truly based on free will. The knowledge that workers accept employment in sweatshops, for instance, does not attend adequately to the alternative options available (or not available) to potential workers when they accept that job. When potential employees have no other viable employment choices available to them, one of the basic conditions for a fair employment contract is violated.[33] Kurt Nutting writes:

The mere existence of expressed consent, or of alternatives, does not, of course suffice to show that there is no coercion. If the highwayman says, "Your money or your life," and I hand over my money, the existence of the alternative does not show that I have not been coerced into handing over the money. In general, to know if an agreement was reached noncoercively, we need to know if the agreement was between parties relatively equal in bargaining power – and this means that neither side faced a significantly "greater evil" than the other if the agreement could not be reached.[34]

Adam Smith noted that, in many cases, workers often face the greater evil (for example, starvation) in the relationship with an employer, who in the

[33] Manuel G. Velasquez, *Business Ethics: Concepts and Cases*, fifth edn. (Upper Saddle River, NJ: Prentice Hall, 2002), 460.
[34] Kurt Nutting, "Work and Freedom in Capitalism," in *Moral Rights in the Workplace*, ed. Gertrude Ezorsky (Albany, NY: State University of New York Press, 1987), 102.

short term might face only the loss of production before another employee can be found.[35]

The market relationship of work involves, among other things, the operation of power among various parties. Nutting claims that the labor relationship always entails coercion,[36] but I differentiate between the morally justifiable power to influence, on the one hand, and coercion, which is the morally illegitimate use of power to influence, on the other. In my frame, coercion is a normative term that signifies inappropriate action or relationship. It is relevant to state that people of minority religious traditions – some who are immigrants to the US in recent years or decades, including Muslims, Hindus, and Latin American Catholics, Pentecostals, and evangelicals – often hold little socioeconomic power and arguably often do not enter into the labor market with the ability to make fully voluntary decisions about employment. They may not, therefore, be in a strong position to make requests for religious understanding or accommodation, not to mention salaries, benefits, and safety measures.[37]

The commitment to dignity and respect limits what demands a firm should make on its employees. To be sure, the work-for-pay relationship has a significant instrumental dimension to it but, at the same time, workers cannot be treated as other "inputs" to the production process, like capital or land, or simply as a means to some economic end.[38] Only while upholding the basic tenets of justice and protecting the dignity of workers can companies pursue profit. Instrumental relations are framed by a fundamental

---

[35] "Many workmen could not subsist a week, few could subsist a month, and scarce any a year without employment. In the long run, the workman may become as necessary to his master as his master is to him; but the necessity is not so immediate." Adam Smith, *An Inquiry into the Nature and Causes of the Wealth of Nations*, ed. R. H. Campbell, A. S. Skinner, and W. B. Todd, Glasgow Edition of the Works and Correspondence of Adam Smith, 2 vols. (New York: Oxford University Press, 1976), I.viii.12, 84.

[36] Nutting, "Work and Freedom in Capitalism," 102–03.

[37] The framework of respectful pluralism argues that all employees, regardless of their socioeconomic status, should be permitted to express their religious identity.

[38] It is important to note that, in the market-based relationship of work, firms are not the only parties that have instrumental goals. Indeed, a variety of actors (or "stakeholders") have their own objectives. For instance, stockholders seek the long-term increase in the value of their stock. They certainly may also desire to contribute to society by making a product available for consumption or by creating employment opportunities for workers. Managers typically desire to maximize their own salary and benefits. Employees pursue a dependable and good salary. Managers and employees alike often seek to find meaningful or fulfilling work, not as a means, but as an end in itself. Indeed, employees often articulate their work in terms of living out their religious, spiritual, or moral obligations. Customers seek affordable, useful goods and services. Neighbors of the company hope that the presence of the business in their community will generate positive outcomes (e.g., employment, community relations, increased tax revenues) with a minimum of negative external effects (e.g., pollution, traffic congestion). For all of these parties, the protection of human dignity of all persons serves as a constraint on the legitimate objectives of market-based relationships.

commitment to dignity and respect in a just society. Thus, we ask: what does a moral commitment to the dignity of persons require of companies and employees in terms of religious expression at work? When persons enter into a market-based relationship of work, how free and welcome are they to express themselves religiously (and in other ways)?

Working conditions and religious expression

Recall that the second circumstance of the workplace assumes that work is a fundamental part of one's identity and that one's sense of dignity is significantly affected by one's work. Many Americans are self-employed and have significant control over their working conditions and ways in which they can express themselves while working. Even more Americans, however, labor as employees, working for companies large and small. In these organizations, what does upholding equal respect and human dignity require – and who is responsible for ensuring these requirements are met? In business ethics, attention to respect and dignity customarily focuses on the guarantee of fair wages and decent working conditions for employees. In legal terms, the latter commitment has been translated into minimum occupational safety and health standards, such as those enforced by OSHA (Occupational Safety and Health Administration) in the United States. In moral terms, some ethicists call for a fuller approach to ensuring that policies and cultures create a workplace in which the dignity of all is acknowledged and working conditions are humane and fair.[39]

Such conditions should be understood, I assert, within a wide view of health and well-being. Manuel D. Velasquez, citing Adam Smith's concern about the human costs of labor, argues that moral attention to working conditions should include a worker's mental as well as physical health.[40] Smith emphasized the ways in which the repetition of a few tasks, under the division of labor, could dull workers' minds and lead to lives of monotony.[41] In an effort to achieve morally acceptable working conditions and employee health, it is necessary to discuss the proper role of religious, spiritual, political, and cultural expression by individuals while at work.

At this point in the argument, a question arises: how vital to an individual's sense of human dignity is the freedom to express one's religious

---

[39] Michael Boylan, *Business Ethics: Basic Ethics in Action* (Upper Saddle River, NJ: Prentice Hall, 2001), 215–17; Velasquez, *Business Ethics*, 457.
[40] Velasquez, *Business Ethics*, 461–62.
[41] Smith, *The Wealth of Nations*, v.i.f.50–54, 781–85. Smith's concern about dulled minds led him to call for public education for the "common people."

identity (or other aspects of one's identity) in the workplace? My moral argument depends upon the understanding – articulated in different ways by differing religious or philosophical traditions – that religious, spiritual, and cultural commitment is a constitutive part of one's identity that cannot be compartmentalized and should not be silenced from explicit expression during work hours. Earlier chapters have presented examples of how employees' fundamental beliefs and actions are evident in multiple kinds of expression.[42] I do not offer a universal account of "how religion is essential to identity in all spheres of life," because I do not believe there is one such account. Further, my argument for respectful pluralism cannot provide a definitive answer to the question of "how much" religion is appropriate in the workplace and what specific dimensions can be legitimately excluded. If the examples and cumulative discussion of earlier chapters are convincing, however, then they add support to my claim that workplace organizations should enable employees explicitly to express their religious identity at work to a significant degree. Not to permit employees to do so in some measure would be a violation of their dignity. The possible contention that employees enter freely into a presumedly voluntary work-for-pay contract must be considered within the prior constraint of the need to guarantee each employee's human dignity. In situations of genuine voluntariness, employees would arguably be less likely than in many present situations to exchange their rights of explicit religious expression for wages.

This argument, based on the respect that is owed to workers and managers because they, as humans, possess dignity, has implications beyond the specific focus on religion and the workplace. Expression based upon other aspects of identity, including gender, race, ethnicity, age, and sexual orientation, similarly should be allowed at work. In addition, workplace rules about employee interaction should be subjected to the moral criterion of the respect due employees as persons.[43]

The argument for significant religious and other expression at work is not based upon the instrumental value of religion or spirituality for the company's level of motivation, quality of communication, or overall productivity. My analysis makes no claims about whether or not permitting such expression will make employees or companies more efficient or profitable.

---

[42] See esp. chs. 4 and 5 above.
[43] Instances of short periods of time on the job when conversation is not permitted may well be acceptable, but policies that forbid outright co-worker conversation during lengthy work shifts, such as those at some large retail department-store chains, are seriously suspect. Barbara Ehrenreich offers a first-hand account of her employment as a Wal-Mart employee and her encounter with such restrictive policies. Barbara Ehrenreich, *Nickel and Dimed: On (Not) Getting by in America* (New York: Metropolitan/Owl Books, Henry Holt and Company, 2001).

The features of respectful pluralism that invite, rather than repress, conflict may well contribute to efficiency, but I do not make that empirical claim. It is also reasonable to assert that allowing employee expression may well help with morale – but such a convenient overlap with efficiency is not necessary to make the policy a morally acceptable one.[44] Instead, the approach argues for a significant degree of employee expression based upon the prior moral obligation not to violate workers' dignity.

The presumption of inclusion, with limiting norms

The following paragraphs state, in the form of a principle and three norms, the essential framework of respectful pluralism. The principle and norms build upon the moral argument based upon the dignity and equal respect of all human beings and depending upon basic political and civil rights and commutative justice. From that perspective, the principle and norms address the circumstances of the contemporary workplace – religious diversity, non-compartmentalization, the workplace as a public site, the contested place of religion in public life, and companies as for-profit enterprises.

The guiding principle of respectful pluralism is termed the *presumption of inclusion*. It can be stated as follows: To the greatest extent, workplace organizations should allow employees to express their religious, spiritual, cultural, political, and other commitments at work, subject to the limiting norms of noncoercion, nondegradation, and nonestablishment, and in consideration of the reasonable instrumental demands of the for-profit enterprise.

The term *presumption of inclusion* contrasts starkly with an understanding of the workplace as a secular sphere. Unlike that view, the principle assumes that non-compartmentalization holds true and that workers can properly bring their religious commitments to work. It places the moral burden of justification on policies that would limit personal expression. The framework does not, however, assert that any and every action by employees or managers is appropriate at work simply because an employee claims that it is a part of his or her identity. Rather, the essential criteria of inclusion and exclusion – the limiting norms – are the same, whether the expression is seen to be religious, gender-based, cultural, political, or otherwise. The essential point is that the moral status of employees, possessing dignity and deserving respect, builds a presumption for a high degree of "personal" expression. Thus, even when workers are engaged in the market relationship

---

[44] See ch. 9 below.

of employment, it is generally permissible for them to express religious and other aspects of their identity. Note that this moral argument exceeds the legal minimums. Title VII of the Civil Rights Act (as amended) protects employees against discrimination and harassment based on many aspects of identity, including religion; but respectful pluralism is more expansive in calling for leadership that respects and allows employees to express their identity.

The first limiting norm is *nondegradation*. This norm prohibits co-workers from employing speech or symbols or otherwise conveying messages directed at particular individuals or groups of co-workers that show clear disrespect for them. As with other dimensions of the framework, this norm requires the exercise of judgment, by applying the moral commitment to uphold the dignity of each employee, in determining what types of expression are degrading or seriously disrespectful to other employees. Certainly, adherence to this norm has the potential to label many forms of religious, cultural, political, and other expression unacceptable.

The second limiting norm, *noncoercion*, suggests that, just as firms should not coerce employees in the employment relationship, employees must not use their power illegitimately to influence co-workers or subordinates. In particular, this norm suggests that employees should not use their position or proximity to colleagues or subordinates to impose their religious, spiritual, or political values on them or to subject them to unwanted invitations in ways that violate their co-workers' human dignity.

The third limiting norm, *nonestablishment*, addresses not individual employees but the workplace organization as an institution. It asserts that, given the circumstance of employee diversity, it is not morally acceptable for a company to endorse, or in any way promote, one particular religious or spiritual worldview over others, even if that worldview is deemed "generic" or is intended to apply to all employees. Upholding the *equal* respect of each worker amidst diversity requires that individual employees be allowed to work within an environment in which leaders can apply the principle and limiting norms of respectful pluralism to all worldviews in a consistent manner. It is important to acknowledge, of course, that all organizations have an organizational culture; some scholars will call any such culture a functional equivalent of a religion. Respectful pluralism is itself a set of ideas for creating a culture that models, as the name suggests, mutual respect amidst diversity.[45] Thus, this criticism has merit. Yet respectful pluralism, while it depends upon substantive moral commitments, is not designed

---

[45] Ibid.

to offer a complete or an exclusive view of truth; rather, its purpose is to encourage co-workers of multiple perspectives and worldviews to communicate with each other and to work together in relative harmony. In short, the framework arguably meets its own criteria of noncoercion and nondegradation, and it respects the various aspects of identity that employees bring to work.

The other limiting consideration acknowledges the legitimate end of profit-seeking by companies. Accordingly, in addition to the moral constraints on personal expression, companies may place other reasonable constraints on expression, as long as they uphold the nonestablishment norm and do not degrade or coerce employees. As should be clear from the entirety of the framework, however, appeals to profitability cannot be made callously as an excuse to exclude all religious or spiritual expression. Further, a company may not make policies that grant the opportunity for one type of expression (for example, religious, spiritual, or political) but exclude another type.[46] Notice that one of the attractive features of respectful pluralism is that it does not require managers or others to determine whether an expression is driven by, or is seen by observers as having, religious, spiritual, or political motivations. Instead, managers and co-workers should apply the tenets of inclusion and limiting norms – which, admittedly, is no simple task. Employers retain legitimate rights to restrain personal expression of various kinds for legitimate safety or efficiency reasons, as long as they do so on an equal basis for all employees. The spirit of the presumption of inclusion, however, does suggest that managers need to have sound reasons to justify any decision not to allow personal expression. That is, the fundamental commitment to equal respect places the moral burden (but not necessarily the legal burden) on the company to show employees why a limit on personal expression is necessary. The legal limitations of Title VII and other federal and state laws are also in place as minimum guarantees against discrimination and harassment.

RESPECTFUL PLURALISM IN OPERATION: PERMISSIBLE
EXPRESSIONS AND LIMITATIONS

A few examples of workplace scenarios related to personal or institutional expression of religion (among other kinds of potential conflict) will give an idea of how respectful pluralism might look in operation.

---

[46] Arguments based on legal reasoning have been successful in rejecting the exclusion of employees' expression merely because it was religious. See examples in ch. 4 above.

When is it morally acceptable for employees to wear their religious garb at work? The presumption of inclusion suggests that respectful pluralism calls for a high level of understanding and flexibility on the part of the employer and co-workers toward religiously motivated dress. After September 11, 2001, Muslim women have faced tremendous problems in the workplace because of their religious obligation to wear *hijab*.[47] Respectful pluralism's approach to such examples requires accommodation – on moral grounds – that goes beyond the standard *de minimis* interpretation of the legal framework required in Title VII of the Civil Rights Act.[48] Given that the workplace is a public or quasi-public institution, the company's decision to exclude women in *hijab* would not only send a message of exclusion to Muslim women, but it would reinforce the idea that Muslims' religious obligations place them outside of US public life. Muslim women who appear in *hijab* must be treated with the same respect accorded other employees; dress codes should be accommodated unless compelling dangers are demonstrated. As a practical matter, examples of suitable compromises abound in which religious persons were able to uphold their commitments while still meeting safety requirements.[49] In rare cases when genuine safety concerns prohibit a person in loose-fitting clothing to hold a position, corporations have a moral obligation beyond *de minimis* costs to find a suitable alternative position for the employee.

As a second example, consider an employee who wishes to hang a religious poster in his or her work area. For instance, a worker wishes to hang a poster that says, "Jesus Saves!" in his cubicle. A few other workers complain about the poster: "It has no place in the office" or "He shouldn't be declaring that his faith is better than mine." In a framework of respectful pluralism, this employee would be allowed to hang such a poster, as long as adherents of other religious and cultural groups are permitted to hang their own respectful posters as well. To be sure, some employees will find the Christian message to be disrespectful, at least in intention. In this author's judgment, this message in isolation is neither coercive nor degrading of persons of other

---

[47] See chapter 4 above for examples of discrimination against women based on their attempts to wear *hijab* at work.

[48] Title VII of the Civil Rights Act (as amended) requires reasonable accommodation of religion by employers unless they show they would face "undue hardship" in doing so. The US Supreme Court decided in *TWA* v. *Hardison* (1977) that demonstrating such an undue hardship was not a high standard to meet. See Michael Wolf, Bruce Friedman, and Daniel Sutherland, *Religion in the Workplace: A Comprehensive Guide to Legal Rights and Responsibilities* (Chicago: Tort and Insurance Practice Section, American Bar Association, 1998), 104–34.

[49] As one example, the Whirlpool Corporation's safety engineers gathered with Muslim women in its manufacturing plant to develop a mutually agreeable policy. James E. Challenger, "Firms Make Room for Different Religions," *Chicago Sun-Times*, May 14, 2000.

faiths; but reasonable persons may disagree, and applications of respectful pluralism will have to be made in any particular setting. Indeed, the very discussion of whether or not something is perceived as coercive or degrading may well be a way to identify tension already latent among co-workers and to produce a beneficial outcome. Critics might say that this kind of debate is a distraction from work. I would make two kinds of argument in response to that criticism: first, I assert that conflicts will arise among workers whether explicit religious messages are allowed or not; second, I would reiterate my claim that, based upon respect for workers, it is impermissible to forbid religious and other expressions at work. Some limit on the number of posters, works of art, and plants, etc., could certainly be established, but those limits should be set and upheld for all persons, regardless of their rank and irrespective of the religious, political, or cultural tradition they reflect. It is not acceptable, however, to prohibit all employees from hanging any decorations or expressions in their work area.

As these examples show, it is incorrect to say that the substantive content of posters and other messages should not be evaluated. The general presumption of permitting religious, political, and other expression is limited morally by the three norms, in addition to relevant legal constraints, especially the legal limits placed on libelous or hate-inspiring speech. The norms of noncoercion and nondegradation require reflection on the substance of the message. It is not necessary, though, to ask whether a given expression is religious or spiritual in nature.

Contrast the Christian poster discussed above with a scenario in which an employee hangs a poster that states, "Homosexuals: repent and turn to Jesus Christ." This message entails a clear condemnation of certain persons' sexual orientation. Since sexual orientation is widely (though admittedly not universally) acknowledged as an important part of human identity, the poster's denigration of a personal identity violates the limiting norm of nondegradation. Whether or not a poster with such a message cites religious scripture (for example, biblical texts) should not make a difference in determining its inclusion or exclusion. An employer's personal view regarding homosexuality is not even relevant in this case; regardless of his or her personal view, an employer should forbid the display of such a poster on the grounds that many employees will interpret the poster's message as degrading to homosexuals. Respectful pluralism focuses on whether the content of the message itself reflects respect or disrespect for human dignity.

This example reveals that not all readers (or employers or employees) will agree with the framework of respectful pluralism. For some religious persons, homosexuality is incompatible with their (religiously, culturally, familially, or politically influenced) understanding of human nature and society. They might argue that respectful pluralism promotes (or is itself a form of) moral relativism because it allows theologically or morally unacceptable behavior to go unquestioned. The view of respectful pluralism does not require workplace leaders even to take a position on the truth or falsity of the message, but, rather, it evaluates the actions and speech of employees in terms of the principle and norms.

The norms that limit the general presumption of inclusion of employee expression apply, in parallel fashion, to political messages as well as religious ones. For instance, employees are welcome to hang an American flag or a poster that states, "God bless America!" Similarly, workers should be allowed to hang flags of other nations as well.[50] It would not be permissible, however, for an employee to hang a poster (or wear a t-shirt or button) that says, "Foreigners, go home!" or, conversely, "Death to America!" Much like the religiously based case above, these messages are directed at a particular group of persons and suggest that their national identity is not welcome in the workplace. These messages fail the nondegradation test.

The second limiting norm within respectful pluralism prohibits situations in which co-workers, regardless of intention, have the effect of coercing other employees through their religious, spiritual, or other expression at work. On this point, consider cases of employees who wish to invite co-workers to religious events.[51] Supporters of the secular workplace would view the extension of *any* religious invitation at work as coercive, that is, as an illegitimate use of one's potential influence and proximity to put pressure on co-workers. Yet, given the importance of religion and the circumstance of non-compartmentalization, it is morally acceptable for employees to invite colleagues to religious events (or political rallies or cultural celebrations, for that matter) as long as they are willing to take no for an answer and then refrain from extending further unwanted invitations. After a person has indicated he or she does not want to receive such invitations, then it is, in fact, coercive (i.e., a violation of the norm of noncoercion) to continue making advances.[52] As with other examples, the line between invitation and

---

[50] One difficult case is whether or not employees could hang a Confederate battle flag in their workspace (see ch. 4 above for a fuller discussion). The framework of respectful pluralism objects to hanging that flag on grounds that, whatever the intentions of the employees who wish to display it, because of its historic ties to slavery and the segregationists who opposed the civil rights movement, the flag has come to signify disrespect for the human dignity of African Americans.

[51] See ch. 4 above for a discussion of recent legal cases that concern the issues of invitation and/or proselytization.

[52] On this distinction, President Clinton's "Guidelines on Religious Exercise and Religious Expression in the Federal Workplace" offers a well-articulated position. William Jefferson Clinton, "Guidelines on Religious Exercise and Religious Expression in the Federal Workplace" (Washington, DC: The White House Office of the Press Secretary, 1997).

proselytization is not always clear-cut, especially since co-workers might be unwilling to state their discomfort at being approached, but the co-worker's genuine ability to say no without fear of negative repercussions is a significant determining factor.

With coercion as with degradation, religious expression is not the only form of expression subject to debate. The colorful case of selling Girl Scout cookies addressed in chapter 4 above and other solicitations in the workplace provide illustrative examples. When an employee approaches a co-worker with the offer to buy some product, whether for a charitable cause or otherwise, that invitation need not necessarily be interpreted as coercive. Many employees might appreciate the opportunity to make a contribution to an organization or to buy the product. Others find the practice to be a terrible abuse of the goodwill of co-workers. As with religiously based invitations, when a boss or supervisor solicits employees to buy a product, the potential for coercion is even greater. Whether or not this is a violation of the noncoercion policy is dependent on the context but, once again, the guiding principle's presumption of inclusion and the ability of the person being approached to decline the offer are important guideposts.

The previous examples concern the first two limiting norms and deal with individual employees who seek to make religious or other kinds of "personal" expression while at work. The third norm, nonestablishment, applies to situations in which the expression is not merely individualistic but in some way reflects or suggests an undue institutional preference for a specific religious worldview. Leaders' individual religious beliefs and actions may easily be mistaken for institutionally supported expression. As a consequence, religious expression by formal leaders in any workplace is potentially more problematic than religious expression by employees who are not formal leaders. That is, because a leader has formal power, a leader's invitations, statements, or actions may be interpreted as unfair to employees of differing commitments, regardless of his or her intention. This point is admittedly a contentious one, especially since most of the spirituality and leadership literature focuses disproportionately on the faith of leaders.[53] The potential for coercion by bosses based upon their formal or positional power is often overlooked in these discussions. Both the Christian establishment view and the generic spirituality view tend to discount this problem, since in different ways each perspective supports the belief that employees generally hold the same set of values held by the manager.

[53] Much of the literature seems to suggest that, if religious values are going to come into the workplace, they will be introduced in a top-down fashion by the leaders. The literature tends to overlook the fact that lower-level employees also seek to live out their faith and often bring their religious identity into the workplace. This is a curious oversight. See ch. 6 above for a more detailed discussion.

Consider a manager who invites employees to a New Age ritual in her office before work once a week. The case would be essentially the same if the boss offered a Bible study class or a yoga session. Employees generally know about the weekly meeting, whether through word-of-mouth, e-mails, or bulletin board invitations. The boss or manager does not intentionally seek to exclude anyone – indeed, she would love for all to come – but she is unabashedly specific in presenting the content of her beliefs and practices. In other words, whether she is a Christian or Hindu or a New Age adherent, many employees would not recognize the meeting's religious/spiritual approach as reflective of their own beliefs and practices. Despite the fact that the manager makes efforts to assure that workers are neither rewarded for participating nor penalized for not attending, it is clear that she comes to know the regular attendees particularly well. Other employees feel they are losing access to her because they are not a part of this intimate circle.

This is a difficult situation, because managers, just like employees, should not have to sacrifice their faith or religious values when they enter the workplace. Yet, in order to avoid even the appearance of favoritism or coercion, the boss should find ways to hold or attend religiously based meetings in contexts other than the workplace. There are at least two possible alternatives. First, she could meet with employees, not in office space, but rather in a setting outside the workplace. (Holding such a meeting for subordinates in her home, however, might still create feelings of favoritism, though such a situation would still be preferable to meeting in her office.) A second alternative would be to attend meetings that lower-level employees hold in their own offices. Even this, however, would not dispel all of the questions about a preferred circle of employees.

This concern about institutional expressions of religion in the workplace also applies to religious symbols employed by companies themselves. The nonestablishment norm implies that neither the effective establishment of a religion nor the creation of a civil–corporate religion is compatible with respectful pluralism.[54] Consideration of an example of effective establishment and an example of civil–corporate religion will support this claim. First, consider a company that wishes to adopt a logo that includes the Christian symbol of a cross or a fish. After all, a member of the board of trustees states, the founder of the company was a strong Christian and believed in putting his faith to work. The company stands for care and service, board members reason, just as Christ embodied love and service. In addition, most of the workforce is Christian and no one objected when

---

[54] Establishment religion and civil–corporate religion are discussed in detail in ch. 6.

the company sponsored various Christian benevolence programs in the past. Surely, such a desire to reflect a religiously based value system can be well intentioned. Yet the practice violates the norm of nonestablishment. It does not attend adequately to the possible public impact that the effective Christian preference could have on the sense of place of non-Christians, particularly, but not exclusively, those in the workforce.

This reasoning applies not only to Christian or Jewish or Muslim expressions of religion. Consider a more generically spiritual approach that may be at least as potentially exclusive or coercive. I have in mind corporate continuing education seminars that require employees to meditate in order to "discover" their spiritual self at work. Leadership scholars have pointed out the potentially problematic nature of such "nontraditional" spiritual training programs, including their "high potential for psychological and legal fallout."[55] Because the framework of respectful pluralism does not depend on whether or not an argument is religious in order to be included or excluded, it is not necessary or relevant to determine whether a particular seminar takes a faith-based or secular approach to meditation, leadership, or professional development. The relevant question is whether or not the potential exists for employees to feel coerced or degraded in such training. In various cases, employees, including those from traditional religious backgrounds, have reported such negative effects. This practice violates the norm of nonestablishment and, in the process, probably violates the other two norms as well.

CONCLUSIONS

These examples do not settle or provide a definitive resolution to the myriad problems of diverse employee expressions in the workplace. Indeed, the framework of respectful pluralism is not meant to be a checklist with easy answers for any workplace. Particular contexts will require uniquely creative solutions to potentially divisive situations. It is also worth noting a few other limitations and further considerations of the framework. The commitment to acknowledge the human dignity of all workers and extend them equal respect – and hence grant employees the right to religious and other expression in the workplace – has implications beyond any one particular firm. Regarding issues of equitable pay or safe and healthy working conditions, the wider legal, social, and cultural context affects the "deal"

---

[55] Mark Lipton, "'New Age' Organizational Training: Tapping Employee Potential or Creating New Problems?" *The Human Resources Professional* 3/2 (1991): 72.

that individual employees and individual firms can negotiate. Analogously, the issue of employees' religious and other expression in the workplace demands a more comprehensive analysis of what opportunities are afforded employees in various workplaces, as well as in public life as a whole, to express aspects of their identity. This analysis should include attention to laws as well as to cultural norms and mores about religious expression. For instance, both the generic spirituality and the Christian establishment views continue to hold sway, not only in the workplace, but also in most aspects of American life today. The basic moral requirements of human dignity and equal respect should be discussed in various aspects of public life, including within religious communities. The attendant issues, then, do not merely call for workplace leadership, but also society-wide leadership concerning the appropriate role of religion in public life. Comparative analyses, such as my examination of India and Singapore, can also shed light on how the wider societal laws and norms impact religion's roles in the workplace.

Many (most) important philosophical and theological discussions about the nature of pluralism – and claims about truth and morality – are not answered by a framework for negotiating differences in the workplace. Indeed, on this point, my account of respectful pluralism seeks to minimize the number of situations in which managers must become theologians or must assess whether or not a religious claim is appropriately grounded or genuinely held. The presumption of inclusion and the limiting norms are designed to avoid making the workplace the context for settling philosophical or theological debates about the truth of religious (or political or cultural) expressions. I have emphasized, however, that the framework is not merely procedural and value-neutral. It is not. Coercion or degradation of employees, whether by the imposition of religious values or by the denial of employees' own religious expression, is unacceptable on moral grounds. The framework calls upon workplace leaders and the whole leadership process to put religious pluralism into practice in order to allow a diverse workforce to work together respectfully and even productively.

As with other forms of diversity, it is difficult to discuss religious expression predominantly in the negative terms of discrimination. (Analysis of discrimination is the most frequent, but not wholly satisfactory, mode of discussing race-based and gender-based diversity in the workplace.) In some cases, religious expression by employees does lead to discrimination against them in the workplace (for example, discrimination against Sikhs men who wear turbans or Jewish men who wear the yarmulke). In other cases, however, religious expression by some can contribute to explicit or implicit discrimination against other employees (for example, institution-sponsored prayers at official workplace functions which fail to acknowledge employees from other traditions). In yet other instances, the relationship between religious expression and discrimination is ambiguous (for example, evangelical Christians who claim to experience discrimination because of their religious expression but in other ways enjoy the fruits of an effective Christian establishment in terms of the working calendar, etc.). My framing of respectful pluralism in constructive terms is intended to move beyond a merely defensive treatment of religion in the workplace. Religiously based and other commitments in a diverse workplace do create the potential for conflict – conflict that the framework of respectful pluralism is designed to orchestrate in ways that are positive for individual employees and the organization as a whole.

The approach of respectful pluralism also allows for a significant *pedagogical* component. That is, the presumption of inclusion of religious and other expression helps create a working environment in which people are able to share information about their religious, spiritual, and moral practices with others to a significant degree. As long as employees enter into the discussion (whether around the water cooler or in open lunchtime forums) in a spirit of respect and noncoercion, then they have an opportunity to learn from one another. The media tend to focus on the divisive nature of religion in public life (and, admittedly, the examples considered above may reinforce that view). The quieter, more mundane discussions at work, in which people share their own personal narratives, religious and otherwise, are less newsworthy but perhaps cumulatively more significant. The most basic point is that the leadership process should enable such conversations to take place on a level playing field that admits many points of view. The playing-field metaphor may be misleading, though, because the approach does not intend to generate competition in any sense.

The limiting norm of nonestablishment does not preclude efforts to create a workplace culture in which individual employees may express their religious commitments. Indeed, although the examples considered in this chapter have emphasized the negotiation of potential conflict among individuals, respectful pluralism offers a proactive approach to building a culture of mutual understanding. Consistent with the framework's presumption of inclusion, the overall approach assumes that, in many or most cases, religion is a healthy, central part of an individual's identity. Workplace organizations can address religious diversity in healthy ways, too.

CHAPTER 9

Leadership for a pluralistic workplace

This concluding chapter considers how a framework of respectful pluralism applies to the study and practice of leadership in diverse organizations. The following pages discuss constructive ways in which individual leaders and the leadership process as a whole can promote an organizational environment that respects the dignity of all employees. Stated succinctly, the effort to shape a workplace marked by respectful pluralism is a matter of good leadership.

This book has made a number of connections with issues that are central to leadership studies, including organizational culture, ethics, spirituality, critical thinking, conflict, diversity, and profitability. The analysis offers strong criticism of overly simplistic treatments of the interrelationships of some of these topics – for example, the interrelationship between a leader's faith and her ethics; between spirituality and profitability; and between religion and organizational culture. In this chapter I consider questions of leadership and provide a tempered account of legitimate links between and among some of these topics. Finally, the chapter provides some key conclusions, limitations, and implications of the analysis undertaken in this book.

ORGANIZATIONAL CULTURE AND LEADERSHIP: ENABLING PLURALISM

In respectful pluralism, the organization itself should not be aligned with any explicitly religious, spiritual, or other comprehensive worldview. Rather, in this moral framework I posit that organizations should allow for significant employee expression of various aspects of their identity on an equal basis. When such a condition exists, we say that *diversity* – a descriptive reality reflecting empirical characteristics of the workforce – has been transformed into *pluralism* – a term that reflects a positive quality of relationships among diverse people. Diana Eck states:

[*P*]*luralism* is not just another word for diversity. It goes beyond mere plurality or diversity to active engagement with that plurality. Pluralism is not a given but must be created. Pluralism requires participation, and attunement to the life and energies of one another.[1]

The realization of respectful pluralism in the workplace does not simply happen, just because managers decree that religious or spiritual establishment is not acceptable or because the CEO distributes a memo stating that individual employees may "bring their religion to work." Rather, leaders, along with employees, must be actively engaged in constructing the conditions of pluralism.

Respectful pluralism should be reflected in a company's culture. Organizational culture results from the intentional and unintentional efforts of leaders and employees to shape their workplace. Scholars who study organizations suggest at least three central points about the relationship of leadership and workplace culture. First, successful organizations tend to have a discernible, distinctive culture that workers, managers, and other stakeholders recognize. That is, employees should understand their own work to be part of an organization with a clear identity and sense of purpose.[2] Second, effective leaders are able to perceive the subtleties of the culture of their organization. They make the effort to understand the prevailing values, language, and norms of relationship-oriented and task-oriented behaviors.[3] Third, leaders do not simply take organizational culture as a given; rather, they learn to develop it and guide it in desired directions.[4] Edgar Schein argues that, although cultures are deeply ingrained in organizations and are not easily altered, the most important task that leaders can perform is to help shape that culture in positive ways.[5]

Leaders can play a vital part in creating an environment of respectful pluralism. They can send clear signals to their employees that religious and other forms of diversity are valued in the company. They can make it apparent that, while they as individuals might uphold their particular religious or spiritual obligations and draw on their beliefs in understanding their work, they do not grant preferential status to their own tradition and they do not make their perspective the official company worldview. Leaders can make and publicize company rules against discrimination and

---

[1] Diana L. Eck, *A New Religious America: How a "Christian Country" Has Now Become the World's Most Religiously Diverse Nation* (San Francisco: Harper San Francisco, 2001), 70.
[2] Terrence E. Deal and Allan A. Kennedy, *Corporate Cultures* (Boston: Addison-Wesley, 1982).
[3] Edgar H. Schein, *Organizational Culture and Leadership*, second edn. (San Francisco: Jossey-Bass, 1992); Deal and Kennedy, *Corporate Cultures*.
[4] Deal and Kennedy, *Corporate Cultures*. [5] Schein, *Organizational Culture and Leadership*.

harassment that exceed the legal minimum requirement. But, even beyond policy dictates, leaders can find appropriate, context-specific methods of communicating respectful pluralism to employees.

Earlier chapters raised a few specific ideas for practices that contribute to a culture of respectful pluralism. As a first example, recall the case of supplemental holiday policies in India's governmental and bank sectors; in many states of India, government and formal private-sector employees are permitted to take two or three paid holidays in addition to the fourteen public national days; the list from which they may choose their supplemental paid leave includes a wide variety of holy days in a number of religious and spiritual traditions.[6] Within the US context, a law firm in Houston, Texas, has implemented a similar practice for its employees. In addition to the basic national holidays observed by the whole firm, each employee at Vinson & Elkins is able to choose two other paid days from a list of religious, cultural, and secular holidays that firm leaders have developed and regularly revise in consultation with employees. For example, a group of Native American employees in the law firm recently worked to determine holidays from their traditions. According to the director of administration at Vinson & Elkins, the firm has opted to employ a list of approved holidays – rather than simply offer more private vacation time – in order "to make a statement that it celebrates its diversity."[7]

This law firm's leaders have made a deliberate choice to acknowledge diverse employees' holy days and festivals. They employ the policy as a way of promoting a culture of pluralism. Employees understand the holiday program to be a part of the firm's organizational values. The firm's values do not reach the level of becoming a form of establishment, however, because the firm falls far short of promoting a comprehensive religious, cultural, or other kind of worldview over others. The approach is based upon a thin set of values, consistent with a culture of respectful pluralism. The administrator's comments suggest that such a policy enables other employees to learn about the diverse backgrounds of the workforce. The policy and resulting culture illustrate the potential value of respectful pluralism's pedagogical dimension. That is, practices reflecting respectful pluralism allow employees to learn about their co-workers and the calendar they observe.

Beyond gaining knowledge about holidays, co-workers can also learn from each other through encounters involving religious dress, objects and

[6] See ch. 7 above.
[7] L. M. Sixel, "Law Firm Gives Holiday Choices," *Houston Chronicle*, May 4, 2001. The firm has decided that all employees who request religious holidays (e.g., Rosh Hashanah) will receive that day off, but, for pragmatic reasons, secular holiday requests are weighed against personnel needs of the firm on that day. Recall the discussion in ch. 4 above that distinguishes between holy days and holidays as communal events and vacations as private ones.

symbols, and religiously based ideas. In workplaces that do not restrict speech about potentially divisive topics, discussions around the water cooler can increase understanding about the religious, spiritual, political, and other beliefs and practices of co-workers. The limiting norms of respectful pluralism help assure that these conversations are nondegrading and noncoercive and that no tradition receives preferential treatment over another. It is unnecessary and unlikely that such informal discussions will frequently focus on any one particular theme, such as religion or spirituality, politics or culture, family, or sports, for that matter. Yet, as long as employees continue to complete their work tasks and converse with each other respectfully, including the proviso of accepting no for an answer to invitations, topics are not off-limits.

As a way of augmenting such spontaneous encounters throughout the working day, company leaders could be more proactive in creating educational opportunities for employees to learn about colleagues. As an example, businesses could permit or support open forums or "brown-bag lunches" in which co-workers talk about their religious, spiritual, cultural, or political beliefs or practices. In order to be compatible with respectful pluralism, these programs would require that company managers or employees schedule such programs on an equal basis for employees of any and all backgrounds. An initiative like a voluntary-attendance forum is a promising way in which to model respect for the dignity of employees of many traditions and worldviews. Critics may contend that such a program would bring only potentially divisive or distracting dimensions of the personal lives of employees to the workplace. My disagreement with this objection is rooted in the moral importance of employees' expression of religious and other aspects of their identity. It also bears repeating that not just any type of program would be permitted; all programs being considered for presentation must be evaluated according to the limiting norms of respectful pluralism in order to disallow potentially coercive or degrading programs.[8]

Ford Motor Company, headquartered in Dearborn, Michigan, a city with one of the highest concentrations of Muslims in the United States, recently conducted an open forum that received significant press coverage. Prior to September 11, 2001, the company had funded interfaith dialogue groups and "a support group for workers of Middle Eastern descent." In response to the September 11 tragedy, a Muslim manager began to hold "impromptu 'Islam 101' courses" for employees. These sessions were so popular that the company worked with the manager to sponsor "An Islamic Perspective on

---

[8] How to deal with the potential problem of employees, who agree in advance to be respectful in their presentation but then use their program as an occasion to proselytize, is a significant practical problem that would have to be addressed in any given context.

the Events of September 11," a meeting attended by about four hundred employees.[9] This example illustrates a number of points consistent with respectful pluralism. First, Dearborn, Michigan, is noteworthy for its high degree of religious and cultural diversity; other US cities are moving, at different speeds, toward this circumstance. Second, in response to this reality – even prior to September 11, 2001 – Ford Motor Company has financed groups to address diversity. Third, employees themselves took initiative to communicate with each other, especially after the terrorist attacks. Finally, Ford again supported this employee initiative aimed at employee understanding and mutual respect.

The Ford example suggests the relevance and potential value of employee groups that in one way or another seek to understand diversity. Companies and employees face choices concerning which kinds of groups are appropriate for a given context. Some groups are interreligious or address other kinds of employee diversity (for example, groups that discuss gender issues or race relations in the workplace). Alternatively, so-called common interest groups can bring together persons sharing an element of identity (for example, all members are Christians, Wiccans, Arab Americans, Libertarians, etc.). Companies may *sponsor* (for example, provide direct or in-kind support) for these groups or they can simply *permit* (and possibly recognize) them as interest groups without providing them substantial support. One type of company-sponsored group is the network group. Network groups often begin as "self-organized social support groups" for minority employees but are embraced by the company as a helpful way to retain and encourage such employees (for example, African Americans or women).[10] Context should dictate when a sponsored network group is or is not appropriate. In general terms, however, given the emphasis in respectful pluralism against institutional promotion of a specific religious or other comprehensive worldview, a company should normally only provide indirect support for religiously based employee groups. There may be cases, however, in which network groups for employees of a minority or marginalized tradition may actually help make the wider organizational culture more equitable for people of all traditions. Indirect support could include permission to post group announcements on a specified bulletin

[9] Danny Hakim, "Ford Motor Workers Get on the Job Training in Religious Tolerance," *New York Times*, November 19, 2001.
[10] Ray Friedman, "The Case of the Religious Network Group," *Harvard Business Review* (1999). This is an interesting hypothetical case, followed by replies from five commentators, that analyzes the dilemmas caused when Christian employees seek to have a "Christian network group" and debates whether such a group is consistent with the company-sponsored status of minority network groups.

board or permission to use the cafeteria or a conference room (when it is not needed for company purposes), provided such permission is granted on an equal basis to all network groups. The company can also offer some of these indirect benefits to shared interest groups (those whose purposes pass muster with the limiting norms) on an equal basis. Employee groups, supported or permitted by companies as the context dictates, can help foster the kind of open encounter that is welcome in an organizational culture of respectful pluralism.

ETHICS AND SPIRITUALITY: CREATING RESPECTFUL CONVERSATIONS

The above examples suggest ways in which the culture of an organization can model the values of respectful pluralism without privileging a specific religious or spiritual comprehensive worldview. Some critics will maintain that respectful pluralism is itself a worldview – one that permits employees to express a variety of religious, moral, and philosophical beliefs and practices in the workplace. The framework does, in fact, entail that moral perspective, and it does so unabashedly. I would argue, however, that this is hardly a comprehensive worldview. It is substantive enough to exclude coercive and degrading expressions in the workplace, but it does not offer full understandings of truth, goodness, or rightness. I assert that the workplace should not be an institution in which leaders make determinations, in any *ultimate* sense, about what is true, or right, or good.[11] On the other hand, given that the workplace is a significant sphere of public encounter, there is moral value, in addition to the more fundamental guarantee of human dignity to each employee, in the pluralistic encounter of diverse employees at work. John Stuart Mill makes a related argument in his seminal work *On Liberty*:

If all [hu]mankind minus one, were of one opinion, and only one person were of the contrary opinion, [hu]mankind would be no more justified in silencing that one person, than he, if he had the power, would be justified in silencing [hu]mankind. Were an opinion a personal possession of no value except to the owner; if to be obstructed in the enjoyment of it were simply a private injury, it would make some difference whether the injury was inflicted only on a few persons or on many. But the peculiar evil of silencing the expression of an opinion is, that it is robbing the human race; posterity as well as the existing generation; those who dissent from

---

[11] This claim applies even to those beliefs and practices excluded by the limiting norms of respectful pluralism. They may well prove to be true, right, or good, but the workplace is not the place to decide that. They are excluded by the value of equal respect as embodied in the limiting norms.

the opinion, still more than those who hold it. If the opinion is right, they are deprived of the opportunity of exchanging an error for truth: if wrong, they lose, what is almost as great a benefit, the clearer perception and livelier impression of truth, produced by its collision with error.[12]

The claim that workplace leaders should not attempt to resolve matters of ultimate truth among various worldviews does not mean that respectful pluralism cannot allow individual employees to share with one another their deepest convictions about how the world is and should be. On the contrary, respectful pluralism enables that encounter to take place. In the above passage, Mill argues against government coercion toward minority viewpoints; respectful pluralism, analogously, argues against company coercion toward employees – either by forbidding religious expression altogether from the workplace or by granting preferential status to one religion or spiritual perspective. The issue goes beyond the prevention of coercion, however, to the establishment of respectful communication across employee difference. The leadership required to achieve this condition entails both the thoughtful, context-specific application of the norms of respectful pluralism and proactive efforts to create an environment in which employees recognize pluralism and respect as fundamental values of their organization.

The creation of a company environment marked by respectful pluralism, I argue, is a moral act. Allowing expression of religious, spiritual, political, and cultural identity reflects respect for employees and it also helps, as Mill contends, a community to engage multiple perspectives. The operation of respectful pluralism is one part of a healthy workplace. There are certainly other dimensions of a morally healthy corporate structure and culture. Joanne Ciulla states:

A moral environment is a system of customs and habits found in daily life that take on a logic of their own. They influence dispositions and sensibilities of people given the structure, tradition, beliefs, leadership, policies, and practices of an organization . . . A healthy moral environment is one where it makes sense to be honest, fair, loyal, forthright, etc.[13]

Ciulla affirms that the moral messages present in a given environment contribute to whether or not employees act *responsibly*. Company leaders should shape an environment that encourages employees to behave responsibly and makes it relatively easy for them to do so. They should leave the acting to

[12] John Stuart Mill, *On Liberty; with The Subjection of Women; and Chapters on Socialism*, ed. Stefan Collini (Cambridge University Press, 1989), 20.
[13] Joanne B. Ciulla, "Messages from the Environment: The Influences of Policies and Practices on Employee Responsibility," in *Communicating Employee Responsibilities and Rights: A Modern Management Mandate*, ed. Chimezie A. B. Osigweh, Yg. (New York: Quorum, 1987), 134.

the employees but should remain vigilant to be sure that no violations are occurring. Similarly, the messages from the environment contribute to whether or not co-workers act *respectfully*. A healthy moral environment facilitates employees' ability to express their religious convictions at work in a noncoercive, nondegrading way. Leaders should maintain a level of vigilance, however, to ensure that employees adhere to the limiting norms in their speech and actions.

Ciulla's article illuminates a second relevant point about leadership efforts to create an environment of respectful pluralism. As her examination of an ethically unhealthy corporation shows, codes of ethics alone cannot create moral environments. She cites unrealistic company demands for productivity that led managers in one large corporation to break "every one of the articles in the company's code of ethics."[14] In a cut-throat environment, no one at the corporation paid more than lip-service to the code of ethics. Analogously, a decree from the human relations officer in favor of the tenets of respectful pluralism will not transform the environment of an organization. The creation of a pluralistic environment requires continued efforts to design policies and a culture that encourages employees to express their identity at work, and to learn, if they choose, from one another. The effort to construct respectful pluralism requires sustained, deliberate leadership.

It is no wonder, then, that some scholars and practitioners prefer a more straightforward connection between ethics and spirituality in which being spiritual, in one sense or another, leads employees to act morally. If organizations become more spiritual in orientation, the assumption is that they will also become more ethical. It is a great deal easier for a president or CEO to declare that his or her values should apply to the company than to work to create a complex, multivocal conversation among managers and employees about what values the company should uphold. Such top-down statements, especially when couched in spiritual or religious terms, run the risks of appearing so hollow as to be meaningless or of conveying the substance of a comprehensive worldview, thereby violating the limiting norm of nonestablishment.

CREATIVE AND CRITICAL THINKING: ENCOURAGING
PLURALISM AND DISSENT

The pluralistic conversations enabled by respectful pluralism might well have a positive influence on their organization, at least over time. Such

---

[14] Ibid., 135.

leaders are able to choose respectful pluralism's long-range benefits over simpler, but more shortsighted, models. Within respectful pluralism, employees can communicate with each other in relative freedom, restricted only by the limiting norms and the reasonable demands of the tasks at hand. The communication generated by spontaneous discussion around the office – and perhaps in open forums and lunch talks – might very well provide fresh ideas or spark discussion of new understandings of a work-related problem. Many authors on leadership and spirituality state that spiritual workers and a spiritual organization tend to be more creative than their secular counterparts.[15] It would certainly be difficult to defend such a claim empirically – especially given the difficulty in measuring spirituality and creativity. Yet it is reasonable to suggest that workplaces in which employees feel invited to express their *diverse* ideas – based upon religious, spiritual, or other aspects of identity – could foster creativity to a greater degree than more restrictive environments.

Along with its potential to promote creativity among employees and managers, respectful pluralism can contribute to an environment that encourages employees to engage in critical thinking. Critical thinking, according to Stephen Brookfield, includes at least four components: naming and questioning assumptions; understanding contextual factors; imagining alternative approaches to problems; and practicing "reflective skepticism."[16] When employees express their deeply held convictions, whether religious, cultural, moral, or otherwise, they draw upon multiple dimensions of their worldview to reflect critically upon company policies and practices. These workers are able to communicate their reasons for working for their company in whatever language is appropriate for them; at the same time, when they object to a work requirement or a company goal, on religious or other grounds, they can articulate their reasons for disagreeing. When employees are free to share their religious and other perspectives, they will sometimes openly support company policies and sometimes offer dissenting opinions. Religious perspectives are thus truly independent of official company worldviews.

For example, persons can fully support the work of their company as doing God's will or as contributing to the common good. Conversely, employees' can make religiously based arguments that call company leaders to

[15] Gordon E. Dehler and M. Ann Welsh, "Spirituality and Organizational Transformation: Implications for the New Management Paradigm," *Journal of Managerial Psychology* 9/6 (1994); John F. Milliman et al., "Spirit and Community at Southwest Airlines: An Investigation of a Spiritual Values-Based Model," *Journal of Organizational Change Management* 12/3 (1999).

[16] Stephen D. Brookfield, *Developing Critical Thinkers: Challenging Adults to Explore Alternative Ways to Thinking and Acting* (San Francisco: Jossey-Bass, 1987).

provide them with higher salaries and more humane working conditions.[17] In between these two positions, many workers are able to support some, perhaps most, aspects of the company's structure, culture, and mission, while offering criticism of other parts. Critical thinking in the workplace includes ongoing, constructive reflection on one's own tasks as well as the wider structure, culture, and mission of the company. As Brookfield argues, critical thinking is a process that involves more than merely cognitive features; for one, it requires that an individual possess self-confidence in order to be willing to challenge fundamental assumptions.[18] Employees can freely exercise critical thinking within the overall healthy, constructive environment of respectful pluralism. The limiting norms would preclude some types of criticism of co-workers and company policies – not for its substance but for the way in which it is communicated (i.e., if it is coercive or degrading).

A company that invites a significant degree of critical thinking by its employees encourages all employees – not just formal leaders – to be active agents. Followers also understand themselves to be vital actors in the company. As Robert Kelly asserts, critical thinking is one of the most important components of effective followers in organizations. Many managers, however, do not have the confidence or the flexibility to promote critical thinking exercises among their employees.[19]

A key sign of the operation of respectful pluralism is the space for employees to offer religiously based dissent from company policies and practices. When religion and spirituality are independent sources of creative and critical thinking, the organizational environment manages not to impose limits upon the substance of what employees can say. Few approaches to religion and the workplace emphasize the space for dissent, however. This feature of respectful pluralism may be one of the most challenging for companies to embrace. Yet, as Kelly, Brookfield, and many other scholars suggest, encouraging critical thinking in all employees and managers can lead to overall productive, healthy working environments.

DIVERSITY: ORCHESTRATING, NOT AVOIDING, CONFLICT

Encouraging critical and creative thinking, especially in a framework of respectful pluralism, requires understanding that conflicts may arise when

---

[17] One prominent group that assists employees to work to change unjust working situations is the National Interfaith Committee for Worker Justice, headquartered in Chicago, Illinois. The group's website may be accessed through http://www.nicwj.org.

[18] Ibid.

[19] Robert E. Kelly, "In Praise of Followers," *Harvard Business Review* (1988).

employees express their divergent perspectives. Like other kinds of difference, religiously based aspects of identity can contribute to tension or misunderstanding among diverse co-workers. The resulting conflict can be destructive or constructive. Leadership approaches to diversity should expand to include and attend to religion as a principal category. Scholars in leadership studies have argued that healthy organizational environments not only seek out common ground but also benefit from respectful, honest conflict. James MacGregor Burns has argued that, in the political sphere, the effective expression of conflicting ideas and policies is a sign of a healthy democratic process.[20] Leaders should not be afraid of conflict, but rather they should encourage open discussion of dissenting views. Barbara Gray compares *collaborative* leadership in organizations to the New England town meeting, where differences are aired in public. She emphasizes how representatives from a variety of conflicting perspectives can be brought together for positive outcomes.[21] Neither Burns nor Gray, however, addresses religious or spiritual diversity directly in his or her respective framework.

In his work on leadership in diverse organizations, John Fernandez stresses the importance of "productive conflict" in which differences are expressed, not avoided. Fernandez cites a number of studies in which "heterogeneous groups" outperform "homogeneous groups" if they benefit from leadership that helps create a context in which members come to know and understand their differences.[22] Similarly, Gill Robinson Hickman suggests that leadership studies utilize the concept of "conflict capital" (echoing conversations of financial capital, human capital, and social capital) through which "a substantially enhanced outcome . . . results from the effort to bring about change among leaders and participants with diverse perspectives."[23]

The positive view toward conflict in the work of Burns, Gray, Fernandez, and Hickman is consistent with the argument for attending to, rather than overlooking, religious and spiritual diversity in the workplace. Leaders should view religiously informed perspectives not only as a source of conflict but also as a potential source of innovation. The starting place is not the common ground or unity typically assumed in prevailing frameworks of

[20] James MacGregor Burns, *Leadership* (New York: Harper Torchbooks, 1978); James MacGregor Burns, "Let the Opposition Speak," *Richmond Alumni Magazine* 64 (2002).

[21] Barbara Gray, *Collaborating: Finding Common Ground for Multiparty Problems* (San Francisco: Jossey-Bass, 1989).

[22] John P. Fernandez with Mary Barr, *The Diversity Advantage: How American Business Can Out-Perform Japanese and European Companies in the Global Marketplace* (New York: Lexington Books, 1993).

[23] Gill R. Hickman, "Leadership and Capacity Building in Organizations," in *Leading Organizations*, ed. Gill R. Hickman (Thousand Oaks, CA: Sage, 1998), 408.

spiritual leadership. Rather, if cooperation, mutual understanding, or even some kind of unity is achieved, it is a result of a leadership process of open dialogue and sharing of ideas, not by assumption or definition. Such a leadership process provides a promising way to understand the appropriate place of spirituality and religion in the workplace.

The work of Ronald A. Heifetz also offers valuable insights for respectful pluralism.[24] Acknowledging the reality and the potentially valuable role of conflict, Heifetz argues that leadership (both with and without authority) requires creating an environment in which participants are uncomfortable with their internal and external conflicts but not so uncomfortable that they cannot address them productively. The task of leadership is not to impose one set of values upon all followers, but to "orchestrate" conflict in order to achieve a desirable outcome. While formal leaders are capable of exerting more influence on the process, leaders with and without authority can help create both a structure and a culture to negotiate conflict. Heifetz rarely considers religious or spiritual diversity as a chief source of conflict, but his theory of adaptive work and orchestration of conflict provides a way to address those forms of diversity within a workforce.

PROFITABILITY AND MORALITY: KEEPING PRIORITIES STRAIGHT

I have emphasized that respectful pluralism is a moral framework that builds upon a conception of human dignity and the significance of religious (and other forms of) commitment in many employees' lives. I make no claim that enacting respectful pluralism will make companies more efficient or profitable. It may not. But companies that make a profit yet fail to create conditions of equal respect for their workers are operating unethically. To be sure, scholars and practitioners may well take issue with some aspects of my framework or some of the examples of its application. Perhaps some will claim I ask companies to go too far in welcoming religion at work. To create such moral debates about what human dignity requires in the workplace is one of the goals of this book.

It is important to reiterate that private-sector companies must generate a profit if they are to continue to operate. The aim of the private-sector company is not to serve, first and foremost, as a public forum. But neither is it to be, first and foremost, a for-profit enterprise. On its most fundamental

---

[24] Ronald A. Heifetz, *Leadership without Easy Answers* (Cambridge, MA: Belknap Press of Harvard University Press, 1994).

level, a company exists as a set of human relationships that are subject to legal and moral constraints. Thus the argument for respectful pluralism depends upon the priority of morality – especially according respect to each employee – over profitability.

There is, nonetheless, reason to believe that the features of respectful pluralism can be consistent with a profitable organization. It is fully acceptable to design a respectful workplace that contributes to profitability; as I have argued, though, the modifier is no small constraint. Scholars of diversity and organizations suggest that there is value (in efficiency terms as well as ethical terms) to confronting conflicts instead of letting them fester among a workforce. They suggest, further, that misunderstandings among workers of diverse backgrounds can lead to a drop in productivity. Leadership scholars have established that the maintenance of high-quality relationships and good communication among employees can ultimately lead to greater productivity than adherence to seemingly straightforward task-oriented processes. Similarly, the encouragement of multiple perspectives, critical thinking, and creativity can be cost-effective. Scholars need to conduct empirical studies to assess the impact of respectful pluralism on factors such as the quality and level of communication, motivation and morale, critical and creative thinking, and workplace relationships. Do improvements in these dimensions make up for the time and effort required to allow workers to express their religious and other commitments at work? That question, which cannot be answered within the scope of this book, is an interesting and important one. The moral argument for respectful pluralism does not, however, depend upon an affirmative answer.

IN CONCLUSION: LIMITATIONS AND IMPLICATIONS

Based upon the descriptive and normative analysis of this book, a rich and complicated picture emerges of religion and the workplace. Respectful pluralism does not solve all of the dilemmas or model all of the complexities; however, it should help spark a critical conversation among scholars and practitioners about the ways in which religion does operate and should operate in the workplace. Throughout the book, I have attempted to be precise in employing language of religious beliefs, ideas, worldviews, convictions, commitments, expressions, rituals, actions, and practices; yet these terms cannot adequately capture the disparate realities of religion's multiple forms. The discussion of the ways in which employees express their religion differently at work also emphasizes that, for some persons, distinctive communities and traditions directly influence their beliefs and actions, while others make no claims to being shaped by organized religion.[25] The book includes no single definition of religion (in the workplace or elsewhere); I hope that the myriad examples, ranging from individual obligations of adherents of minority traditions to institutional establishment of a majority tradition, manage to reflect the diversity of religious expression. Undoubtedly I have overlooked many other important examples. More research, including fieldwork, is needed to document religious encounters in changing American workplaces.

I have also sought to acknowledge, through disparate examples, that private-sector workplaces themselves are quite varied. Further analysis is necessary to describe how organizational size, structure, culture, history, and industry or sector affect the relationship between the workplace and religion. Large corporations with labor forces in the tens or hundreds of thousands certainly have different personnel policies and cultures than small local businesses. Employees in firms with successful collaborative leadership and positive labor-management relations will tend to view religion and spirituality in a different way than employees in firms with a history of labor-management distrust and tension. Is religion a source of mutual support or a source of prophetic dissent? Religiously influenced speech and action can play either role, depending not only on the nature of the religion but also on the nature of the organization. The central ideas of respectful pluralism – the presumption of inclusion and the limiting norms – are flexible enough to have application in various organizational settings.

In addition to complexities resulting from a variety of religious forms and organizational settings, the comparative analysis of the USA, India, and Singapore suggests that political–legal contexts also play a large role in understanding religion in the workplace. Indeed, the cross-national examination reveals that scholars often take for granted such things as the laws concerning civil rights and national holidays in their discussions of religion and spirituality at work. My reference to US debates over religious institutions and the state, within the First Amendment framework, reinforces the point that the operation of religion in the workplace occurs within a legal context. A moral framework like respectful pluralism must understand the minimum conditions that are guaranteed by law. It is also worth noting that in the US (as well as in India) legal structure varies according to both state and local laws that supplement and apply national law. In addition, throughout the book I have identified the importance of understanding the role of religious ideas in public life beyond the workplace itself – the ways

---

[25] See ch. 5 above.

in which, for instance, civil religion, culturally established Christianity, generic spirituality, and secularism continue to compete in many spheres of society. These and other historical and contemporary factors frame the context of the workplace and the religious beliefs and practices of employees.

For the purposes of this book, it is not necessary to distinguish those aspects of belief or practice that are religious from those that are spiritual. It is important, however, to demonstrate that the current trend among employees, consultants, and scholars alike to draw simple dichotomies between religion and spirituality is flawed.[26] Workplace leadership should develop a consistent approach to employee expression in the workplace, whether it be religious, spiritual, political, or cultural in nature. Religion, like spirituality, is not a priori either divisive or unifying. What is important, from the perspective of the organization, is the way in which beliefs are articulated or actions are undertaken. Given the presumption of inclusion, ideas and actions are welcome unless they violate a limiting norm. Many, but not all, practices labeled as spiritual are welcome at work; the same is true of religious expression. Notwithstanding my strong critique, the religious–spiritual dichotomy may well prove useful to scholars and practitioners who wish to make an empirical study of the relationship of employees' at-work behaviors to their regular involvement with religious institutions outside of work; such a study would have to recognize that people identifying as *religious* include individuals in addition to those who are religious participants. Fascinating research questions also remain about how the term *spiritual* appeals, in disparate ways, to many religious participants as well as persons who self-identify as "spiritual, but not religious."[27]

My framework argues that scholars must be careful to differentiate individual-level and institutional-level issues when analyzing any aspect of values and culture. The language of organizational spirituality and spiritual leadership at work blurs this line inappropriately. It enables an organization to gloss over religious, spiritual, and moral differences among its employees, and it can lead an organization to require employees to participate in actions that conflict with their personal convictions. The limiting norm of nonestablishment is designed to protect against such situations. No framework, of course, can remove all potential conflicts of identity or loyalty for employees. Some people may find the values of respectful pluralism – values which are based upon the assumptions of the equal dignity of all persons

---

[26] See ch. 3 above.
[27] Robert C. Fuller (Robert C. Fuller, *Spiritual, but Not Religious: Understanding Unchurched America* [Oxford University Press, 2001]) offers an important analysis of the non-religious side of this divide.

and tolerance of people from various comprehensive worldviews – to be morally unacceptable.

Compared with the secular, generic spirituality, and establishment Christianity approaches to the workplace, my framework pays more attention to the potential conflicts between employees' religious, spiritual, and moral commitments, on the one hand, and their employee responsibilities, on the other. For some employees, this challenge manifests itself as competing loyalties to two institutions – the congregation and the company. Both establishment and spirituality models seek to reduce or mask these tensions in different ways.[28] It is fully appropriate and potentially valuable for scholars and practitioners to reflect upon how members of particular religious communities can and should "take their faith to work."[29] These examinations should pay more attention than earlier analyses have paid to the question of how employees negotiate the *internal* conflicts they experience when such competing pressures arise. Some of these tensions may well have analogies with other issues of balancing work- and nonwork time, such as work–family conflicts. The emphasis on conflict in my framework thus not only pertains to tensions that can arise among members of a diverse workforce; it also calls for consideration of the competing loyalties within individual persons who navigate – and seek to integrate – various spheres of life.

The faith of followers is just as important as – and in many ways raises fewer problems than – the religious expression of formal leaders. The pluralistic model of the workplace creates space in which employees from various levels of the organization can be moral agents – and can even express dissenting perspectives – while on the job. The spirituality or religion of a workplace does not come from the top and trickle down. Leaders, formal and otherwise, do play a crucial role in shaping and maintaining a structure and culture of respectful pluralism, but all employees actively engage in such a condition. It is too simple to say that workplace leadership is responsible for creating a *process* or *procedure* by which all employees can communicate their *substantive* beliefs and commitments.[30] Yet this statement does communicate the general idea that the employees, not the organization, should generate the multiple, sometimes complementary and sometimes competing, expressions.

---

[28] See ch. 6 above.
[29] One recent book that explores these issues from the perspective of predominantly white Christian congregations in the US is Laura L. Nash and Scotty McClennan, *Church on Sunday, Work on Monday: The Challenge of Fusing Christian Values with Business Life* (San Francisco: Jossey-Bass, 2001).
[30] The process itself contains the substantive values of respectful pluralism.

In this book I have engaged scholarship in various fields in the effort to understand the interrelationships of religion and the workplace. It is my hope that scholars in religious studies have found ideas that will enable them to expand our understanding of the workplace as an important public context in which religion, in all its diversity, operates. I invite philosophers, theologians, and ethicists of specific traditions to develop perspectives on work, business ethics, and organizational leadership that address the challenge of workforce diversity. I encourage scholars of management and leadership studies to understand religion, in its multiple and potentially conflictual forms, as an important part of many employees' identities that should be respected rather than avoided, reduced, or exploited. Expanding our understanding of religion and the workplace will require an interdisciplinary and interreligious conversation marked by respectful engagement among diverse perspectives.

Bibliography

Abe, Masao. "Buddhism." In *Our Religions*, edited by Arvind Sharma, 69–137. San Francisco: Harper San Francisco, 1993.

Aeppel, Timothy. "Juggling Act: More Plants Go 24/7, and Workers Are Left at Sixes and Sevens." *Wall Street Journal*, July 24, 2001, A1, A6.

Albanese, Catherine L. *America: Religions and Religion*. Third edn. Belmont, CA: Wadsworth, 1999.

Austin, Allan D. *African Muslims in Antebellum America: A Sourcebook*. Vol. 5, *Critical Studies on Black Life and Culture*. New York: Garland Publishers, 1984.

Ballon, Marc. "For Most Firms, Business as Usual on Martin Luther King Holiday." *Los Angeles Times*, January 15, 2000, 1.

"Ban on American Flags Lifted." *United Press International Wire Service*, September 17, 2001.

Barber, Benjamin R. *Jihad Vs. McWorld*. New York: Ballantine Books, 1995.

Barrett, David B., George T. Kurian, and Todd M. Johnson. *World Christian Encyclopedia: A Comparative Survey of Churches and Religions in the Modern World*. Second edn. 2 vols. New York: Oxford University Press, 2001.

Barth, Karl. *Church Dogmatics: The Doctrine of Creation, the Creature*. Translated by J. K. S. Reid, et al. Edited by T. F. Torrance and G. W. Bromiley. 4 vols. Vol. 3/3. Edinburgh: T. & T. Clark, 1960.

Bell, Elizabeth. "Central Valley Town Gropes with Specter of Hate Slaying; Arab American Shot in His Reedley Store." *San Francisco Chronicle*, October 4, 2001, A3.

Bellah, Robert N. "Civil Religion in America." *Daedalus* 96 (1967): 1–21.

"Comment [on Robert Mathisen's Essay, 'Twenty Years after Bellah: Whatever Happened to Civil Religion?' *Sociological Analysis* 50/2 (1989): 129–46]." *Sociological Analysis* 50/2 (1989): 147.

Habits of the Heart: Individualism and Commitment in American Life. Berkeley, CA: University of California Press, 1985.

Bhindi, Narottam and Patrick Duignan. "Leadership for a New Century: Authenticity, Intentionality, Spirituality and Sensibility." *Educational Management & Administration* 25/2 (1997): 117–32.

Biberman, Jerry and Michael Whitty. "Editorial: Twenty-First Century Spiritual Paradigms/Possibilities for Organizational Transformation." *Journal of Organizational Change Management* 12/3 (1999): 180–74.

"A Postmodern Spiritual Future for Work." *Journal of Organizational Change Management* 10/2 (1997): 130–38.

Biberman, Jerry, Michael Whitty, and Lee Robbins. "Lessons from Oz: Balance and Wholeness in Organizations." *Journal of Organizational Change Management* 12/3 (1999): 243–54.

Billitteri, Thomas J. "Finding the Spirit at Work: In Their Quest for Peace and Fulfillment, Today's Harried Workers Can Get Help from Many New Books." *Publishers Weekly*, May 19, 1997, 46, 48, 50, 52–53.

Blair, Jayson. "Sears Agrees to Change Sabbath Work Policy." *New York Times*, April 5, 2000, 7.

Blank, Renee and Sandra Slipp. *Voices of Diversity: Real People Talk about Problems and Solutions in a Workplace Where Everyone Is Not Alike.* New York: Amacom, 1994.

Bolman, Lee G. and Terrence E. Deal. *Leading with Soul: An Uncommon Journey of Spirit.* First edn. San Francisco: Jossey-Bass, 1995.

Boylan, Michael. *Business Ethics: Basic Ethics in Action.* Upper Saddle River, NJ: Prentice Hall, 2001.

Bredemeier, Kenneth. "Dealing with Politics in the Office." *Washington Post*, November 15, 2000, 1.

Brookfield, Stephen D. *Developing Critical Thinkers: Challenging Adults to Explore Alternative Ways to Thinking and Acting.* San Francisco: Jossey-Bass, 1987.

Buchanan, Constance. *Choosing to Lead: Women and the Crisis of American Values.* Boston: Beacon Press, 1996.

Burns, James MacGregor. *Leadership.* New York: Harper Torchbooks, 1978.

"Let the Opposition Speak." *Richmond Alumni Magazine* 64 (2002): 26–27.

Burritt, Chris. "New Colors Unify Emblem of Division." *Atlanta Journal and Constitution*, November 26, 1997, 8.

Buultjens, Ralph. "India: Religion, Political Legitimacy, and the Secular State." *The Annals of the American Academy of PSS* 483 (1986): 93–109.

Buxton, R. F. "Sunday." In *The New Westminster Dictionary of Liturgy and Worship*, edited by J. G. Davies, 499–500. Philadelphia: Westminster Press, 1986.

Cacioppe, Ron. "Creating Spirit at Work: Re-Visioning Organization Development and Leadership – Part I." *Leadership & Organization Development Journal* 21/1 (2000): 48–54.

Calvin, John. *Institutes of the Christian Religion.* Translated by F. L. Battles. Edited by J. T. McNeill. London: S.C.M. Press, 1961.

Carter, Stephen L. *The Culture of Disbelief: How American Law and Politics Trivialize Religious Devotion.* New York: Basic Books, 1993.

Cavanagh, Gerald F. "Spirituality for Managers: Context and Critique." *Journal of Organizational Change Management* 12/3 (1999): 186–99.

Challenger, James E. "Firms Make Room for Different Religions." *Chicago Sun–Times*, May 14, 2000, 5.

Chaves, Mark. *Ordaining Women: Culture and Conflict in Religious Organizations.* Cambridge, MA: Harvard University Press, 1999.

Chong, Terence. "Asian Values and Confucian Ethics: Malay Singaporeans' Dilemma." *Journal of Contemporary Asia* 32/3 (2002): 394–406.

Chua Beng Huat and Kian-Woon Kwok. "Social Pluralism in Singapore." In *The Politics of Multiculturalism: Pluralism and Citizenship in Malaysia, Singapore, and Indonesia*, edited by Robert W. Hefner, 86–125. Honolulu: University of Hawai'i Press, 2001.

Chua Lee Hoong. "Code Red? Code Green? Code Orange!" *The Straits Times*, October 16, 2002.

Ciucci, William. "Muslims Finding a Place; Some in Richmond Area Content with Employer Accommodations." *Richmond Times-Dispatch*, May 30, 2001, C1.

Ciulla, Joanne B. "Leadership and the Problem of Bogus Empowerment." In *Ethics: The Heart of Leadership*, edited by Joanne B. Ciulla, 63–86. Westport, CT: Praeger, 1998.

"Leadership Ethics: Mapping the Territory." In *Ethics: The Heart of Leadership*, edited by Joanne B. Ciulla, 3–25. Westport, CT: Praeger, 1998.

"Messages from the Environment: The Influences of Policies and Practices on Employee Responsibility." In *Communicating Employee Responsibilities and Rights: A Modern Management Mandate*, edited by Chimezie A. B. Osigweh, Yg., 133–40. New York: Quorum, 1987.

The Working Life: The Promise and Betrayal of Modern Work. New York: Times Books/Random House, 2000.

Clinton, William Jefferson. "Guidelines on Religious Exercise and Religious Expression in the Federal Workplace." Washington, DC: The White House Office of the Press Secretary, 1997.

Cohen, Arthur Allen. *The Myth of the Judeo-Christian Tradition*. New York: Harper & Row, 1969.

"Company, Employee at Odds over Religious Dress Code." *Fort Worth Star Telegram*, August 8, 1999, 2.

"Confederate Flag Supporters Agree to End Protest at Aluminum Plant." *Associated Press State & Local Wire*, September 15, 2000.

Conger, Jay Alden, ed. *Spirit at Work: Discovering the Spirituality in Leadership*. First edn. The Jossey-Bass Management series. San Francisco: Jossey-Bass, 1994.

Coolidge, Donald. "A Demanding Time for Chaplains Who Give at the Office." *Christian Science Monitor*, January 2, 2002, 2.

Cooper, Glenda. "A Muslim Family in N.Y. Fears for a Son Who Loved America." *New York Times*, September 18, 2001, A22.

Couto, Richard. "Narrative, Free Space, and Political Leadership in Social Movements." *Journal of Politics* 55 (1993): 57–79.

Covey, Stephen R. *The Seven Habits of Highly Effective People*. New York: Simon & Schuster, 1989.

Covey, Stephen R., A. Roger Merrill, and Rebecca R. Merrill. *First Things First*. New York: Simon & Schuster, 1994.

Cox, Harvey. "The Market as God: Living in the New Dispensation." *Atlantic Monthly* 283/3 (1999): 18–23.

Davila, Florangela. "Electrical Worker Sues for Right to Practice Religion – Growing Muslim Population Has Sparked Similar Cases." *Seattle Times*, August 15, 1998, A7.

Davis, S. *Managing Corporate Culture*. Cambridge, MA: Ballinger, Inc., 1986.

Deal, Terrence E. and Allan A. Kennedy. *Corporate Cultures*. Boston: Addison-Wesley, 1982.

Dehler, Gordon E. and M. Ann Welsh. "Spirituality and Organizational Transformation: Implications for the New Management Paradigm." *Journal of Managerial Psychology* 9/6 (1994): 17–26.

De Lange, Nicholas. *An Introduction to Judaism*. Cambridge University Press, 2000.

Diehl, William E. "Sharing Personal Faith at Work." In *Faith in Leadership: How Leaders Live Out Their Faith in Their Work – and Why It Matters*, edited by Robert J. Banks and Kimberly Powell, 140–56. San Francisco: Jossey-Bass, 2000.

Thank God It's Monday! Philadelphia: Fortress Press, 1982.

Dugger, Celia. "More Than 200 Die in 3 Days of Riots in Western India." *New York Times*, March 2, 2002, 1.

Dykstra, Craig. *Growing in the Life of Faith: Education and Christian Practices*. Louisville, KY: Geneva Press, 1999.

Easterlin, Richard J. "Does Economic Growth Improve the Human Lot?" In *Nations and Households in Economic Growth: Essays in Honour of Moses Abramowitz*, edited by Paul A. David and Melvin W. Reder, 89–125. New York: Academic Press, 1974.

"Does Money Buy Happiness?" *The Public Interest* 30 (1973): 3–10.

"Will Raising the Incomes of All Increase the Happiness of All?" *Journal of Economic Behavior and Organization* 27 (1995): 35–47.

Eck, Diana L. *Encountering God: A Spiritual Journey from Bozeman to Banaras*. Boston: Beacon Press, 1993.

A New Religious America: How a "Christian Country" Has Now Become the World's Most Religiously Diverse Nation. San Francisco: Harper San Francisco, 2001.

Eck, Diana L. and the Pluralism Project at Harvard University. *On Common Ground: World Religions in America CD-Rom*. New York: Columbia University Press, 1997.

Eck, Diana L., Rebecca K. Gould, and Douglas A. Hicks. "Encountering Religious Diversity: Historical Perspectives." In *On Common Ground: World Religions in America CD-Rom*. New York: Columbia University Press, 1997.

Eckstein, Sandra. "Boss, Workers in Clash over Prayer; Muslims Who Sought Five-Minute Break from College Park Assembly Line Were Refused, Left Jobs." *Atlanta Journal and Constitution*, January 26, 2001, 1C.

Ehrenreich, Barbara. *Nickel and Dimed: On (Not) Getting by in America*. New York: Metropolitan/Owl Books, Henry Holt and Company, 2001.

Epstein, Richard A. "In Defense of the Contract at Will." In *Ethical Theory and Business*. Sixth edn. Edited by Tom L. Beauchamp and Norman E. Bowie, 275–83. Upper Saddle River, NJ: Prentice Hall, 2001.

Ettenborough, Kelly, Adam Klawonn, and Christina Leonard. "Valley Mourns Apparent Backlash Killing." *Arizona Republic*, September 17, 2001.

Everett, William Johnson. "Religion and Federal Republicanism: Cases from India's Struggle." *Journal of Church and State* 37 (1995): 61–85.

Fairholm, Gilbert W. *Perspectives on Leadership: From the Science of Management to Its Spiritual Heart.* Westport, CT: Quorum, 1998.

Farley, Margaret A. *Personal Commitments: Beginning, Keeping, Changing.* San Francisco: Harper & Row, 1986.

Fernandez, John P., with Mary Barr. *The Diversity Advantage: How American Business Can Out-Perform Japanese and European Companies in the Global Marketplace.* New York: Lexington Books, 1993.

"Flight Diverted Due to Confusion over Prayer." *Reuters Online*, October 15, 2001.

Flowers, Ronald B. *That Godless Court?: Supreme Court Decisions on Church–State Relationships.* First edn. Louisville, KY: Westminster John Knox Press, 1994.

Frank, Robert. *Luxury Fever: Why Money Fails to Satisfy in an Age of Affluence.* New York: Free Press, 1999.

Freedman, Dan. "Terror Suspects Place Islam under New Lens; Some Say Prisons Are Fertile Ground for Radical Muslims." *Milwaukee Journal Sentinel*, July 7, 2002, 14A.

Friedman, Milton. *Capitalism and Freedom.* University of Chicago Press, 1962.

Friedman, Ray. "The Case of the Religious Network Group." *Harvard Business Review* (1999): 28–40.

Fuller, Robert C. *Religion and the Life Cycle.* Philadelphia: Fortress Press, 1988.

  Spiritual, but Not Religious: Understanding Unchurched America. Oxford University Press, 2001.

Galanter, Marc. *Competing Equalities: Law and the Backward Classes in India.* Delhi: Oxford University Press, 1984.

Gallup, George and D. Michael Lindsay. *Surveying the Religious Landscape: Trends in U.S. Beliefs.* Harrisburg, PA: Morehouse Publishers, 1999.

Goldberg, Beverly. "Aide Says She Was Fired for Wearing a Cross." *American Libraries*, March 2002, 21–22.

Gray, Barbara. *Collaborating: Finding Common Ground for Multiparty Problems.* San Francisco: Jossey-Bass, 1989.

Greenleaf, Robert K. *Servant Leadership: A Journey into the Nature of Legitimate Power and Greatness.* New York: Paulist Press, 1977.

Grish, Kristina. "Christian Activewear Labels Practice What They Preach (T-Shirts with Religious Messages)." *Sporting Goods Business*, April 16, 1999, 25.

Gunther, Marc. "God & Business." *Fortune*, July 9, 2001, 58–60.

Gutiérrez, Gustavo. *A Theology of Liberation: History, Politics, and Salvation.* Translated by C. Inda and J. Eagleson. Maryknoll, NY: Orbis Books, 1973.

Hakim, Danny. "Ford Motor Workers Get on the Job Training in Religious Tolerance." *New York Times*, November 19, 2001, 6.

Handy, Robert T. "A Decisive Turn in the Civil Religion Debate." *Theology Today* 37/3 (1980): 342–50.

Hardin, Patricia. "What's Your Sign?: Companies Use Otherworldly Assessment Methods to Choose the Right Employees." *Personnel Journal*, 74/9 (September 1995), 66–67.

Hauerwas, Stanley. *A Community of Character: Toward a Constructive Christian Social Ethic.* University of Notre Dame Press, 1981.

Hauerwas, Stanley and William H. Willimon. *Resident Aliens: Life in the Christian Colony.* Nashville, TN: Abingdon, 1989.

Hawley, John Stratton. "Teaching the Hindu Tradition." In *Teaching the Introductory Course in Religious Studies: A Sourcebook,* edited by Mark Juergensmeyer, 37–48. Atlanta, GA: Scholars Press, 1991.

Hefner, Robert W. "Introduction: Multiculturalism and Citizenship in Malaysia, Singapore, and Indonesia." In *The Politics of Multiculturalism: Pluralism and Citizenship in Malaysia, Singapore, and Indonesia,* edited by Robert W. Hefner, 1–58. Honolulu: University of Hawai'i Press, 2001.

Heifetz, Ronald A. *Leadership without Easy Answers.* Cambridge, MA: Belknap Press of Harvard University Press, 1994.

Herberg, Will. *Protestant–Catholic–Jew: An Essay in American Religious Sociology.* Garden City, NY: Doubleday & Company, 1960.

Hickman, Gill Robinson, "Leadership and Capacity Building in Organizations." In *Leading Organizations,* edited by Gill R. Hickman, 405–09. Thousand Oaks, CA: Sage, 1998.

Hickman, Gill Robinson, ed. *Leading Organizations: Perspectives for a New Era.* Thousand Oaks, CA: Sage, 1998.

Hickman, Gill Robinson and Dalton S. Lee. *Managing Human Resources in the Public Sector: A Shared Responsibility.* Fort Worth: Harcourt College Publishers, 2001.

Hickman, Gill Robinson and Georgia Sorenson. "Invisible Leadership: Acts on Behalf of a Common Purpose." In *Building Leadership Bridges,* edited by C. Cherrey and L. R. Matusak, 7–24. College Park, MD: James MacGregor Burns Academy of Leadership, 2002.

Hicks, Douglas A. *Inequality and Christian Ethics.* New Studies in Christian Ethics 16. Cambridge University Press, 2000.

"Inequality, Globalization, and Leadership: 'Keeping Up with the Joneses' across National Boundaries." *Annual of the Society of Christian Ethics* 21 (2001): 63–80.

"Religion and Respectful Pluralism in the Workplace: A Constructive Framework." *Journal of Religious Leadership* 2/1 (2003).

"Spiritual and Religious Diversity in the Workplace: Implications for Leadership." *Leadership Quarterly* 13 (2002): 379–96.

"Workplace Understanding without 'Secret Santa.'" *Providence Journal,* December 18, 2001.

Higginbotham, Evelyn Brooks. *Righteous Discontent: The Women's Movement in the Black Baptist Church, 1880–1920.* Cambridge, MA: Harvard University Press, 1993.

Hinkelammert, Franz J. *The Ideological Weapons of Death: A Theological Critique of Capitalism.* Translated by Phillip Berryman. Maryknoll, NY: Orbis Books, 1986.

Hochschild, Arlie. *The Time Bind: When Work Becomes Home and Home Becomes Work.* New York: Metropolitan Books, 1997.

Hoffman, Brett. "Spirituality at Work: Employers Finding Ways to Integrate Religion into the Workplace." *Fort Worth Star Telegram*, June 30, 2001, 3.

Holly, Derrill. "Muslim Group Settles Religious Headgear Dispute." *Associated Press State & Local Wire*, April 28, 1999.

Hopfl, Heather. "The Making of the Corporate Acolyte: Some Thoughts on Charismatic Leadership and the Reality of Organizational Commitment." *Journal of Management Studies* 29/1 (1992): 23–33.

Hopkins, Thomas J. *The Hindu Religious Tradition.* The Religious Life of Man series, edited by Frederick J. Streng. Belmont, CA: Wadsworth, 1971.

Hughes, Richard L., Robert C. Ginnett, and Gordon J. Curphy. *Leadership: Enhancing the Lessons of Experience.* Third edn. Boston: Irwin McGraw-Hill, 1999.

Hunter, James Davison and Os Guinness, eds. *Articles of Faith, Articles of Peace: The Religious Liberty Clauses and the American Public Philosophy.* Washington, DC: Brookings Institution, 1990.

Ibrahim, Nabil A., Leslie W. Rue, Patricia P. McDougall, and G. Robert Greene. "Characteristics and Practices of 'Christian-Based' Companies." *Journal of Business Ethics* 10 (1991): 123–32.

"Jailers Are Studying Islam as Ranks of Inmate Converts Grow; Faith Encourages Less Violence, One Muslim Says." *St. Louis Post-Dispatch*, April 12, 1999, D2.

Jaworski, Joseph. *Synchronicity: The Inner Path of Leadership.* Edited by Betty S. Flowers. First edn. San Francisco: Berrett-Koehler Publishers, 1996.

Johnson, Craig E. *Meeting the Ethical Challenges of Leadership: Casting Shadow or Light.* San Francisco: Sage, 2001.

"Judge Asked to Rule on Complaint against Hewlett-Packard." *Associated Press State & Local Wire*, April 6, 2001.

Kant, Immanuel. "An Answer to the Question: What Is Enlightenment?" In *Kant: Political Writings*, edited by Hans Reiss, 54–60. Cambridge Texts in the History of Political Thought. Cambridge University Press, 1991.

Kanungo, Rabindra N. and Manuel Mendonca. "What Leaders Cannot Do Without: The Spiritual Dimensions of Leadership." In *Spirit at Work: Discovering the Spirituality in Leadership*, edited by Jay Alden Conger, 162–98. San Francisco: Jossey-Bass, 1994.

Kelly, Robert E. "In Praise of Followers." *Harvard Business Review* (1988).

Khun Eng Kuah. "Maintaining an Ethno-Religious Harmony in Singapore." *Journal of Contemporary Asia* 28/1 (1998): 103–21.

Kidder, Rushorth M. *Shared Values for a Troubled World: Conversations with Men and Women of Conscience.* San Franciso: Jossey-Bass, 1994.

King, Ralph. "If Looks Could Kill." *Asiaweek.com*, November 30, 2001.

King, Sandra W. and David M. Nichol. "A Burgeoning Interest in Spirituality and the Workplace: Exploring the Factors Driving It." *Business Research Yearbook* (1999): 718–27.

Konz, Gregory N. P. and Frances X. Ryan. "Maintaining an Organizational Spirituality: No Easy Task." *Journal of Organizational Change Management* 12/3 (1999): 200–10.

Krugman, Paul. "For Richer." *New York Times Magazine*, October 20, 2002, 62–72.

Kung, Hans and Karl-Josef Kuschel, eds. *A Global Ethic: The Declaration of the Parliament of the World's Religions*. New York: Continuum, 1993.

Kurtz, Janell, Elaine Davis, and Jo Ann Asquith. "Religious Beliefs Get New Attention." *HR Focus*, July 1996, 12–13.

Laabs, Jennifer J. "Balancing Spirituality and Work." *Personnel Journal* 74/9 (1995): 60–76.

Lee, Chris and Ron Zemke. "The Search for Spirit in the Workplace." *Training* 30/6 (1993): 21–28.

Lewis, Diane E. "Workplace Bias Claims Jump after Sept. 11." *Boston Globe*, November 22, 2001, 1.

Lipton, Mark. " 'New Age' Organizational Training: Tapping Employee Potential or Creating New Problems?" *Human Resources Professional* 3/2 (1991): 72–76.

MacIntyre, Alisdair. *After Virtue*. University of Notre Dame Press, 1981.

"Made in Heaven: Christian Retailing." *The Economist*, May 23, 1998, 63.

Mallory, Maria. "Balancing Faith at Work: Employees, Firms Must Weigh Belief Vs. Offending Others." *Atlanta Journal and Constitution*, April 8, 2001, 1R.

Marty, Martin E. "Two Kinds of Two Kinds of Civil Religion." In *American Civil Religion*, edited by Russell E. Richey and Donald G. Jones, 139–57. New York: Harper & Row, 1974.

Maslow, Abraham H. *Motivation and Personality*. New York: Harper, 1954.

McFadden, Robert D. "In a Stadium of Heroes, Prayers for the Fallen and Solace for Those Left Behind." *New York Times*, September 24, 2001, B7.

McPhee, Mike. "Sabbath Observer Wins Suit on Firing Pueblan; Awarded $2.25 Million." *Denver Post*, July 18, 2001, A1.

Miklave, Matthew T. and A. Jonathan Trafimow. "Is There Room for Promise Keepers in the Dress Code?" *Workforce* 79/9 (2000): 124.

Mill, John Stuart. *On Liberty; with The Subjection of Women; and Chapters on Socialism*. Edited by Stefan Collini. Cambridge University Press, 1989.

Miller, Martin and Gina Piccalo. "For Some, an Unflagging Discomfort about Flying the Stars and Stripes." *Los Angeles Times*, September 18, 2001, 1.

Milliman, John F., Jeffery Ferguson, David Trickett, and Bruce Condemi. "Spirit and Community at Southwest Airlines: An Investigation of a Spiritual Values-Based Model." *Journal of Organizational Change Management* 12/3 (1999): 221–33.

Mitroff, Ian I. and Elizabeth A. Denton. *A Spiritual Audit of Corporate America: A Hard Look at Spirituality, Religion, and Values in the Workplace*. First edn., The Warren Bennis signature series. San Francisco: Jossey-Bass, 1999.

"A Study of Spirituality in the Workplace." *Sloan Management Review* (Summer 1999): 83–92.

Mohn, Tanya. "Office Artwork Brings Out the Critic in Employees." *New York Times*, January 31, 2001, 10.

Mooney, Tom. "Charges against Sikh Dropped." *Providence Journal*, October 26, 2001, A-01.

Morris, Aldon. "The Black Church in the Civil Rights Movement: The SCLC as the Decentralized, Radical Arm of the Black Church." In *Disruptive Religion: The Force of Faith in Social Movement Activism*, edited by Christian Smith, 29–46. New York: Routledge, 1996.

Nash, Laura L. *Believers in Business*. Nashville, TN: Thomas Nelson Publishers, 1994.

Nash, Laura L. and Scotty McClennan. *Church on Sunday, Work on Monday: The Challenge of Fusing Christian Values with Business Life*. San Francisco: Jossey-Bass, 2001.

Nasr, Seyyed Hossein. "Islam." In *Our Religions*, edited by Arvind Sharma, 425–532. San Francisco: Harper San Francisco, 1993.

National Conference of Catholic Bishops. *Economic Justice for All: Pastoral Letter on Catholic Social Teaching and the U.S. Economy*. Washington, DC: United States Catholic Conference, 1986.

Neal, Judith A. "Spirituality in Management Education: A Guide to Resources." *Journal of Management Education* 21/1 (1997): 121–39.

Neuborne, Ellen. "Charity Begins at Work: Parents Work the Workplace as Fund-Raisers." *USA Today*, January 22, 1997, 1B.

Niebuhr, Gustav. "Christian Arabs, Too, Are Harassed." *New York Times*, October 15, 2001, A16.

"Studies Suggest Lower Count for Number of U.S. Muslims." *New York Times*, October 25, 2001, A16.

Niebuhr, H. Richard. *Christ and Culture*. First edn. New York: Harper & Row, 1951.

Nimer, Mohamed. "Accommodating Diversity: The Status of Muslim Civil Rights in the United States 2001." Washington DC: Council on American–Islamic Relations, 2001.

Nix, William. *Transforming Your Workplace for Christ*. Nashville, TN: Broadman and Holman, 1997.

Norton-Taylor, Duncan. "Businessmen on Their Knees." *Fortune*, October 1953, 140–41, 248, 253–54, 256.

Nussbaum, Martha. *Poetic Justice: The Literary Imagination in Public Life*. Boston: Beacon Press, 1995.

Nutting, Kurt. "Work and Freedom in Capitalism." In *Moral Rights in the Workplace*, edited by Gertrude Ezorsky, 97–104. Albany, NY: State University of New York Press, 1987.

Pantham, Thomas. "Indian Secularism and Its Critics: Some Reflections." *Review of Politics* 59/3 (1997): 523–40.

Pattison, Stephen. *The Faith of the Managers: When Management Becomes Religion*. London: Cassell, 1997.

"Recognizing Leaders' Hidden Beliefs." In *Faith in Leadership: How Leaders Live Out Their Faith in Their Work – and Why It Matters*, edited by Robert J. Banks and Kimberly Powell, 169–81. San Francisco: Jossey-Bass, 2000.

Pava, Moses L. "Religious Business Ethics and Political Liberalism: An Integrative Approach." *Journal of Business Ethics* 17 (1998): 1633–52.

Perina, Kaja. "Covenant Marriage: A New Marital Contract." *Psychology Today* 35/2 (2002): 18.

Pierce, Gregory F. *Spirituality@Work: 10 Ways to Balance Your Life on-the-Job.* Chicago: Loyola Press, 2001.

Plas, Jeanne M. *Person-Centered Leadership: An American Approach to Participatory Management.* Thousand Oaks, CA: Sage, 1996.

Plumner, Robyn. "Don't Let Patriotism Get Out of Hand." *Milwaukee Journal Sentinel,* November 15, 2001, 19A.

Putnam, Robert D. *Bowling Alone: The Collapse and Revival of American Community.* New York: Simon & Schuster, 2000.

Raboteau, Albert J. *Slave Religion: The "Invisible Institution" in the Antebellum South.* Oxford University Press, 1980.

Rauschenbusch, Walter. *Christianizing the Social Order.* New York: Macmillan, 1912.

Rawls, John. "The Idea of Public Reason Revisited." *University of Chicago Law Review* 64 (1997): 765–807.

Political Liberalism. The John Dewey Essays in Philosophy 4. New York: Columbia University Press, 1993.

A Theory of Justice. Cambridge, MA: Harvard University Press, 1971.

Rey, Jay. "Settlement Reached in Case on Religious Discrimination." *Buffalo News,* January 6, 2001, 3B.

Robinson, Gill D. "Person-Centered Management." *Black Women of Achievement Magazine* 1 (1988): 1.

Robinson, Jo Ann Gibson. *The Montgomery Bus Boycott and the Women Who Started It.* Edited by David J. Garrow. Knoxville, TN: University of Tennessee Press, 1987.

Robinson, Richard H. and Willard L. Johnson. *The Buddhist Tradition: A Historical Introduction.* Third edn. The Religious Life of Man series. Edited by Frederick J. Streng. Belmont, CA: Wadsworth, 1982.

Roof, Wade Clark. *A Generation of Seekers: The Spiritual Journeys of the Baby Boom Generation.* San Francisco: Harper San Francisco, 1993.

The Spiritual Marketplace: Baby Boomers and the Remaking of American Religion. Princeton University Press, 1999.

Rosier, Katherine Brown, and Scott L. Feld. "Covenant Marriage: A New Alternative for Traditional Families." *Journal of Comparative Family Studies* 31/3 (2000): 385–94.

Rousseau, Jean-Jacques. *The Social Contract.* Translated by Judith R. Masters. Edited by Roger D. Masters. New York: St. Martin's Press, 1978.

Sanchez, Rene and Bill Broadway. "A Kinship of Grief: With Prayers and Patriotism, a Nation Comes Together." *Washington Post,* September 15, 2001, A1.

Sandel, Michael J. "Freedom of Conscience or Freedom of Choice?" In *Articles of Faith, Articles of Peace,* edited by James Davison Hunter and Os Guinness, 74–92. Washington, DC: Brookings Institution, 1990.

Liberalism and the Limits of Justice. Cambridge: Cambridge University Press, 1982.

Schein, Edgar H. *Organizational Culture and Leadership.* Second edn. San Francisco: Jossey-Bass, 1992.

Schleiermacher, Friedrich. *On Religion: Speeches to Its Cultured Despisers.* Translated by R. Crouter. Cambridge University Press, 1996.

Schopf, Josh. "Religious Activity and Proselytization in the Workplace: The Murky Line between Healthy Expression and Unlawful Harassment." *Columbia Journal of Law and Social Problems* 31/1 (1997): 39–59.

Schor, Juliet. *The Overworked American: The Unexpected Decline of Leisure.* New York: Basic Books, 1992.

Sen, Amartya. "Description as Choice." *Oxford Economic Papers* 32 (1980): 353–69.

"Equality of What?" In *The Tanner Lectures on Human Values.* Edited by S. McMurrin. Salt Lake City: Utah University Press and Cambridge University Press, 1980.

"Goals, Commitment, and Identity." *Journal of Law, Economics, and Organization* 1/2 (1985): 341–55.

"Rational Fools: A Critique of the Behavioural Foundations of Economic Theory." *Philosophy and Public Affairs* 6 (1977): 317–44.

"The Threats to Secular India." *New York Review of Books* (1993): 26–32.

Sharma, Arvind. "Hinduism." In *Our Religions,* edited by Arvind Sharma, 1–67. San Francisco: Harper San Francisco, 1993.

Shoop, Julie Gannon. "Keeping the Faith: Advocates Seek Protection for Religious Rights at Work." *Trial* 33/11 (1997): 12–14.

Sixel, L. M. "Law Firm Gives Holiday Choices." *Houston Chronicle,* May 4, 2001, 1.

"To Some, Soliciting Sales at Work Is a Crummy Idea." *Houston Chronicle,* January 22, 1996, 1.

Smart, Ninian. "The Pros and Cons of Thinking of Religion as Tradition." In *Teaching the Introductory Course in Religious Studies: A Sourcebook,* edited by Mark Juergensmeyer. Atlanta: Scholars Press, 1991.

Smith, Adam. *An Inquiry into the Nature and Causes of the Wealth of Nations.* Edited by R. H. Campbell, A. S. Skinner, and W. B. Todd. Glasgow Edition of the Works and Correspondence of Adam Smith. 2 vols. New York: Oxford University Press, 1976.

The Theory of Moral Sentiments. Translated by D. D. Raphael and A. L. Macfie. Glasgow Edition of the Works and Correspondence of Adam Smith. New York: Oxford University Press, 1976.

Smith, Christian. "Correcting a Curious Neglect, or Bringing Religion Back In." In *Disruptive Religion: The Force of Faith in Social Movement Activism,* edited by Christian Smith, 1–25. New York: Routledge, 1996.

Society for Human Resource Management Issues Management Program. "Religion in the Workplace Mini-Survey." Alexandria, VA: Society for Human Resource Management, 1997.

Sullivan, Pat McHenry. "Workplace Thinking Has Been Altar-Ed." *San Francisco Examiner,* November 28, 1999, 5.

Tamney, Joseph B. "Conservative Government and Support for the Religious Institution in Singapore: An Uneasy Alliance." *Sociological Analysis* 53/2 (1992): 201–17.

"Religion and the State in Singapore." *Journal of Church and State* 30 (1988): 109–28.

Taylor, Charles. "Religion in a Free Society." In *Articles of Faith, Articles of Peace*, edited by James Davison Hunter and Os Guinness, 93–113. Washington, DC: Brookings Institution, 1990.

Taylor, Frederick Winslow. *The Principles of Scientific Management*. New York: W. W. Norton, 1911.

Tharamangalam, Joseph. "Religious Pluralism and the Theory and Practice of Secularism: Reflections on the Indian Experience." *Journal of Asian and African Studies* 24/3–4 (1989): 198–212.

Thiemann, Ronald F. *Religion in Public Life: A Dilemma for Democracy*. Washington, DC: Georgetown University Press, 1996.

Tillich, Paul. *Systematic Theology*. Vol. 1. University of Chicago Press, 1951.

Tischler, Len. "The Growing Interest in Spirituality in Business: A Long-Term Socio-Economic Explanation." *Journal of Organizational Change Management* 12/4 (1999): 273–79.

Tocqueville, Alexis de. *Democracy in America*. Translated by George Lawrence. Edited by J. P. Mayer. New York: HarperPerennial, 1969.

Tourish, Dennis and Ashly Pinnington. "Transformational Leadership, Corporate Cultism, and the Spirituality Paradigm: An Unholy Trinity in the Workplace?" *Human Relations* 55/2 (2002): 147–72.

Tu Wei-ming. "Confucianism." In *Our Religions*, edited by Arvind Sharma, 139–227. San Francisco: Harper San Francisco, 1993.

Turnbull, Lornet. "Mixing Work, Religion Requires Flexibility by Workers." *Columbus Dispatch*, October 4, 1999, 10.

"Unions Act to Allay Fears of Anti-Muslim Bias." *Straits Times*, September 26, 2002.

"Unions Push for Panel to Prevent Discrimination against Moslems." *Deutsche Presse-Agentur*, October 12, 2002.

Velasquez, Manuel G. *Business Ethics: Concepts and Cases*. Fifth edn. Upper Saddle River, NJ: Prentice Hall, 2002.

Wakin, Daniel J. "Seeing Heresy in a Service for Sept. 11; Pastor is under Fire for Interfaith Prayers." *New York Times*, February 8, 2002.

Waldman, Amy. "Gunmen Raid Hindu Temple Complex in India, Killing 29." *New York Times*, September 25, 2002, 8.

"Wal-Mart Settles Worker's Religious Bias Suit." *St. Louis Post-Dispatch*, August 23, 1995, 3C.

Walzer, Michael. *Spheres of Justice: A Defense of Pluralism and Equality*. New York: Basic Books, 1983.

Werhane, Patricia H. and Tara J. Radin. "Employment at Will and Due Process." In *Ethical Theory and Business*. Sixth edn., edited by Tom L. Beauchamp and Norman E. Bowie, 266–75. Upper Saddle River, NJ: Prentice Hall, 2001.

Williams, Benjamin D. "Humility and Vision in the Life of the Effective Leader." In *Faith in Leadership: How Leaders Live Out Their Faith in Their Work – and Why It Matters*, edited by Robert J. Banks and Kimberly Powell, 62–76. San Francisco: Jossey-Bass, 2000.

Wolf, Michael, Bruce Friedman, and Daniel Sutherland. *Religion in the Workplace: A Comprehensive Guide to Legal Rights and Responsibilities.* Chicago: Tort and Insurance Practice Section, American Bar Association, 1998.

Wolpert, Stanley. *A New History of India.* Sixth edn. New York: Oxford University Press, 2000.

Wolterstorff, Nicholas. *Until Justice and Peace Embrace.* Grand Rapids, MI: Eerdmans, 1983.

"Workers Say Company Ignored Hate Campaign." *Los Angeles Times*, August 1, 2001, 8.

Wren, J. Thomas and Marc J. Swatez. "The Historical and Contemporary Contexts of Leadership: A Conceptual Model." In *The Leader's Companion: Insights on Leadership through the Ages*, edited by J. Thomas Wren, 245–52. New York: Free Press, 1995.

Wuthnow, Robert. *After Heaven: Spirituality in America Since the 1950s.* Berkeley, CA: University of California Press, 1998.

God and Mammon in America. New York: Free Press, 1994.

Wuthnow, Robert and John H. Evans, eds. *The Quiet Hand of God: Faith-Based Activism and the Public Role of Mainline Protestantism.* Berkeley, CA: University of California Press, 2002.

Yearley, Lee H. *Mencius and Aquinas: Theories of Virtue and Conceptions of Courage.* Albany, NY: State University of New York Press, 1990.

Yeo, Alicia, Arlina Arshad, and Sue Ann Chia. "Religious Code Goes Beyond Keeping Peace." *Straits Times*, October 16, 2002.

Young, Iris Marion. *Justice and the Politics of Difference.* Princeton University Press, 1990.

Yukl, Gary. *Leadership in Organizations.* Fifth edn. Upper Saddle River, NJ: Prentice Hall, 2002.

Index